Social Studies and
Young Children

Social Studies and Young Children

Eucabeth A. Odhiambo
Shippensburg University

J. Kent Chrisman
Shippensburg University

Laureen Nelson
Shippensburg University

PEARSON

Boston   Columbus   Indianapolis   New York   San Francisco   Hoboken
Amsterdam   Cape Town   Dubai   London   Madrid   Milan   Munich   Paris   Montreal   Toronto
Delhi   Mexico City   Sao Paulo   Sydney   Hong Kong   Seoul   Singapore   Taipei   Tokyo

President and Editorial Director: Jeffery W. Johnston
Senior Acquisitions Editor: Julie Peters
Program Manager: Megan Moffo
Project Manager: Mary Beth Finch
Editorial Assistant: Andrea Hall
Marketing Manager: Margaret Waples
Executive Field Marketing Manager: Krista Clark
Senior Product Marketing Manager: Christopher Barry
Procurement Specialist: Deidra Skahill
Senior Art Director: Diane Lorenzo

Cover Designer: Melissa Welch/StudioMontage
Cover Art: michaeljung/Shutterstock
Media Project Manager: Allison Longley
Full-Service Project Management: Cenveo® Publisher Services
Composition: Cenveo Publisher Services
Printer/Binder: LSC Communications, Inc.
Cover Printer: LSC Communications, Inc.
Text Font: ITC New Baskerville Std

Credits and acknowledgments for material borrowed from other sources and reproduced, with permission, in this textbook appear on the appropriate page within the text.

Every effort has been made to provide accurate and current Internet information in this book. However, the Internet and information posted on it are constantly changing, so it is inevitable that some of the Internet addresses listed in this textbook will change.

Library of Congress Cataloging-in-Publication Data
Odhiambo, Eucabeth A.
  Social studies and young children / Eucabeth A. Odhiambo, Shippensburg University J. Kent Chrisman, Shippensburg University, Laureen Nelson, Shippensburg University.
     pages cm
  ISBN 978-0-13-355073-3
 1. Social sciences—Study and teaching (Early childhood)—United States. I. Chrisman, J. Kent. II. Nelson, Laureen. III. Title.
  LB1139.5.S64O34 2014
  372.83—dc23

ISBN 10: 0-13-355073-7
ISBN 13: 978-0-13-355073-3

Preface

Young children learn best when they have authentic and age-appropriate experiences with a broad range of people, ideas, activities, and materials. This book offers this type of framework to college and university students who are preparing to be teachers. The book is based on developmentally appropriate practice (DAP) in the social studies. The research and theoretical base support the belief that teachers of young children must recognize and embrace children's individual development and the factors that influence those differences. Thus, this book seeks to assist and guide pre-service and in-service teachers with ways to teach social studies in early childhood environments in many settings.

This book also emphasizes that social studies happens everywhere, every day, and with everyone. A major goal in the textbook is to demonstrate how the standards (NCSS and NAEYC) can be integrated into the daily curriculum—emphasizing throughout that learning does not happen in compartments or silos but rather together and sometimes simultaneously.

KEY FEATURES OF THIS TEXT

The content-related chapters have the following key features that make it easy to use the book not only as an information resource but also as an activity resource:

- *Big idea charts* summarize the key ideas in the chapter, giving the reader classroom applications and the standards met. This feature allows the reader to understand what he/she can expect in the rest of the chapter.

- *Adaptations for English language learners figures* incorporate best practices for all young learners and focus those practices on helping linguistically diverse students to learn in a variety of ways.

- *Accommodations for children with diverse needs figures* promote appropriate methods, materials, and interactions for children with special needs.

- *Sample activities* are integrated through each of the chapter narratives and are highlighted in lesson planning sections. Nearly all chapters have a section with sample activities that the preservice teacher or in-service teacher can use.
- *Connections to Literacy* sections provide examples of trade fiction and nonfiction books that can be used with social studies topics and integrated with literacy and other subject areas.
- *Resources* sections provide a list of additional sources that can be used either as background information or for use with children.
- *Home/School Connection boxes* are included to emphasize the importance of the home to each child's learning experience and to provide ways to engage the families.
- *Learning centers* sections are included to emphasize the importance of play for young children's learning. These sections provide ideas for practical applications in classroom settings.

ACKNOWLEDGMENTS

First and foremost, we wish to recognize Pearson Higher Education for its commitment to education. Pearson's vision and dedication have contributed to improved understanding of teaching social studies and continue to support teachers in their efforts to teach children social studies.

This book is a collaborative endeavor by many individuals. We are grateful to Julie Peters, our Senior Acquisitions Editor, who provided invaluable guidance and support. Her exceptional feedback, suggestions, and editing were instrumental in producing this book. We would like to thank many others for their contributions: Their tireless efforts, attention to detail, and encouragement brought this book to successful completion.

We are grateful to our reviewers and want to express our sincere appreciation for their insightful critiques, suggestions, and ability to help us see issues from multiple perspectives. They include the following: Natalie Young, Northern Illinois University; Lynn S. Kline, The University of Akron; and John P. Broome, University of Mary Washington.

We sincerely appreciate several others who helped with gathering children's photos and artifacts for preparation of the book. Those include the following: families of children at the Grace B. Luhrs Elementary

University School and Hamilton Heights Elementary School; Konnie Serr, first-grade teacher; and Lisa Cline, Administrative Assistant.

Finally, we would like to thank our readers for their dedication and commitment to improving the quality of teaching social studies to young children in ways that come naturally to them. Providing them with thoughtful lessons, hands-on activities, and important discussions helps them make sense—in developmentally appropriate ways—of the world in which they live.

About the Authors

Dr. Eucabeth Odhiambo is a member of the Department of Teacher Education faculty at Shippensburg University. She has served the education community in a variety of positions during the past 25 years. As a classroom teacher she worked with kindergarten and second through eighth grades. She teaches undergraduate and graduate courses in the Early Childhood and Curriculum and Instruction programs, as well as child development and social studies methods. She is also involved in student teacher supervision. She has made numerous professional presentations at local, state, national, and international conferences. Dr. Odhiambo has authored publications on teaching, pre-service training, and diversity.

Dr. Laureen E. Nelson is a member of the Department of Teacher Education faculty at Shippensburg University. She has served the early childhood field in a variety of capacities over the past 25 years. She has been a classroom teacher, a preschool teacher and director, and a faculty member teaching both undergraduate and graduate courses in the Early Childhood program and the Curriculum and Instruction program. She currently teaches child development and assessment courses in the Early Childhood undergraduate program, as well as early childhood curriculum and assessment, leadership in early childhood education, and social and emotional development in early childhood in the graduate program. She has made presentations on teaching math and social studies to young learners at local, state, national, and international conferences and has co-authored publications on teaching math to young learners.

Dr. J. Kent Chrisman is a professor of early childhood education at Shippensburg University and has published books related to families, professional development, and mathematics for young children. He is currently co-authoring a three-volume encyclopedia of early childhood education. Dr. Chrisman has been a preschool assistant teacher, family services director, and director of Lab Schools in Texas and Pennsylvania. He has also served as president of state AEYC affiliates in Texas, Kentucky, and Pennsylvania and was appointed to the Early Learning Council by the governor of Pennsylvania. He continues to present at conferences and workshops in addition to teaching graduate and undergraduate courses in early childhood education.

Table of Contents

Social Studies and Young Children

1 Understanding the Development of Social Studies Concepts and Young Children

Learning Outcomes

After reading this you should be able to:

- Explain the process of learning about social studies through the theories and research of Piaget, Erikson, Ainsworth, Kohlberg/Gilligan, and Vygotsky.

- Explain what is meant by developmentally appropriate practices in social studies.

- Describe general characteristics of children in various stages and how they learn social studies.

- Explain how children's literature can be used to support learning of social studies.

- Describe the types of adaptations that can be planned for English language learners (ELL) and children with special needs that might help them acquire social studies concepts.

- Explain how to involve families/caregivers in supporting the acquisition of social studies skills at home.

Standards Addressed in this Chapter

NCSS Standards

The National Council for the Social Studies (NCSS) has organized social studies into 10 broad interrelated and holistic themes. Those addressed in each of the upcoming chapters will be in bold:

1. Culture
2. Time, continuity, and change
3. People, places, and environments
4. Individual development and identity
5. Individuals, groups, and institutions
6. Power, authority, and governance
7. Production, distribution, and consumption
8. Science, technology, and society
9. Global connections
10. Civic ideals and practices (NCSS, 2010)

Source: National curriculum standards for social studies: A framework for teaching, learning and assessment. Silver Spring, MD: National Council for the Social Studies.

SOCIAL STUDIES EDUCATION GOALS

Welcome to the world of helping young children learn about themselves, each other, and the broader community. Helping young children gain social skills and social understanding requires both knowledge of social studies content and comprehension of child development. To provide you with both of these, we use nationally recognized sources as our framework in this textbook. Two major sources are the National Council for Social Studies (NCSS) standards (see sidebar) and the National Association for the Education of Young Children (NAEYC) principles of developmentally appropriate practice (Copple & Bredekamp, 2009; see Figure 1.1 for a summary of influential theories and researchers). Melendez, Beck, and Fletcher (2000) have summarized five goals that will also be crucial to remember throughout this text:

1. ***Individual development.*** Young children are developing in the areas of *self-esteem* and *self-concept,* which are impacted by the people around them—other children, teachers, caregivers, and families—who in turn influence their character. Individual development takes place while interacting with others, whether in play or other activities. In these situations, young children can learn to solve problems, cope with strong emotions, and learn to

David Kostelnik/Pearson

David Kostelnik/Pearson

negotiate. Additionally, teachers can foster individual development in the way they interact and communicate with children.

2. *Social and civic competence.* Young children at a very early age are interacting with people around them. Their knowledge, skills, and attitudes about the people and community around them are critical for future interactions. To promote this competence, children in the primary grades should learn about their communities. The basis of this knowledge and skill can start in the classroom community and expand as the children grow older.

3. *Knowledge-based concept of social reality.* Classroom activities provide experiences that allow children to acquire and develop ideas about their social reality, encouraging a variety of ways to look at, and value, diversity.

4. *Appreciation and respect for human diversity.* Human diversity exists everywhere. Young children need to value differences that exist around them, such as physical and cultural variations. Classroom discussions, experiences, interactions, and activities must cultivate the knowledge of and, consequently, the appreciation of and respect for diversity. Through an effective social studies curriculum, teachers will foster appreciation for these differences.

5. *Global citizenship.* The idea of being a part of the world needs to take root and flourish in the awareness of young children as they grow. Thus teachers are to engender in children "a sense of responsibility for their acts and for their impact on others" (Melendez et al., p. 27).

The NCSS themes guide teachers in deriving content that can be further categorized into the subject areas of geography, history, economics, and civics/political science. Throughout these themes is also an underlying awareness of and appreciation for multicultural education. Both content and strategy must lead to the following teaching goals:

Creating a caring community of learners
Enhancing development and learning

Planning curriculum that will lead to the achievement
of important goals

Assessing children's development and learning

SETTING THE STAGE FOR LEARNING

The theories discussed here center on learning in social contexts, as
related to the development of young children (birth through third
grade). It is important to remember that learning must be discussed
with a clear and strong focus on both research and theoretical base.
Teachers must understand theory because theory guides and informs
practice. Being grounded in research and theory provides a solid foundation for making learning relevant and age appropriate.

The theorists and researchers most often mentioned in the early
development of social skills are the following:

Jean Piaget

Lev Vygotsky

Erik Erickson

Mary Ainsworth

Lawrence Kohlberg and Carol Gilligan

Urie Bronfenbrenner

Figure 1.1 presents a brief overview of their theories and research
as they relate to children's development of social understanding; a
brief example of application is given:

Figure 1.1
Theories and Applications.

Theorist/ Researcher	Terms Associated with This Theory as It Relates to Social Studies	Example of an Application
Jean Piaget and Barbel Inhelder (1969)	Development occurs in stages. In early childhood these are named the Sensory-Perceptual-Motor, Preoperational, and Concrete Operational Stages. Some characteristics of the Preoperational stage include **egocentrism,** difficulty in **decentering**, and perspective-taking.	Teachers of young children must be aware that children's thinking is focused on meeting their own needs and that they require help in understanding the needs of others. This ability grows over time with assistance from caring adults.

(*continued*)

Figure 1.1
(*continued*)

Theorist/ Researcher	Terms Associated with This Theory as It Relates to Social Studies	Example of an Application
Erik Erikson (1950)	Human development proceeds through a series of social stage crises that must be resolved successfully for optimal growth and development.	Teachers of young children will need to provide environments that support children as they work to resolve these crises. Examples include:
	In the early years these are called: Trust vs. Mistrust	Provide infant rooms that are responsive to babies' language and physical needs (diaper changing routines that have rich language and interaction).
	Autonomy vs. Shame and Doubt	Make sure that toddler rooms allow children to move, explore, and gain skills in interacting in safe ways (toilet-training routines that are individualized, spaces that are challenging but not overwhelming, and so on).
	Initiative vs. Guilt	Incorporate preschool experiences that continue to expand language development and help children build on new skills in movement, problem-solving, and interactions in both group times and center times. *Note:* Play begins a major vehicle here to develop both self-regulation and executive functioning (Bodrova and Leong, 1996).
		Kindergarten and primary grades provide children with transitioning opportunities to move from early childhood settings into school-age settings (Pianta & Kraft-Sayre. 2003).
	Industry vs. Inferiority	Classrooms continue to provide age-appropriate materials and activities that support the growth of social skills (such as projects, family engagement, use of home language, use of both fiction and nonfiction sources, and so on).
		Primary grade children in elementary school are given opportunities to practice decision-making without explicit adult control. These scaffolded opportunities promote the growth of **autonomy**, perseverance, and integrity.

Theorist/ Researcher	Terms Associated with This Theory as It Relates to Social Studies	Example of an Application
Lev Vygotsky (1978)	Sociocultural theory states that young children's learning is influenced by both the immediate community and the larger social/historical context. Major terms include:	Families, community, and society influence what children learn and how they learn it. Examples include the ways that families teach each other about child rearing and guidance methods as well as large government programs such as Head Start and No Child Left Behind.
	Zone of Proximal Development (ZPD) Tools	Vygotsky's theory states that learning occurs first with the help of others or with the help of tools; then gradually children reach a level of independence after practicing a new skill.
		One of the major components of the ZPD is that of recursion, in which learning seems to be forgotten and children need time and practice to return to skills acquired earlier. Play and projects in the primary grades help children remember the terms and concepts learned earlier.
Mary Ainsworth (1989)	**Attachment** theory indicates that all humans need and benefit from close, intimate relationships in infancy.	Infants and toddlers need responsive adults who can provide supportive, consistent interactions that promote children's explorations of the world. It is vital that the same adults interact with babies and toddlers over a long period of time to build rapport, trust, and so on.
		Alice Honig (2010) has written and presented extensively about the many ways attachment theory can be implemented with very young children.
Urie Bronfenbrenner (1975)	Bioecological theory centers on understanding that spheres of influence surround each child, involving the family, community, school, local government, broader influences, and so forth, and that these spheres interact with each other and with the child.	Classroom teachers should understand that a child's home and neighborhood form a basis for understanding social studies concepts.
Lawrence Kohlberg (1981) and Carol Gilligan (1982)	Kohlberg's theory of the stages of **moral development** holds that rules and laws increasingly lead to decisions based on ethics. Gilligan's work on moral decision-making is based on caring relationships.	Classroom practices help children come to understand the need for caring about each other, resolving differences through both rules and fair interactions. Examples of such practices have been described by other authors such as Nell Noddings, Dan Gartrell, and the Center for Social and Emotional Foundations for Early Learning (CSEFEL).

To further your understanding of the typical characteristics of child development, review Figures 1.2 through 1.5. As you read, reflect on your current knowledge of child development and how it applies to children's learning of social studies.

Figure 1.2

General Characteristics of Children from Birth to Age 3.

Characteristics of Children 0–3 Years Old	How Teachers Can Help
0–9 months: • Use the sense of smell, sight, hearing, touch, and taste to learn about the world around them. • Engage with familiar people, that is, smile, laugh, gaze, grin, coo, reach out, and hold tight. • Learn through movement.	• Be involved in responsive interaction. • Interact, converse with the baby. • Provide pleasurable routines. • Balance between carry and cuddle and floor or firm surface time.
8–18 months: • Able to move. • Exploration as a key to learning. • More interest in their peers. • More attached to adults they love. • More responsive to communication.	• Play and talk to infants. • Make eye contact and use gestures. • Encourage interest in language by reading to infants. • Use slow speech, enunciate words. • Repeat words—names, objects, and actions. • Support peer interactions. • Provide health and safety. • Provide room to roam for infants learning to be mobile.
16–36 months (toddlers): • Identity. • Desire for independence and control. • Increased desire to explore. • Need for security. • Imitate adults. • Fascinated by words. • Enjoy hearing stories about people and things they know. • Love to categorize objects. • Seek out friends, enjoy play, and engage in group activities. • Learn the meaning of being a girl or boy and notice differences between girls and boys.	• Know the family well. • Greet toddler and family warmly. • Use a warm and caring tone of interaction and touch to demonstrate that children are valued. • Give choices where possible. • Introduce social guidelines. • Organize an environment that will foster chances for control as toddlers participate in various activities. • Frequently read to toddlers. • Comfort toddlers.

Figure 1.3
General Characteristics of 3- to 5-Year-Old Children.

Characteristics of Children 3–5 Years Old	How Teachers Can Help
• Physically very active—play, running, dance, dramatic play, outdoors. • Hearing well developed. • Continuing development of gross motor skills. • Fine motor skills not developed. Difficulty with writing, drawing, cutting. • Need planned physical activities in order to improve physical development. • Socially, more interactions with peers. • Often develop close friendships with caring teachers (Howes & Richie, 2002). • Emotional development—increased understanding of their own emotions, such as anger, sadness, fear.	• Plenty of hands-on activities. • Plan physical activities indoors and outdoors. • Provide a variety of objects, such as buttons, zippers, beads to string, and drawing and painting supplies, to help improve their fine motor skills. • Promote a sense of community by model caring and respectful language, class projects, class meetings. • To promote literacy and language development, engage children in conversations and in listening to others.

Figure 1.4
General Characteristics of 5- and 6-Year-Old Children.

Characteristics of Children 5 and 6 Years Old	How Teachers Can Help
• Physical development—kindergarteners are doing actions in all areas that are more complex than those performed by children in the 3–5 bracket; for example, they are running faster, have improved cognition, and demonstrate improved social relationships. • More developed fine motor skills, such as writing, drawing, and so on. • Social and emotional development—are more able to apply internal control and monitor their actions, are better at cooperative interaction, and are better at preventing conflict. • Increased interest in friendships and the ability to make and keep friends.	• Teach physical skills and offer opportunities to play in which children can use new physical skills. • Create an environment that offers time to practice fine and gross motor skills. • Model whatever it is that you want children to follow, such as empathy and understanding.

Figure 1.5
General Characteristics of 6- to 8-Year-Old Children.

Characteristics of Children 6–8 Years Old	How Teachers Can Help
• Overall growth occurs in all areas of the body, with improved gross and motor skills.	• Create a supportive and safe environment.
• Refine gross skills, such as running and jumping, and motor skills, such as drawing and reading.	• Work together with children to develop classroom rules.
• They have better understanding of relationships, that is, how to make and maintain relationships and what can affect others.	
• Exhibit concept acquisition and reason.	
• They are able to self-regulate their thoughts and attention, plan and organize, retain and recall information.	
• Rules are absolute and students are more concerned about pleasing the teacher—"good boy, good girl mentality."	

DEVELOPMENTALLY APPROPRIATE PRACTICES IN SOCIAL STUDIES

The home environment, the community, and the school are the major places where each child's social learning experience can be broadened (Mindes, 2005). Social studies begins at birth and develops with each experience. Thus a developmentally appropriate practices model calls for

- Using curriculum founded on everyday familiar experiences to foster learning (social skills in groups; interactions during play; children's ideas about their world; common words used in social practices such as greetings, hygiene, eating, and so on)

- Involving children in experiences that expand and extend their understanding of democracy (building abilities to cooperate within a group, turn-taking, negotiating, listening, and so on)

Restorative Justice Practices in Early Childhood Programs

Central to social studies are concepts of justice, fairness, and citizenship. Classroom methods to teach these concepts are sometimes collectively referred to as "restorative justice" strategies. Listed below are some classroom practices that promote these concepts in age-appropriate ways:

- Problem-solving discussions at group time meetings
- Conflict resolution meetings
- Dialogue between conflicting parties
- Increasing victim awareness
- Restorative justice conversations

Positive behavior approaches

- Talking about behavior without blaming
- Seeing misbehavior as an opportunity for learning
- Modeling conflict resolution strategies
- Teaching and supporting self-regulation approaches
- Curriculum focus on relationship building and conflict prevention
- Nurture groups and approaches
- Playground strategies that encourage safe play
- Teaching resiliency
- Respecting rights of everyone

Sustainability in Early Childhood Education

Sustainability as a topic in early childhood curricula is still emerging. However, it relates to many of the same themes as others that have been discussed previously in this chapter (e.g. justice, economics, and fairness). Helping children begin to understand and then to act on concepts related to the big topics of sustaining the environment, natural resources, accessibility, technology, and so on, for all people, can be integrated into classrooms on a regular basis (saving water, reusing paper, and recycling many materials, for instance). Davis (2010) includes articles from a variety of authors in her book *Young Children and the Environment: Early Education for Sustainability* that give both broad reasons and practical ways to include sustainability concepts in programs for young children. Including sustainability themes and activities in the early years enables children to understand even more complex issues in later grades.

Metacognition and Children's Understanding of Social Studies Concepts

Metacognition refers to one's ability to think about one's own thinking (Flavell, 1977). In *Growing Minds* (2012), Karen Capraro describes a process that worked with second graders. They first recorded their current thinking (**schema**) or knowledge about a topic; then they generated questions about the topic. She then taught her class ways to think about their questions and began to define this as inferring. The last step was to recognize the new knowledge they had gained.

This model, named SQiNK (schema, questions, inferring, new knowledge) by the children, also helps you think about how to teach the social studies concepts in this book. Thinking both about your own thinking and about how children think will be repeating themes.

Supporting your understanding of children's development with appropriate theoretical grounding is a focus of this first chapter. By gaining a deep knowledge of both individual and age-typical development, classroom teachers are better able to plan social studies content and strategies that convey the central concepts in the social studies curriculum. This chapter introduces the themes of the National Council for the Social Studies (NCSS), and these themes continue throughout the text.

HOME/SCHOOL CONNECTION

Home and school relations must be built and maintained for each age group. However, it is particularly critical for caregivers of infants and toddlers. It is important that the infant care teacher value the information provided by the family and, at the same time, that the family value the knowledge and personality of the child care teacher. This partnership provides a growing relationship that will in turn benefit the child. Communication must be ongoing, with the infant care teacher and the parents sharing information about sleeping, eating, playing, elimination patterns, and learning.

The infant care teacher must make an effort to learn more about the culture of the family, particularly when the home culture is different from that of the teacher. It is also important because childrearing perspectives differ. The child care teacher must be able to consider and openly discuss with the family differences and similarities in caring for their child.

Toddlers need support as they continue to grow. Sharing new developments and interests allows both parents and care teachers to support the toddler. Knowing and understanding the family creates continuity of care between home and child care, which allows the child to thrive and at the same time gain teacher and parental support.

Early childhood settings should be a place where parents are welcome to participate—to read to children and share their skills or just observe children in action. Teachers should initiate conversations regarding differences in perspectives so that they forge a strong partnership with parents. The teacher can support the family by making a picture book or a list of words for older children in the family's language, which can be used to communicate with the child. Younger children will need to hear familiar words that hold specific meaning to them. Furthermore, this will open a way to future communication and may gain help the teacher might need from the family. At this stage, social studies has a lot to do with teaching children about relationships and their environment both at home and at school.

In the primary grades, family involvement has traditionally moved to a parent-teacher conference event, an occasional open house, or a PTA meeting. Some research, however, indicates that a more comprehensive family engagement model is much more powerful in creating school and home environments that support children's academic success.

(*continued*)

Joyce Epstein (2001) has identified the following six major components for family engagement:

Parenting

Communicating

Volunteering

Learning at home

Decision-making

Collaborating with the community

ACCOMMODATIONS FOR CHILDREN WITH DIVERSE NEEDS

Providing proper and just educational accommodations for children with diverse needs is an important part of the educational process. Each chapter will include figures presenting appropriate adaptations for these students: those for English language learners, or ELL (Figure 1.6), and those for students with special needs (Figure 1.7).

Figure 1.6
Adaptations for ELL.

Adaptations for English Language Learners

It is most important for teachers to understand the home culture and home language of the child. Families should be encouraged to share their perspectives regarding child care, childrearing, learning, problem-solving, and socializing. Teachers should be willing to actively listen and discuss differences and similarities. These discussions should result in compromises and agreements on the best way to promote the child's growth and development. Schools should facilitate communications for parents who do not speak English by recruiting bilingual staff or using translators where needed throughout the day, such as in classrooms, conferences, and meetings.

Here are some specific strategies:

- Use picture books or lists of words in the family's language.
- Present pictures with captions in both the family's language and English for older children (kindergarten through primary age).

- For younger children (infants and toddlers), just using words or pointing to pictures will create the necessary familiarity.
- Engaging ELL and children who are behind in vocabulary and other language skills in additional conversations will support comprehension.
- Engage children with hands-on materials that will provide further language development in more meaningful ways than just auditory instruction.
- Connect sensory experiences (touching, smelling, seeing, tasting, hearing) with both English and home language terms.

Teachers should spend additional time and use multiple strategies to help English language learners with academic language. This is also referred to as "cognitive academic language proficiency," or CALP (Cummins, 2008). Academic language consists of those words and terms that are used in school but not typically in homes or in the community and is therefore more challenging in ELL populations. Academic language is critical for success in school because it ties directly to learning content in each subject.

Goldenberg (2006) recommends the following instructional supports:

1. Strategic use of the primary language.
2. Consistent expectations, instruction, and routines.
3. Extended explanations and opportunities for practice.
4. Physical gestures and visual cues.
5. Focusing on the similarities/differences between English and the home language.
6. Building on the home language and skills.
7. Target vocabulary and check comprehension frequently.
8. Paraphrase students' language and encourage them to expand.

In planning and implementing strategies, it is helpful to bear in mind the stages of English language learners (Krashen & Terrell, 1983):

Stage 1: The Silent/Receptive or Preproduction Stage
Lasts up to six months

Stage II: The Early Production Stage
Lasts for another six months

Figure 1.6
(*continued*)

Stage III: The Speech Emergence Stage
Lasts for one or more years

Stage IV: The Intermediate Language Proficiency Stage
Last for another year

Stage V: The Advanced Proficiency Stage
Lasts 3 to 5 years

Figure 1.7
Adaptations for Children with Special Needs.

Adaptations for Children with Special Needs

Children identified with special needs often require the same experiences as typically developing children to acquire social studies skills. However, teachers must understand each child's background in order to make adequate and relevant adaptations. Adaptations for children with special needs can better take place when caregivers, teachers, and families develop and maintain mutual respect and two-way communication. Special needs may be noticed at infancy or may come to light as the child grows. Either way, families and caregivers/teachers have to work together to ensure provision of suitable adaptations.

Here are some examples of adaptations:

- Adaptations for older children (preschool, kindergarten, or primary grade children) must be specific to their unique needs and not based on a rigid interpretation of the chronological age of the child (e.g., because he is seven he *must* do this).
- Movement programs can help children with gross motor development disabilities (Pica, 2004).

CONNECTIONS TO LITERACY

Children's books provide developmentally appropriate ways to learn about social studies. There are many books available that foster geography, history, civics, and economics skills and concepts. The NCSS, in conjunction with the Children's Book Council (CBC), annually publishes a list that can be used as a guide to selecting good books. The following are some pointers to keep in mind when searching for books (Melendez et al., 2000):

- Review the themes of social studies so that you are aware of the relevant topics, such as geography, history, economics, and diversity.
- Choose books with clear illustrations and good details of concepts.
- Read the story beforehand to make sure it is appropriate for the age level you teach and to assess language level and clarity of descriptions.
- Consider all genres, including folktales, poetry, and song picture books.

Including a variety of multicultural/multiethnic books, songs, and experiences promotes children's understanding of diversity, in their classroom as well as their community. Specific books and literacy strategies related to teaching social studies content will be mentioned in other chapters.

ASSESSING PREKINDERGARTEN AND KINDERGARTEN CHILDREN'S DEVELOPMENT AND LEARNING

Assessment is done for the following reasons:

1. To meet the developmental and learning needs of each child.
2. To evaluate and improve program effectiveness.
3. To screen and identify children with potential disabilities or special needs.

Screening needs to be done when children enter the program. Decisions should be made based on information provided by families and collected through observing each child. Anecdotal notes are useful in reminding the teacher of specific observations. Observations must be done in the following developmental domains: physical, cognitive, social, and emotional. The teacher can find many opportunities to observe a child in an effort to assess him/her, for example, during play, games, center time, discussions, and one on one time with the teacher. For kindergarten and primary grade children, written, paper-pencil tests and other products are collected and used to adjust instruction on a day-to-day basis. Assessment must be made on an ongoing basis "at regular intervals throughout the year" (Copple & Bredekamp, 2009, p. 179) and should be integrated into the teaching and curriculum (Copple & Bredekamp, 2009). Teachers need to ensure that assessment is consistent with developmental and learning goals in the curriculum and that it matches the age, development, and culture of the child (Copple & Bredekamp, 2009). It is important for teachers to share the assessments with families; in that way they are able to work together to help the child progress.

SAMPLE ACTIVITY

The upcoming chapters will provide suggestions for effective and enjoyable activities. Here is one for the teacher who is learning about the different theories of development.

Making Observations

Observe children in different age groups, from infancy through primary age, in a family setting or school environment, and then identify the developmental characteristics outlined by the theorists and researchers mentioned in this chapter.

RESOURCES

Teachers have some useful sources to tap into as they learn about developmentally appropriate ways to teach social studies. Two of the most helpful are listed below:

- Center for the Social and Emotional Foundations of Early Learning: csefel.vanderbilt.edu/
- NAEYC: Young Children (YC), Guidance Matters column: naeyc.org/

Suzanne Clouzeau/Pearson

Assessing Learning Outcomes

- Explain the process of learning through the theories of Piaget, Erikson, Ainsworth, Kohlberg/Gilligan, Bronfenbrenner, and Vygotsky.
- Explain developmentally appropriate practices in social studies.
- Describe general characteristics of children in various stages and how they learn social studies.
- Explain the general social, physical, cognitive, and emotional stages of development that children go through and how the stages could impact the learning of social studies.
- Explain how children's literature can be used to support learning of social studies.
- Describe the types of adaptations that can be planned for English language learners (ELL) and children with special needs that might help them acquire social studies concepts.
- Explain how to involve families/caregivers in supporting the acquisition of social skills at home and in supporting teachers of young children.

References

Ainsworth, M. (1989). Attachments beyond infancy. *American Psychologist, 44,* 709–716.

Bodrova, E., & Leong, D. (1996). *Tools of mind: The Vygotskian approach to early childhood.* Upper Saddle River, NJ: Prentice Hall.

Bronfenbrenner, U. (1975). *Influences on human development.* New York, NY: Holt, Rinehart and Winston.

Capraro, K.. (2012). *Growing minds: Building strong cognitive foundations in early childhood.* Washington, DC: National Association for the Education of Young Children (NAEYC).

Copple C., & Bredekamp, S. (Eds.). (2009). *Developmentally appropriate practice in early childhood programs* (3rd ed.). Washington, DC: National Association for the Education of Young Children (NAEYC).

Cummins, J. (2008). BICS and CALP: Empirical and theoretical status of the distinction. In B. Street & N. H. Hornberger (Eds.), *Encyclopedia of language and education* (2nd ed., Vol. 2, pp. 71–83). New York: Springer Science + Business Media.

Davis, J. M. (2010). *Young children and the environment: Early education for sustainability.* Port Melbourne, Australia: Cambridge University Press.

Epstein, J. L. (2001). *School, family, and community partnerships.* Boulder, CO: Westview Press.

Erikson, E. (1950). *Childhood and society.* New York, NY: W. W. Norton.

Flavell, J. H. (1977). *Cognitive development.* Englewood Cliffs, NJ: Prentice Hall.

Gilligan, C. (1982). *In a different voice.* Cambridge, MA: Harvard University Press.

Goldenberg, C. (2006). Improving achievement for English learners: What research tells us. *Education Week, 25*(43), 34–36.

Honig, A. (2010). *Little kids, big worries: Stress-busting tips for early childhood classrooms.* Baltimore, MD: Brooks Publishers.

Howes, C., & Richie, S. (2002). *A matter of trust: Connecting teachers and learners in the early childhood classroom.* New York, NY: Teachers College Press.

Kohlberg, L. (1981). *Essays on moral development, Vol. I: The philosophy of moral development.* San Francisco, CA: Harper & Row.

Krashen, S., & Terrell, T. D. (1983). *The natural approach: Language acquisition in the classroom.* London, England: Prentice Hall.

Melendez, W. R., Beck, V., & Fletcher, M. (2000). *Teaching social studies in early education.* Albany, NY: Delmar Thomson.

Mindes, G. (2005). Social studies in today's early childhood curricula. *Young Child NAEYC, 60*(5), 12–18

Piaget, J., & Inhelder, B. (1969). *The psychology of the child.* New York, NY: Basic Books.

Pianta, R., and Kraft-Sayre, M. (2003). *Successful kindergarten transition: Your guide to connecting children, families & schools.* Baltimore, MD: Brookes Publishing Co.

Pica, R. (2004). *Experiences in movement: Birth to age eight* (3rd ed.). Clifton Park, NY: Delmar Learning.

Vygotsky, L. (1978). *Mind in society: The development of higher psychological processes.* Cambridge, MA: Harvard University Press.

2 Planning Social Studies Activities with Young Children

Learning Outcomes

After reading this chapter you should be able to:

- Discuss the rationale for teaching young children social studies.
- Discuss how to engage families in planning curriculum.
- Explain various teaching strategies for planning social studies activities.
- Outline themes and projects that can be used throughout the year for children ages 0 through 8.

NCSS Standards

The National Council for the Social Studies (NCSS) has organized social studies into 10 broad interrelated holistic themes. Those addressed in this chapter are in bold:

1. **Culture**
2. Time, continuity, and change
3. **People, places, and environments**
4. **Individual development and identity**
5. Individuals, groups, and institutions
6. **Power, authority, and governance**
7. Production, distribution, and consumption
8. Science, technology, and society
9. Global connections
10. Civic ideals and practices (NCSS, 2005)

NAEYC Standards

The following NAEYC Standards for Professional Preparation Programs are addressed in this chapter:

Standard 4. Teaching and Learning

4b. Using developmentally effective approaches

4c. Understanding content knowledge in early education

DEVELOPMENTAL BASIS FOR TEACHING CHILDREN SOCIAL STUDIES

The National Council for the Social Studies (NCSS) affirms that "The aim of social studies is the promotion of civic competence—the knowledge, intellectual processes, and democratic dispositions required of students to be active and engaged participants of public life" (NCSS, 2005, p. 9). The NCSS emphasizes that "civic competence rests on this commitment to democratic values, and requires the abilities to use knowledge about one's community, nation, and world; apply inquiry processes, and employ skills of data collection and analysis, collaboration, decision-making and problem-solving" (NCSS, 2005, p. 9). For young children to understand their world, they must first begin to understand their place in it. This begins with learning about their surroundings, their families, their communities, and their connection to the outside world.

It is true that children are born into social studies. We are all social beings who belong to society. The way we live and relate to others in society starts early in life, between conception and eight years. During this time we learn our identity, and our perspective of others takes shape (Melendez, Beck, & Fletcher, 2000). At every stage of development—whether infant, toddler, preschool, or primary age—children look around and try to make sense of the social and physical environment. Through experiences in school, children are able to develop mainstream social behaviors and values (Mindes, 2005).

Teaching social studies and making the content relevant and appropriate depend on the age and stage of development and certainly on family and cultural background in both school and child care settings. People, places, and environment (NCSS, theme 3) for 3-year-olds might mean immediate family, whereas power, authority, and governance (NCSS, theme 6) for the third grader might mean the local mayor.

Carla Mestas/Pearson

"For each age group—infant, toddler, preschool and primary—social interactions form the foundation for building curriculum" (Mindes, 2005, p. 15).

Social studies content connects to children's lives and can be integrated with basic aspects of subject areas such as geography, history, and civics/political science. These areas can be connected to events and activities in children's daily lives and can be learned through projects, activities, field trips, and class discussions. (*Note:* Reading fiction and non-fiction as well as writing can be incorporated into each type of activity.)

Teachers can support children's understanding of democratic processes and attitudes in concrete, experiential ways. Furthermore, "young people who are knowledgeable, skillful, and committed to democracy are necessary to sustaining and improving our democratic way of life, and participating as members of a global community" (NCSS, 2005, p. 9). These skills are considered life-long learning opportunities that afford children the social opportunities necessary to find success as community members and employable adults.

CONSIDERATIONS IN PLANNING THE SOCIAL STUDIES CURRICULUM

Teachers will plan daily, weekly, and unit lessons that will promote achievement of social studies goals that students should reach at each level and stage of development.

Developmentally appropriate curriculum planning must address the following considerations:

1. Recognition of what children should know, understand, and be able to do physically, socially, emotionally, and cognitively.
2. Alignment with state/district/program standards.
3. Clearly defined goals that families can understand.
4. Use of a curriculum framework implemented through a variety of assessments to enable each child to reach the curriculum goals.
5. Use of children's interests in planning.
6. Experiences that include in-depth, focused, and challenging learning opportunities.

Backward Design

In using the Backward Design method, Wiggins and McTighe (2005) remind us that teachers are designers, crafting learning experiences, always mindful of our audiences. In an effort to make learning more effective, teachers should use standards and curriculum to outline what learners need to be able to know and do. Therefore, the three stages of Backward Design include

Stage 1: Identify desired results. What are the specific learning goals? What do we want children to know and understand at the end of this lesson? Is the content meaningful?

Stage 2: Determine acceptable evidence. What is it that children will do that will demonstrate their understanding of this particular content? Determining what will be meaningful evidence demonstrated at the close of the lesson will allow the teacher to plan more effectively.

Stage 3: Planning stage for learning experiences and instruction. Having worked through Stage 1 (establishing goals and appropriateness of information) and Stage 2 (identifying how children may demonstrate their understanding) allows teachers to plan the most appropriate instructional activities. In this stage, and with the knowledge gained in the first two stages, teachers will ask, What activities will equip students with the needed knowledge and skills? (Wiggins & McTighe, 2005).

An example illustrates how Backward Design works. Using the topic of scarcity and choice for second graders, we may first analyze what it is we want children to know and understand about the topic.

Stage 1: Concepts such as the meaning of limited resources, natural and human resources, needs taking precedence over wants, and the difference between adult spending and child spending would be key understandings for this age group.

Stage 2: Discuss the resource of water. Where does it come from when it comes out of the faucet? What is a drought? Examining the differences between dirt that has no water and dirt that is watered would allow for comparisons. How are children able to express and explain limited resources? How do they see people as resources? What do we do when we need someone of a certain expertise (e.g., a plumber, a doctor, a florist)? How can children demonstrate accessing human resources? Have children sort and classify needs and wants into a physical space or graphic organizer, while engaging in conversations about how they make the decision of where to place items. For instance, what are some differences between what adults spend their money on and what children spend their money on? Creating a book together or engaging in a sorting activity will help children carefully consider these groupings.

Stage 3: Now teachers will consider the activities they will implement to give children opportunities to create and demonstrate the evidence of understanding in Stage 1. Some activity ideas may include the following: While filling a watering can for plants in the room, the teacher may ask children where the water comes from. As the children share ideas, the teacher can guide them into a brainstorming session that will lead to understanding that water is a limited resource and is directly related to the amount of rainfall in each area. A walking tour around the building may allow children to see gutters along a roofline that funnel water into a rain barrel used in the school garden, or to examine a hose nozzle that keeps a hose from leaking, which prevents water from being wasted. The class could create a map or chart of water conservation in their town, including water towers and information from workers who protect the water systems.

Designing lessons in this way maximizes the successful outcome of expectations for learners while also providing activities that meet various levels of understanding.

APPLYING STANDARDS TO SOCIAL STUDIES PLANNING

Standards give classroom teachers an organizational basis for teaching children. They provide an overall plan that is based on professional expertise and deliberation. The National Council for the Social Studies (NCSS) is the national organization that provides curriculum guidelines around which teachers for young children can organize their social studies curriculum. According to the NCSS, these standards for both pre-service and in-service teachers "provide professional support for the advocacy of social studies; introduce them to the nature and purpose of social studies; allow the planning of instruction consistent with long-range purposes of social studies" (NCSS, 2010, p. 11).

NCSS can be accessed online at the organization's website, National Council for the Social Studies (socialstudies.org). Many states provide their own curriculum frameworks and standards. School districts typically provide a curriculum that has been adopted by the school board as well.

GOALS AND LEARNING OBJECTIVES

Preparation and planning in advance constitute one of the most important tasks for teaching social studies to young children. The first step in planning is to identify the standards required for the topic for the defined time period, which will help the teacher align the lesson to meet the goals. Goals are broad outlines of what the teacher wants the children to learn by the end of a unit, or by the end of several lessons.

Goals may include program goals that are established by the early childhood program or school district. These often set broad expectations for children but also provide a framework for planning and interacting at the school. One example of program goals in an early childhood program can be found in the "Integrated Approach Design" (Howard, 1975). The program components in this plan include integrity, openness, autonomy, and problem-solving. These are very appropriate for goal-setting in a social studies curriculum.

Recently, Marilou Hyson (2008) and others have written about learning approaches. Although these are not typically viewed as program goals, they certainly need to be considered in planning. Here are the approaches (Pennsylvania Early Learning Standards website):

- Initiative and curiosity
- Engagement and persistence
- Reasoning and problem-solving
- Flexibility, risk-taking, and responsibility
- Imagination, creativity, and invention

Early childhood programs in the United States do not have one universal form or format for lesson planning. However, *intentionality* has become a commonly used phrase in many childcare, preschool, and kindergarten programs. Intentionality in planning expresses the understanding that the teacher has planned specifically for the children in the class and also for the content. Balancing these two factors can be challenging when planning for group times, small groups, learning centers, and outside play.

Intentionality includes selecting songs and books that introduce an aspect of social studies that the teacher has chosen. Examples include books or stories about social situations, families, or wants and needs. In learning centers, intentionality includes infusing props that provide support for scaffolding social studies ideas. Use of props about communities (farms, cities, and so on) is a powerful way to introduce social studies concepts with young children through play.

Use of Objectives

Another way to plan involves highlighting objectives for each lesson or activity from the goals. Unlike broad program goals, objectives are designed to be measurable and specific (Figure 2.1). They determine what the assessment will be like. Objectives and assessment must be directly aligned and remain so throughout the lesson.

Bloom's Taxonomy

Before discussing yearly planning, units, and weekly and daily planning for social studies, it is important to understand more about objectives. Bloom's taxonomy (1956) provides a hierarchy of educational objectives that is divided into three domains; *cognitive, affective,* and *psychomotor* (Figures 2.2 and 2.3). Each of the domains is subdivided into levels

Figure 2.1
Examples of Goals and Objectives.

Examples of Kindergarten Standards, Goals, and Objectives

Standard 5.1: Principles and Documents of Government

Goals

A. Identify the visible roles that government serves.
B. Identify the purposes of rules and laws.

Objectives Examples

The learner will:

- **Discuss** how rules help society and why rules are in place.
- **Identify** rules in school related to fire drills, lunch, walking in the halls, bus safety, classroom, playground, and so on.
- **Explain** what happens when rules are broken.
- **Suggest** several rules that could make the classroom or the school a better place to work and play.
- **Demonstrate** understanding the need to follow classroom and school procedures.

Figure 2.2
Bloom's Taxonomy, Original and Revised.

Lorin Anderson, a former student of Bloom, revisited the cognitive domain in the learning taxonomy in the mid-1990s and made some changes, with perhaps the two most prominent ones being (1) a change in the names in the six categories from noun to verb forms, and (2) a slight rearrangement of them (Pohl, 2000). This new taxonomy reflects a more active form of thinking and is perhaps more accurate.

Original Domain	Revised Domain
Evaluation	Creating
Synthesis	Evaluating
Analysis	Analyzing
Application	Applying
Comprehension	Understanding
Knowledge	Remembering

Figure 2.3
The Three Domains.

Cognitive Domain (Knowledge)	Affective Domain (Attitude)	Psychomotor Domain (Skill)
1. Knowledge	1. Receiving	1. Perception
2. Comprehension	2. Responding	2. Set
3. Application	3. Valuing	3. Guided response
4. Analysis	4. Organization	4. Mechanism
5. Synthesis	5. Internalizing values (characterization)	5. Complex overt response
6. Evaluation		6. Adaptation
		7. Origination

ranging from the simplest to the highest levels of knowledge. These levels are helpful when deciding on what level of objective the teacher wants and needs to teach.

Social studies objectives tend to revolve around **cognitive** and **affective** domains. Cognitive objectives measure knowledge outcomes (Figure 2.4), whereas affective objectives measure emotional and social

Figure 2.4
Cognitive Learning Objective Verbs and Sample Product.

Level of Complexity	Meaning	Examples of Verbs to Use in Objectives	Sample Product
Remember (knowledge)	Recollection, recognition of information	Choose, name, define, record, describe, repeat, list, select, label, memorize, match	Create concept maps and Venn diagrams; name states
Understand (comprehension)	Understanding, interpretation, extrapolation of information	Describe, explain, discuss, identify, demonstrate, illustrate, extend, interpret, rewrite, summarize	Write a description of the directions you use to get to school; draw an accompanying map; design a compass rose
Apply	Using information, concept in new situations	Apply, illustrate, make, explain, use, demonstrate, interpret, solve, dramatize	Dramatize a historical event after reading a story about the event; dress as a character
Analyze	Breaking down information into parts	Classify, categorize, analyze, compare, contrast, diagram, examine, criticize, investigate	Develop a graph of methods classmates use to get to school; tally results to compare data
Evaluate (synthesis)	Developing and applying standards for making judgments	Judge, criticize, defend, estimate, compare	Develop and use criteria (rubric) to review classmates' social studies projects
Create (synthesis)	Developing new product and ideas using learned information	Compose, design, create, develop, formulate, make, hypothesize, plan, produce, construct	Write own song, skit, or story; paint a historical event or figure

Figure 2.5
Tic-Tac-Toe Activity.

Draw a detailed map of the school (Evaluation/Creating level)	State five ways to solve a disagreement (Knowledge/ Remembering level)	Create demographic data from classmates and create a data table (Synthesis/Evaluating level)
Define key words from the social studies unit (Knowledge/ Remembering level)	Review the concepts in the social studies unit (Comprehension/ Understanding level)	Use some of the ideas in the social studies community story to write your own (Application /Applying level)
Analyze and edit your partner's draft of a social studies report and then exchange (Analysis/Analyzing level)	Develop a game based on social studies concepts from this unit (Evaluation/Creating level)	Organize a timeline from memory (Synthesis/Evaluating level)

outcomes (Bloom, 1984). The third is **psychomotor,** which measures physical movement, coordination, and the use of motor skills, including sensory cues, to guide motor activity.

An Example of How to Implement Bloom's Taxonomy in a Social Studies Lesson

Figure 2.5 presents an example of how to incorporate a variety of strategies that include each of Bloom's taxonomy categories.

The benefit of teaching with these types of activities is that they allow children to develop and use differing levels of understanding in a social studies curriculum.

YEARLY, WEEKLY, AND LESSON PLANNING

Integrating children's needs, interests, and abilities with the curriculum goals and objectives promotes retention of the content. The outcome of the plan ends up being both content-driven and child-centered. By planning from an overarching set of goals and objectives, which is also informed by the children's interests, teachers are more prepared to make important connections. When the main idea of the planning is completed, time and focus can be specifically tailored to individuals or groups of children.

Yearly Planning

It is important to look at material the teacher needs to cover throughout the year. Planning in advance for the year gives the teacher an opportunity to look carefully at developmentally appropriate practices through activities that are meaningful for children and allow them to connect to their social surroundings. The state standards and NSCSS standards form the basis for writing such plans. These documents provide information and topics that are developmentally appropriate for the grade level being taught. The teacher is then able to gain an overview of the skills and concepts needed for the level of attainment expected both before and after the present grade level. This process also presents the opportunity to organize topics and align them to other subjects. Cross-curricular planning and thematic units are discussed below.

Weekly Planning

It is common to find teachers who do not plan for the year. They go week by week, making decisions considerably close to when they need to present the lesson. The problem with this kind of planning is that it leaves no room for eventualities. By mapping out the requirements for the year, teachers are better able to plan meaningful lessons and not feel rushed in their implementation. This kind of proactive planning does not rule out the flexibility of adjusting plans at the last minute; it is always beneficial to make the most of spontaneous opportunities and to pay close attention to situations that children find interesting and exciting. These kinds of changes or add-ons should always complement the core, planned lesson.

The best way to address yearly planning is to list the standards required by the state and then countercheck if they are similar to those of NSSC. The option is then available to add those that may not appear in the state standards. Because the standards have been arranged in the order in which they can be logically taught, the teacher then simply needs to align them against a particular month in the year to maximize opportunities for the students.

Unit and Lesson Planning

Unit plans are a series of lesson plans that deal with one topic, which may be taught for one week or even up to a month. Breaking down the lessons allows for purposeful action and for making the most of time by both balancing depth in the lesson and appropriately linking it to the next course of learning (Figure 2.6). Defined as *Scope and Sequence*, such purpose in planning maximizes learning opportunities. Lesson plans can then be prepared based on the unit concepts that the students must know. Units and lesson plans become easier to prepare once yearly plans have been completed. To make sure that all important aspects are covered and included in the lesson, consider the following:

1. National, state, and district standards: Is this concept included in these standards?

2. Objectives: What do the students need to know and do (including higher level thinking like Bloom's)?

3. Product/assessment: How will the students demonstrate what they know?

4. Prior knowledge: What do the students already know?

5. Lesson presentation through differentiation: In what developmentally appropriate ways will the lesson be presented to address all students' learning needs?

6. Process: What materials and activities will be used in teaching and practicing the skills required?

7. Lesson sequence: Are the timeline and instructional sequence, which are critical to students' abilities to make connections, taken into consideration?

8. Culturally responsive teaching considerations: Does the lesson address diversity, equity, collaboration, diverse voices, culture, and families? (It is necessary to approach all lessons with anti-bias significance; anti-bias teaching is extensively addressed in Chapter 8.)

Figure 2.6
Sample Lesson Plan Format.

Weekly Plan:	
Date:_____	
Standards:	
Approaches:	Activities:
Initiative:	
Curiosity:	
Reasoning:	
Invention:	
Meeting Special Needs:	
Assessment(s):	
Differentiation:	
Family Engagement:	

THE ROLES OF CHILDREN AND FAMILIES IN PLANNING

Involving Children in Planning

Both the teacher and children benefit when they plan together. Teachers benefit because children who have been involved in planning are more motivated to learn, often take responsibility for their learning, and are able to self-assess based on the learning goals discussed with them. Children benefit because they feel empowered. Intentional planning maintains standards and objectives while taking into consideration children's interests. It allows children to share in the conversation about what they would like to learn, such as choice of centers and projects. When planning, consider the following:

- Play: Where? Who? What?
- Things they would like to learn more about
- Places they would like to visit for a field trip

The K-W-L chart is one tool that can be formally used to involve children in learning.

K—what they *know* about the topic or concept; understanding their prior knowledge is key to planning the lesson

W—what they *want* to learn about the topic

L—what they *learned* about the concept

Opportunities to involve children in planning are plentiful. These opportunities usually come about during the morning meeting, as the class may be sharing current events, topics of interest, or general problem-solving and questions.

Engaging Families in Planning

Families are, and always should be, an integral part of teaching young children. They play an important role in implementing curriculum and supporting new understandings for early learners. Especially in regard to culturally responsive teaching, families play a key part in the process. Seeking information from families and caregivers is useful in the following ways:

1. Families may have ideas that may be useful for your lessons.
2. Families become a source that one may use to tailor the curriculum to the unique needs of a group of children.

3. Teachers may include family preferences and ideas in the curriculum, making the curriculum relevant to students' lives.

4. It helps demonstrate to families that their ideas are valued.

5. It gives families the opportunity to get directly involved in the classroom.

   To gather information from families, the following methods may be used:

1. Collect information through email, a school or personal website, blogs, social media, as well as traditional phone calls and notes. In this electronic era, there are many additional ways to share information.

2. Get to know families through face-to-face meetings. These can take place by appointment, on back-to-school nights, at open houses, during parent-teacher conferences, and in some cases during drop-off and pick-up times.

3. Send a simple questionnaire home with the children to give families opportunities to express ideas and goals as well as traditions and celebrations they would like to share.

Note: Below are examples of special considerations for adaption to family needs:

• Awareness that not all families have access to or use email

• Awareness that not all families can come to the school due to work schedules, transportation, health issues, past history with that school or program, and so on

INTEGRATING SOCIAL STUDIES INTO OTHER CURRICULUM AREAS

Many teachers are frustrated by the fact that they do not have enough time in the schedule to teach social studies. Conversely, they are aware of the importance of teaching social studies. Integrating social studies into other curriculum areas has specific advantages:

1. It provides an interesting interdisciplinary way of teaching social studies.

2. It allows children to look at content and experiences from a variety of perspectives.

3. It helps portray the reality of life as an integrated experience.

Life is not compartmentalized. Things work together. We live in an environment that is affected by past, present, and future, for example. Time must be measured and counted. Thus, history and math come together at that point. As students learn social studies through other subject areas such as math, language, arts, and music, their view of the world becomes more realistic and connected.

Teachers can plan curriculum experiences that integrate children's learning across the subject areas. Such areas include language, literacy, mathematics, social studies, science, art, music, physical education, and health.

APPROPRIATE TEACHING STRATEGIES

Thematic Units

One way of teaching social studies is by integrating the topics with other subject areas through the use of themes. A theme can be a topic or idea that draws a number of relevant concepts from a variety of subject areas. Thematic units are organized to reflect the fact that areas of learning or knowledge are connected. Building on the ideas, experiences and words with which children are already familiar helps deepen their understanding. Expanding on their interests by listening to thoughts is an effective way to plan. Thus thematic units bring learning ideas together so children can see the connection between concepts and skills. Developmentally appropriate practices therefore encourage an integrated planning and teaching approach.

Elements of Thematic Teaching

Thematic teaching makes it possible for teachers to build interesting, challenging, and meaningful curriculum. Thematic units allow teachers to find and build on student interest. Teachers are then able to plan a developmentally appropriate curriculum at a challenging level and in ways that help children find meaning.

Following are steps the teacher can take for a successful thematic unit outcome:

1. **Choose a theme:** When choosing a theme, consider the recommended standards and the areas that are of interest to the children for that grade level. Base each unit on a specific learning outcome. For example, when building a unit, start from a topic such as the rainforest, democracy, or money. The teacher's

interest and knowledge should be taken into consideration. This helps the teacher clarify what he/she already knows, and what areas he/she has to learn about in order to teach the topic in an accurate and meaningful way.

2. **Break down the topics:** Using a simple graphic organizer such as a web or concept map, break down the topic into different subject areas so that there is a visual representation of the topics. This adds clarity and shows the connections between subject areas. Here is an opportunity for students to contribute to topics by sharing their areas of interest. It also helps to make sure there are no duplications of topics within the same subject area. See Figure 2.7.

Figure 2.7
Themes of Interest for Young Children.

Preschool, Kindergarten, and Primary Ages

- Places people live
- Toys and games
- Families
- Friends
- Our community
- Food we eat
- Alike and different
- Holidays and celebrations
- Five senses
- Music
- Heroes and "sheroes"
- Weather
- Animals
- Dance and movement
- Pets
- My body
- Colors
- Community Helpers
- Maps

3. **Plan for resources:** After the topics have been related to subject matter, select materials and resources that are available in order to implement the thematic unit. Successful thematic learning leans heavily on the use of a variety of resource materials, such as blocks, books, dolls, maps, artifacts, pictures, and costumes. Consider using human resources such as colleagues, parents, families, community, and technology in the form of Internet and multimedia.

4. **Assessment:** Plan for a variety of assessments in advance by putting together an assessment plan. This will help guide the lesson, starting with a pre-assessment such as a KWL (verbal or otherwise, depending on the children's age). Once the teacher has a grasp of what students know about a given topic, the daily planning takes on a more targeted dimension. The teacher can build on what students already know and focus on what they don't know or are not familiar with. The advantage of this approach is that more time can then be spent on unfamiliar areas. Additionally, ongoing assessment of what the students have accomplished must take place. Use of children's work, anecdotal records, checklists, and photographs helps to track the course of the theme being studied (Melendez et al., 2000). Melendez et al. (2000) suggest that a culminating experience, such as another concept map, should be ongoing in order to demonstrate the progress achieved. Another option is to build on the original concept map. As additional information is added to an original concept map, it should be written in a different color so the class can see at a glance the new information they have gathered.

Themes in Preschool

During the preschool years, social studies instruction is most often related to social competence.

Children's knowledge of social studies builds on and is integrated with the development of social skills which are taught and learned through everyday events in the classroom. Examples include supporting children's social skill development in morning meetings, helping to set classroom procedures and giving suggestions for the smooth functioning of the classroom community. This builds competence and confidence in working in a group.

Organizing and planning well-run learning centers allows teacher the opportunity to watch children interacting with others. Teachers can also expand and engage to add to understandings of social concepts. Elena Bodrova and Deborah Leong (2003) have discovered through their research that play often produces a greater amount of "executive functioning" and "self-regulation." This may at first seem counterintuitive until children at play are observed. During play times, children must organize themselves, their time, and the objects with which they want to play. This leads to an increased ability to stay organized. Play also benefits the growth of self-regulation by allowing children to practice roles. This practicing of roles has inherent rules embedded in the play that structure the process naturally but lead to greater internal control, while also building key vocabulary and negotiation skills.

Themes in Kindergarten

For kindergarten children, themes tied to their interests are particularly engaging. As they begin to work together toward common goals, they are building important social and language skills. Having a common goal, whether problem-solving or creating a project, encourages children to develop deeper and more critical thinking. Experience using informal tools and inventive spelling techniques through authentic hands-on experiences eases children into the more complex skills they will use later on.

Strategies for Primary Grades

Themes can include moving from informal to formal measurement in math, because at this age they are developing an understanding of addition, subtraction, whole numbers, geometry shapes, base-ten numeration system and place-value, measurements, multiplication, division, fractions concepts, and properties of two-dimensional shapes. In literacy they continue to develop phonemic awareness and print, which means they begin to use conventional spelling and writing mechanics. Thus, writing stories, making observations, reading books and copying words, drawing maps, and constructing models all become part of the thematic units. The use of technology also becomes an important learning tool at this age and is easily woven into thematic learning.

Project Approach

The creation of projects is another strategy for teaching children social studies. Children are able to study topics in their area of interest for an extended period. Project topics can combine the teacher's interest and the student's interest. It can be group work or individual. Several or all children could have the same interest and work on it individually. "The teacher's role is to facilitate by providing resources and materials and support children's interests and help organize their interests into viable investigations" (Melendez et al., 2000, p. 95).

Depending on the age and abilities of the class, examples of projects may include, for example, different types of houses, mapping of the school or local community, and locating active volcanoes on a web search and identifying the country. Topics can be found in a variety of sources:

1. The curriculum
2. Suggestions from children based on their experiences
3. The local community
4. Current events
5. Different places in the local community, state, region, world
6. Families (traditions, countries of origin, and so on)

Preschool Years

Projects can be integrated in various activities of the day, such as dramatic play, during which the teacher can provide materials such as blocks, books, writing materials, manipulatives, dramatic play props, art, and modeling materials that are relevant to the project of their interest. The daily schedule can encourage social learning by including many opportunities for conversation, play and negotiation. Projects can be simple or complex, a one-time attempt, or something created over time.

Kindergarten

Projects can be integrated during center time, where children will find resources relevant to the project. At this age children can be encouraged to work in small groups and at learning centers. With a variety of teaching strategies, such as specific feedback, encouragement, the modeling of skills and individualized scaffolding, teachers can guide children to learning information through projects and other methods. At this age their work can be represented in the form of drawing, writing, dictating, and making charts. The teacher is able to use these opportunities to deepen children's learning. Basic aspects of geography, history, and civics/political science can be introduced. Creating a classroom store complete with signage, pretend money, supplies, job opportunities, and authentic materials is one example of a project.

Rotating accessories through the block center can introduce different social studies concepts (floor maps of different land masses such as lakes, beaches, or hills/community scenes/traffic signs). Floor maps can be made easily with a vinyl tablecloth and a permanent marker, or they may be purchased from a variety of early childhood product companies such as Constructive Playthings or Lakeshore. Young children appreciate the opportunity to have ongoing projects, and it can be difficult for them to stop when "time is up." Teachers should consider allowing children to save projects (if space allows) and to continue with them at the next available time. This is important in helping children to sustain high levels of interest and more complex thinking.

Primary Grades

Organizing projects in primary grades may take more deliberate planning and executing to make it age-appropriate and challenging. Children at this stage may be able to concentrate and focus for a sustained amount of time. They are often more aware of time as well. The teacher can direct them to take time to work on their projects without interruption or the need to break. However, because concentration is still developing, some children will not be able to concentrate for longer periods of time. It is helpful to suggest a different activity to allow for variety that individual children may need. Aspects of geography, history, economics and civics/political science are stepped up a level. A project of producing a class newsletter, to which children contribute in a variety of ways, is one possibility. Newsletters can be electronic or hard-copy.

Asking students a series of questions allows the teacher to assess prior knowledge and levels of interest and guides the entire class regarding what everyone would like to know about the topic under discussion. Here are examples of questions related to the topic of pets:

* What animals can be pets? (What makes an animal a pet?)
* What are some pets we keep at home?
* What animals are not considered pets?
* How do we take care of pets?
* Where do we get pets?
* What do we do when our pets are sick?
* How do we feed our pets?

- When do we feed our pets?
- What kind of foods do we feed our pets?
- Where do we take our pets for walks?
- Do all pets go for walks?
- How are pets similar or different?
- What are my favorite pets?
- What do I like about my pet?
- Does everyone have a pet?

This structure guides the lesson and maximizes learning and investigative time while steering the lesson in a meaningful direction. Teachers must also incorporate play into lessons. The next step may be looking for appropriate books, materials, and play themes. Connecting real ideas to play experiences allows children to master material, recall experiences, and engage in the scaffolding of learning at the next level. The play environment is most conducive to learning, as children are likely to be relaxed and inquisitive and to view themselves as capable learners.

Learning Centers and Dramatic Play

Another effective teaching strategy involves play. Play is the center of development for a child. Opportunities for play are an essential part of many things that children do during their day. Materials and props are adequately placed so that children are able to reflect on and recreate their experiences. Play is an important part of the curriculum and includes board games, circle games, building blocks, puzzles, and outdoor play (Cooper & Dever, 2001; Levin, 2000).

Drama is combining play with content. Teachers can organize dramatic play by preparing the environment for such learning; this is accomplished by establishing learning interest centers and organized topics for primary age children. Learning centers provide children with an opportunity for learning while they are playing only that which the center themes have been organized to reflect. Thus, learning centers can be defined as areas in the classroom where students go to learn a specific topic. Learning centers are organized in a way that each center represents one idea, concept, or part of a topic. The point is that learning centers, overall, should offer a range of learning ideas. Social studies centers reflecting a particular theme are a place where children can go and spend extended periods of time Learning centers give

Dramatic play learning centers.

children opportunities to make their own discoveries and to investigate their own interests, as well as the interests of others. For primary age children, learning centers are more structured, more defined in their lesson purpose. Directions may require that they complete a variety of assessments.

Setting Up Learning Centers

As with any content, social studies learning centers must be organized to reflect the theme and topic selected by the teacher. Even though children have the freedom to select their activities, there must be organization. Consideration should be given to the following in order to create and carry out successful centers:

1. Students' developmental needs, such as ability, culture and family, community, interests
2. Appropriate theme (See Figure 2.8 for theme ideas.)
3. Topic relevant to the theme
4. Objectives, first general and then specific
5. Relevant materials that go with the topic

Figure 2.8
Learning Centers: Names and Types.

Learning centers have many names	Types of learning centers
Learning area	Reference
Learning station	Travel
Interest area	What's new?
Center	Neighborhood/Community
	Before and now
	Sand and water
	Blocks
	Dramatic play
	Special (topical)
	Library
	Writing
	Art
	Drawing and painting
	Construction
	Sewing and weaving
	Woodworking
	Cutting and pasting
	Modeling

Adapted from Melendez et al., 2000; Seefeldt et al., 2010.

6. Age-appropriate directions (teacher must model), a preview before the project begins, visual direction charts that may be added to the space, a review after center time

7. A plan for assessment

Melendez et al. (2000) say that "Clarity about a center's purposes guides teachers in what to observe as children respond and react to materials. Through informed observations, teachers monitor the progress achieved, both individually and as a group" (Melendez et al., 2000, pp. 97–98).

Arts and Creative Expression

Art and creative expression go hand in hand with social studies. Art can be included as a way of expressing any part of a social studies topic.

Art and creative expressive forms include dramatic play, music, dance, and visual arts. Gross and fine motor skill development must be considered with regard to how much children are capable of doing. Activities need to be monitored with an understanding of skill level expectations so children do not become frustrated in their attempts to participate. Children should be allowed to explore art often and in various ways.

Incorporating Art in Preschool and Kindergarten

Ways to include art is to display it in the classroom, even allowing children to determine the location and arrangement; to arrange for demonstrations and visits from guest artists; and to visit museums and other public displays of art both in person and virtually. Students should be given opportunities to explore various art media and freely use them to demonstrate and expand their ideas. Plan art experiences to support children's expression of their own ideas about the world and of their own illustrations.

Incorporating Art in Primary Grades

Children in this age range are able to get involved in more complex tasks and need to be given the materials and time to do so. Small projects such as making picture books and story boards or making videos can incorporate various social studies themes. Studying famous artists, their origins and place in history, and specialized media can be a meaningful social studies lesson for children. Ultimately, the focus is on the process rather than on a product.

Music

A variety of music genres can be appropriately integrated into all subject areas, social studies included. It can bring the child's culture into the classroom. For example, cultural songs can be used, as well as songs about kindness and working together; instruments from different parts of the world may be explored; and traditions connected to the music may be highlighted. Throughout the day, songs can be used for transition times; at the same time, the words may even express specific values. It is often through songs that children learn about the world around them, whether connecting to each other or singing about animals, or letters and numbers—the possibilities are endless—and songs are typically of high interest, especially when associated with movement. As children get older, they begin to connect even more with the contemporary music of their culture and find a mutual interest with peers who like the same music.

Role-Playing, Puppets

Most children love to role-play. Through role-playing activities, children strengthen problem-solving skills as they self-talk and practice in a safe environment. Vygotsky referenced self-talk as a stage of learning in which children talk to themselves and talk through the steps of problem-solving. Role-play can be encouraged during time spent at various centers or as a group when children are assigned a character. Teachers should never insist that children participate in role-playing; they should always be allowed to simply watch others. After watching, most children are eager to join in, but there will still be a few who do not feel comfortable acting out different scenarios, and that should be all right in the safe environment of a caring classroom. For young children, social studies–related topics such as friendship, sharing, negotiating, fairness, and empathy can be practiced during role-playing. These are behaviors to be encouraged both in class and at home. Primary age children are able to role-play by making up their own words and scenarios or even memorizing a few words from a familiar scenario (for example, *The Three Little Pigs*).

Puppets are great tools for role-playing. For example, the teacher can be the puppet character talking to the child, or the children can be the puppet handlers. Puppets need to be accessible at different centers so that children can role-play on their own. Children will mimic the teacher; thus providing the puppets will aid in the modeled learning process. Both role-play and puppets allow children to explore feelings in a safe environment free of the emotionally charged feelings they may face during a peer encounter. The following are ways in which children can portray concepts through dramatization: dress up and role-play, storytelling, song and dance, simulation, interviews, advertisement, and short play.

Games

Games are an integral part of socialization for children. Most enjoy playing together in both the free play of spontaneous games and organized games. The teacher will be able to involve children in games that are related to social studies. Guessing games, board games for primary age children, and games made on the computer with social studies themes are all possibilities. All encourage turn-taking and engaging with peers.

Figure 2.9
Healthy and Developmentally Appropriate Access to Technology and Screen Media.

Age (years)	Time Limit for Technology and Screen Media Usage
0 – 2	0 media and screen time
2 and above	1–2 hours in general
2 – 5	30 minutes or less, half-day program
	1 hour or less, full-day program

Adapted from recommendations by The American Academy of Pediatrics, 2009, 2010, 2011a, 2011b; the White House Task Force on Childhood Obesity, 2010; Funk, Brouwer, Curtiss, & Mc-Broom, 2009; Campaign for a Commercial-Free Childhood, 2010; Birch, Parker, & Burns, 2011; and Institute of Medicine of the National Academies, 2011.)

Technology and Interactive Media in the Classroom

Technology is now an integral part of many classrooms. For example, the computer with its access to the Internet has become accessible to many students, if not at school then at home. It is "important to apply principles of development and learning when considering the use of technology and new media" (NAEYC & Fred Rogers Center, 2012, p. 1) (Figure 2.9). In making decisions to use media, it is important to understand the difference between various media and what should be used in the classroom. Figure 2.10 lists some types of interactive and

Figure 2.10
Types of Interactive and Noninteractive Media.

Interactive Media	Noninteractive Media
Digital and analog materials	- Certain television programs
- Software programs	- Videos, DVDs
- Applications (apps)	- Streaming media
- Broadcast and streaming media	
- Some children's television programming	
- E-books	
- Internet	
- Other forms of content designed to facilitate active and creative use by young children	
- Content that encourage social engagement	

Adapted from NAEYC & Fred Rogers Center for Early Learning and Children's Media Joint Statement (2012). Technology and Interactive Media as Tools in Early Childhood Programs Serving Children from Birth through Age 8. http://www.naeyc.org/files/naeyc/file/positions/PS_technology_WEB2.pdf

noninteractive media. NAEYC & Fred Rogers Center for Early Learning and Children's Media (2012) emphasizes that "Non-interactive media can lead to passive viewing and overexposure to screen time for young children and are not substitutes for interactive and engaging uses of digital media or for interactions with adults and other children" (p. 2).

There are programs in which children can directly use the computer to listen, read, and interact with pictures and information, and there are others that integrate technology more subtly. The Internet has become an expansive resource for almost anything in the classroom. It can provide visual experiences for children who otherwise may not be exposed to the topic at hand. Various technologies can be used for purposes such as teaching content, assessing learning, creating products, and engaging learners. The SMART Board provides direct access and at the same time projected access to the Internet.

For social studies this can mean "traveling" to different parts of the world. Video can also be used for video conferencing, Skype, and participating in webinars with other people locally and beyond. Children can listen to social studies–related themes and then create their own videos. Using story boards for social studies themes, students can record videos to present and report to others. The Internet carries pictures and video images of people, animals, land forms, and remote locations, all of which support themes in social studies.

Video Productions

Video productions represent an interesting way to engage children in learning social studies. Videos can be used to learn social studies in numerous ways. Using a digital video camera, students can document and interpret historical topics. Through video productions students are able to work together as a group and also become involved with the community, such as through interviews (NCSS, themes 2, 3, 4, and 5). Short video productions are often used to teach new material or review information. However, guidelines listed for high-quality media should be evaluated for age appropriateness, quality of content (including diversity), and viewing time.

Television

Television has use in the classroom, but care must be taken to make sure that what children are watching contributes to their learning. DVDs and videos normally target specific topics that have been recorded. In social studies a plethora of appropriate topics can be viewed through TV. Current events constitute a very important aspect of social studies. Current events can be used to launch many topics and make them personal and relevant to children's lives (environmental studies, poverty, diseases, geographical concepts, economics, and so on). The teacher can record specific news items and documentaries. National Geographic features and clips from shows like "Where in the world is Carmen Sandiego?" can be viewed this way or via the Internet (NCSS themes 2, 3, 4, and 5).

iPads

Just like the computer, iPads are a tool that can greatly enhance the use of technology for teaching social studies. Certain characteristics of the iPad make it a versatile tool: size, rich graphics, an intuitive touch screen, and fast processing speed. The fact that it is possible to use applications that allow for creativity and critical thinking is important. Students can use their iPads for homework, blogging, reading assignments, and projects. Even with young children, apps can prove useful; for example, the iTunes website (itunes.apple.com) offers some apps through which toddlers and preschool children can learn about modes of transportation such as trucks and cars.

It is the teacher's job to research various resources before using them with the students. Caution must be taken here. Opinions vary as to whether technology impacts achievement, especially as new technology is rolled out and finds its way into the classroom. The teacher must consider how much technology to use and whether it will enhance student learning. Furthermore, teachers must evaluate apps before using them. The following are factors teachers must take into consideration when choosing apps for children:

- Does the app meet the content, curriculum, and standards requirements?
- Does the app have a high level of sound and image quality?
- How long does the app run and is it age-appropriate?
- "How interactive is the activity?" (Geist, 2014)—that is, does it promote critical thinking and problem-solving?

See the Resources section for a list of apps and other Internet resources.

Other Instructional Strategies for Teaching Social Studies

Group Discussions

Group discussions are a necessity in the classroom. This is where brainstorming takes place for choosing topics that children are interested in. Group discussion is a great way to talk about information that children are already learning and new knowledge they are beginning to process. Group discussion is also useful as a starting point to get children thinking about a topic and establishing ideas of what they want to do for their projects. Apart from discussing the topic, children get to learn other skills, such as listening to others, respecting others' opinions, and understanding different perspectives. It is an opportunity for the teacher to present and practice discussion rules. Children get to share their experiences of topics and points of curiosity. Much learning takes place during discussions. Planned discussion as well as spontaneous discussions should be frequent events in the classroom.

Field Trips

Field trips provide the actualization of concepts that have been learned in the classroom, often used as culminating activities. Children learn

Lisa Cline

by seeing and experiencing things. Therefore, field trips are significant in the learning process. Places to visit, such as local museums, senior centers, community workplaces, arboretums, farms, community stores, fire stations, and town libraries, offer children wonderful extensions to their studies in the classrooms. For every social studies concept being taught, it is likely that children can go on a field trip—if not to the actual place where the concept originated, then at least to a place where that information is displayed, such as a museum. Opportunities for field trips abound, and sometimes teachers simply need to be creative. Field trips do not need to cost much money. Parents can be an enormous help with ideas, supervision, and planning. The teacher should make major decisions about field trips very early in planning (see Figure 2.11) and include them in the yearly calendar. Virtual field trips via the Internet are a cost-saving back-up but do not replace an actual visit. Use the *Selected Predeveloped Virtual Field Trip Sites* table from *Making and Taking Virtual Field Trips in Pre-K and the Primary Grades* by Dennis J. Kirchen at the naeyc.org website.

Figure 2.11
Planning Guide for the Field Trip.

Planning and Executing a Field Trip	
Advance planning:	**On the day of the trip:**
1. Plan a year ahead.	12. Hold a class meeting to remind students of your expectations for their learning and behavior. For primary age children, provide written information for what they should not miss; use key words for young children.
2. Address a specific objective for the field trip.	
3. Visit the field trip area before you take the children there. This will help you with planning for what you need.	
4. Seek administrative approval by providing a proposal.	13. Have all the children use the rest room before you leave.
5. Write to parents detailing the trip. Send permission slips to be returned a week before the trip.	14. Go over your "to do" list.
6. Confirm your chaperones.	**After the trip:**
7. Remind students to dress comfortably, shoes and all.	15. Allow students to share their observations and reactions to the field trip.
8. Assign one chaperone to a small group of children.	16. Guide them through completing the assignment.
9. Prepare name tags.	**Field trip evaluation:**
10. Leave copies of permission slips at school, and carry originals with you on the trip.	17. Find out if students met learning objectives and expectations.
11. Prepare and take along an emergency kit.	18. What went well? What did not go well? What could you change on future trips?
	19. What was student feedback?

LEARNING PREFERENCES AND DIFFERENTIATION

Learning Preferences

Children learn in different ways. These learning differences impact how students learn and the way they should be taught (see Figure 2.12 for suggested learning strategies). Students differ in the following ways: experience, culture, language, gender, interests, readiness to learn, modes of learning, speed of learning, support systems for learning, self-awareness as a learner, confidence as a learner, and independence as a learner.

Differentiation

Tomlinson and Imbeau (2010) define and describe the key elements of differentiation as the responsibility of teachers to make sure that all children have a chance to learn content in the best way possible. The classroom practice of differentiation requires that the three curriculum areas of content, process, and product (which are based on

Figure 2.12
Learning Strategies.

Additional Learning Strategies

1. Graphic organizers, semantic maps
2. Models, manipulatives
3. Language tools—metaphors, analogies, and similes
4. Mnemonic devices
5. Movement
6. Cooperative learning
7. Storytelling
8. Writing and journals
9. Interactive bulletin boards
10. Exhibits
11. Service-learning
12. Story boards
13. Guest speakers
14. Case studies
15. Archeological digs

three categories of student need and variance—readiness, interest, and learning profile) must be modified.

- Content: the knowledge, understanding, and skills teachers want students to learn.
- Process: how the student comes to understand or make sense of the content through sense-making activities.
- Product: how students demonstrate what they have come to know, understand, and are able to do after an extended period of learning presented through authentic assessments.
- Learner need and variance are based on

  - Readiness: a student's current level of knowledge, understanding, and skills. High-quality teaching should positively impact the condition of readiness.
  - Interest: that which engages, motivates, and involves students.
  - Learning profile: the ways students prefer to learn, explore, or express content; shaped by four elements—learning style, intelligence preference, gender, culture (Tomlinson & Imbeau, 2010).

ACCOMMODATIONS FOR CHILDREN WITH DIVERSE NEEDS

In planning the social studies curriculum, accommodations must be made for children with diverse needs. Teaching social studies to young children must incorporate adaptations for English language learners (ELL) (Figure 2.13) and adaptations for children with special needs (Figure 2.14).

HOME/SCHOOL CONNECTION

Some strategies require more home/school connection than others. For example, projects, field trips, centers, guests, and writing letters and making phone calls will make it necessary to keep parents informed and at the same time solicit their involvement. Always find ways to involve parents: asking a parent to come and share a game with the class, read a favorite story, share a family tradition, cook, or simply save recyclables to send in for a future project can bring the richness of family to a classroom community.

Figure 2.13
Adaptations for ELL.

Adaptations for English Language Learners

Resource accessibility is vital for hands-on social studies activities. Resources should be at the level where children can reach them and also labeled so that children who are ELL can find and access what they need. Allowing children a choice of centers, working individually or in a group, is an option all children should have.

Provide big letters and labeled items for children learning a new language. Allow children to use pictures and drawings if they cannot recall the words. Use group activities so that ELL students learn in a comfortable environment and at the same time learn from native speakers. Avoid individual speaking assignments in front of a group until children feel comfortable doing so (this may take several times). Joining in with others allows a student to hear classmates reciting a song or poem. For example, allow an ELL student to work with a small group of English-speaking peers.

Teachers should be mindful to consistently and explicitly present academic language. Repeated encounters with academic language increase the ELL's learning of those words. For example, a "word wall" where words have pictures associated with them, reading books, and being involved in experiences that emphasize the use of specific academic language are all helpful.

Figure 2.14
Adaptations for Children with Special Needs.

Adaptations for Children with Special Needs

Children with special needs can be given parts that are easier for them to handle; for example, children with a speech difficulty may just use body movement during a finger play or song activity. Children with fine motor difficulties may need larger or smaller tools. Remember that resources should be at the level where children can reach them and also labeled so that children who have special needs can find and access what they need.

SAMPLE ACTIVITIES

A number of activities serve to highlight important social studies concepts. Below are some effective options:

- *Dress up and role-play:* Dress up as a historical figure and role-play the character by demonstrating his/her achievements or contributions with accents or gestures that characterize the historical figure. Let the class guess "who" you are.
- *Storytelling:* Tell a story in any area of social studies, such as family history, history of technology, or an important local, regional, national, or international event.
- *Sing and dance:* Choose a song or dance that teaches social studies contents.
- *Simulation:* Simulation lends itself to teaching economics, civics, and government. Topics might include voting, civic processes such as how a bill becomes a law, and so on.
- *Interview:* Act out a show similar to a TV interview. The interview should focus on a specific topic, event, or situation in a historical figure's life, on the community, or on national leaders.
- *Advertise:* Dramatize a TV commercial. Contents could include introducing the function of the product, explaining the advantage of the product over its counterparts, developing commercial slogans, and highlighting unique features that impress the consumer (economics).
- *Short play:* Developing a short play is a powerful tool applicable to all social studies content. Typical examples are "Underground Railroad," "The First U.S. Flag Maker," "Boston Tea Party," "The First Thanksgiving," and so on.
- *Stories that can be acted out:* *Legend of the Bluebonnet: An Old Tale of Texas* by Tomie dePaola

Songs

- "Lift Every Voice and Sing" by James W. Johnson
- "Follow the Drinking Gourd" by Jeanette Winter

Read aloud for art

- *My Name Is Georgia: A Portrait* by Jeanette Winter
- *Diego* by Jeanette Winter

- *Leonardo and the Flying Boy: A Story about Leonardo Da Vinci* by Laurence Anholt
- *Picasso and the Girl with a Ponytail: A Story about Pablo Picasso* by Laurence Anholt

RESOURCES

The following resources offer valuable assistance in planning the teaching of social studies:

- *Block Play* by Elisabeth S. Hirsch
- *The Creative Curriculum for Preschool*, 5th ed., by <u>Diane Trister Dodge</u>, <u>Laura J. Colker</u>, and <u>Cate Heroman</u>
- Websites for selected social studies topics: Google Earth (earth.google.com); National Archives (archives.gov); National Gallery of Art (nga.gov); Annenberg Learner (learner.org); Pinterest (pinterest.com); National Geographic Kids (kids.nationalgeographic.com/kids/); Money Instructor (moneyinstructor.com/elementary.asp); Scholastic (teacher.scholastic.com); Kidsites for history (kidsites.com/sites-edu/)
- Social Studies and the Young Learner (SSYL): teaching ideas, lesson plans, and handouts written by and for K–6 elementary educators (socialstudies.org/).
- Social studies apps, transportation: iTunes (itunes.apple.com/us/app/means-transportation-interactive/)

Technology Resources

Technology resources are plentiful and available for download (Figure 2.15).

The following apps are free (these are just a few of the hundreds of apps out there):

- Atlas for iPad
- Constitution for iPad
- Declaration for iPad
- The Magic of Reality
- American Museum of Natural History
- More apps can be found on Pinterest (pinterest.com).

Figure 2.15
Apps for Children by Grade Level, Pre-kindergarten through Fourth Grade.

Preschool	Kindergarten Apps	First Grade	Second Grade	Third and Fourth Grades
ABC ZooBorns	Britannica Kids: Volcanoes	Barefoot World Atlas	Barefoot World Atlas	The Magic of Reality
Leo's Pad 2: Educational App for Preschoolers	Britannica Kids: Ancient Egypt	Khan Academy	World Atlas by National Geographic	Barefoot World Atlas
Little Farmer	Britannica Kids: Rainforests		Historic Places	Khan Academy
	Britannica Kids: Solar System		Geocaching	World Atlas by National Geographic
			Britannica Kids: Ancient Egypt	Presidents vs. Aliens
			Stack the Countries	Historic Places
			BrainPOP	Geocaching
				Britannica Kids: Ancient Egypt
				Stack the Countries
				Stack the States

Based on http://www.mindleaptech.com/apps/language-arts/brain-pop/

Assessing Learning Outcomes

- Discuss the rationale for teaching children social studies.
- Explain how you would engage families when using any of the following teaching strategies: project approach; learning centers; dramatic play; arts and creative expression; technology in the classroom; computer and Internet; videos.
- Discuss how to engage families in planning curriculum.
- Explain each of the following teaching strategies and provide examples of how you would use them with varying age groups: project approach; learning centers; dramatic play; arts and creative expression; technology in the classroom; computer and Internet; videos.

References

American Academy of Pediatrics (AAP). (2009). Policy statement—media violence. *Pediatrics, 124*(5), 1495–1503. Retrieved from www.pediatrics.org/cgi/doi/10.1542/peds.2009-2146

American Academy of Pediatrics. (2010). Policy statement—media education. *Pediatrics, 126*(5), 1012–1017. Retrieved from www.pediatrics.org/cgi/doi/10.1542/peds.2010-1636

American Academy of Pediatrics. (2011a, June 13). Council on Communications and Media letter to the National Association for the Education of Young Children.

American Academy of Pediatrics. (2011b). Policy statement—media use by children younger than 2 years. *Pediatrics, 128*(5), 1–7. Retrieved from http://pediatrics.aappublications.org/content/early/2011/10/12/peds.2011-1753

Birch, L. L, Parker, L., & Burns, A. (Eds.). (2011). *Early childhood obesity prevention policies*. Washington, DC: National Academies Press. Retrieved from www.iom.edu/Reports/2011/Early-Childhood-Obesity-Prevention-Policies.aspx

Bloom, B. S. (1956). *Taxonomy of educational objectives, handbook I: The cognitive domain.* New York: David McKay.

Bloom, B.S., Krathwohl, D.R., Masia, B. (1984). *Taxonomy of educational objectives.* New York, NY: Pearson/Longman Publishers.

Bodrova, E., & Leong, D. J. (2003). The importance of being playful. *The First Years of School, 60*(7), 50–53.

Campaign for a Commercial-Free Childhood. (2010, July 26). CCFC letter to Jerlean Daniel, Executive Director, National Association for the Education of Young Children. Retrieved from www.commercialfreechildhood.org/pdf/naeycletter.pdf

Cooper, J., & Dever, M. T. (2001). Social-dramatic play as a vehicle for curriculum integration in first grade. *Young Children, 56*, 58–63.

Copple, C., & Bredekamp, S. (Eds.). (2009). *Developmentally appropriate practice in early childhood programs: Serving children from birth through Age 8* (3rd ed.). Washington, DC: National Association for the Education of Young Children (NAEYC).

Funk, J. B., Brouwer, J., Curtiss, K., & McBroom, E. (2009). Parents of preschoolers: Expert media recommendations and ratings knowledge, media-effects beliefs, and monitoring practices." *Pediatrics, 123*(3), 981–988. Retrieved from http://pediatrics.aappublications.org/content/123/3/981.short

Geist, E. (2014). Using tablet computers with toddlers and young preschoolers. *The Journal of the National Association for the Education of Young Children, 69*(1), 58–63.

Howard, A. E. (1975). *The integrated approach design for early childhood programs.* Nacogdoches, TX: Early Childhood Consultants.

Hyson, M. (2008). *Enthusiastic and engaged learners: Approaches to learning in early childhood education.* New York, NY: Teachers College Press.

Institute of Medicine of the National Academies. (2011). *Early childhood obesity prevention policies: Goals, recommendations, and potential actions.* Washington, DC: Author. Retrieved from www.iom.edu/~/media/Files/Report%20Files/2011/Early-Childhood-Obesity-Prevention-Policies/Young%20Child%20Obesity%202011%20Recommendations.pdf

Kirchen, D. (2011). Making and taking virtual field trips in pre-k and the primary grades. *Young Children, 66*(6), 22–26.

Levin, D. E. (2000). Learning about the world through play. *Early Childhood Today, 15,* 56–67.

Melendez, R. W., Beck, V., & Fletcher, M. (2000). *Teaching social studies in early education.* Albany, NY: Delmar Thomson Learning.

Mindes, G. (2005). Social studies in today's early childhood curricula. *Young Children, 60*(5), 12–17.

National Association for the Education of Young Children (NAEYC) & Fred Rogers Center for Early Learning and Children's Media at Saint Vincent College. (2012). Technology and Interactive Media as Tools in Early Childhood Programs Serving Children from Birth through Age 8. Joint position statement. Washington, DC: National Association for the Education of Young Children (NAEYC). Retrieved from www.naeyc.org/content/technology-and-young-children

National Council for the Social Studies (NCSS). (2005). *Curriculum standards for social studies.* Upper Saddle River, NJ: Merrill Prentice Hall.

National Council for the Social Studies (NCSS). (2010). *National curriculum standards for social studies: A framework for teaching, learning, and assessment.* Silver Spring, MD: NCSS.

PA Keys, Office of Child Development and Early Learning. Pennsylvania Early Learning Standards. Harrisburg, PA.

Pohl, M. (2000). *Learning to think, thinking to learn.* Cheltenham VIC: Hawker Brownlow Education.

Seefeldt, C., Castle, S., & Falconer, R. C. (2010). *Social studies for the preschool/primary child.* (8th ed.). Upper Saddle River, NJ: Merrill Prentice Hall.

Tomlinson, C. A., & Imbeau, M. D. (2010). *Leading and managing a differentiated classroom.* Alexandria, VA: Association for Supervision and Curriculum Development (ASCD).

White House Task Force on Childhood Obesity. (2010). *Solving the problem of childhood obesity within a generation.* Washington, DC: Office of the President of the United States. Retrieved from www.letsmove.gov/sites/letsmove.gov/files/TaskForce_on_ Childhood_Obesity_May2010_FullReport.pdf

Wiggins, G., & McTighe, J. (2005). *Understanding by design.* Alexandria, VA: Association for Supervision and Curriculum Development (ASCD).

3 Child Development, Families, and Communities in the Social Studies Context

Learning Outcomes

After reading this chapter you should be able to:

- Describe the developmental basis for teaching child development, families, and communities in the social studies context.
- Outline the main aspects of a community.
- Create lesson plans for teaching child development, families, and communities in the social studies context.
- Describe how to create opportunities that involve families, English language learners (ELL), and children with special needs.
- Provide experiences in which children are able to bring specific abilities, interests, and talents as they work with others to make decisions and solve problems.
- Discuss the importance of rules and norms in the community.

Big Ideas for Chapter 3: Child Development, Families, and Communities	Classroom Application	Standards Met
Recognition of each child as a unique person	Use of each child's name in the classroom (e.g., graphs of interest surveys throughout the year such as teeth lost and favorite foods)	Individual development and identity (NCSS 4)
Help each child see himself/herself as part of a family and community	Inclusion of families in some class activities and involvement of invited community members for special events	Individuals, groups, and institutions (NCSS 5)

THE CONCEPT OF COMMUNITY
FOR YOUNG CHILDREN

Social studies for young children is a daily experience. Teaching social studies to children who are in the early years of their development must begin with an understanding that their focus on self is typical and the goal for teachers is to increase and support a developing awareness of others. "Personal identity is shaped by family, peers, culture, and institutional influences" (NCSS, 2010, p. 76). This means that they need to learn what constitutes community and their role in it. However, the family and immediate community represent the beginning point from which children can build understanding and connect to their community and learn how to view themselves as part of the community. According to NCSS standard 5, they also must begin to understand how their community influences them through the effects, for example, of families, schools, religious institutions, government agencies, financial institutions, and civic groups on their lives (NCSS, 2005, p. 78). It is therefore the responsibility of both families and educators to help children learn about themselves, their community, and the part they play in their immediate surroundings. Understanding community allows children the opportunity to begin seeing how communities may differ; this, in turn, helps develop perspective and an awareness of the views of others.

The importance of the community concept is outlined in the following statement by the National Council for Social Studies:

> The early years are the ideal time for children to understand democratic norms and values (justice, equality, etc.) in terms of smaller entities (the family, classroom, community). Applying these concepts to the nation and the world will be easier if one understands and appreciates them on a smaller scale. (NCSS, 1988)

TEACHING INDIVIDUAL DEVELOPMENT, IDENTITY, AND COMMUNITY TO YOUNG CHILDREN

We are all social beings who belong to society. The way we live and relate to others in society starts during the early years of our lives. Between conception and 8 years, we learn our identity, and our perspective of others takes shape (Melendez, Beck, & Fletcher, 2000).

The Infant Years (0–3 years)

Community for young children is reflected in their immediate surroundings. For infants this involves interactions with family, caregivers, and peers. Infants develop trust, self-confidence, and emotional security when their needs are met predictably and consistently.

Meeting physical and emotional needs while engaging in reciprocal conversation builds trust that enables infants to calmly interact with their environment. Exploration allows infants to learn about themselves and their environment. Early childhood caregivers must provide opportunities for infants to explore and engage in meaningful interactions with peers. Engaging infants and toddlers in songs and activities (e.g., peek-a-boo, patty-cake) allows them to interact in a positive way.

Play and exploration should be encouraged through supportive adult behaviors (e.g., expanding rich language for infants, providing a variety of both physical and social interactions). Caregivers should play with infants in ways that are appropriate for their age, bearing in mind their interests and physical and emotional tolerance level. Another way to show warmth and caring is through touch, such as pats, hugs, and holding the child.

Infants and toddlers must be respected as persons in order to "develop confidence in their abilities which leads to increased self-esteem" (Copple & Bredekamp, 2009, p. 93). For example, the teacher should allow children to manage on their own but provide support as needed. The teacher can respect each child's preferences for object, foods, and people and can allow choices with limited options, such as choosing between mashed potatoes or bread for a meal. Having choices empowers children, enabling them to feel they have some control personally and to begin to see themselves as capable decision makers. As these children become older, making choices also encourages them to weigh pros and cons (e.g., spending a small amount of money saved on an item for immediate gratification versus saving for something of real value to them or even saving for a "rainy day"). Such opportunities can provide lifelong lessons.

Adult playing with infant.

Preschool (3–5 years)

For 3- to 5-year-olds, interaction with community broadens and becomes more complex. Many children begin to see both home and preschool as their community, complete with different community members, caregivers, and teachers who can expand their sense of community by including a variety of community experiences. As children of this age often enjoy role-playing, they will begin to imitate the roles of their **community helpers**, and this provides an opportunity to extend their view of who is in their community.

They are much more aware of their peers and adults in their lives. Their understanding of community is linked to their social connections and skills. At this age their social skills continue to develop through making friends, solving conflicts, and cooperating with their friends. Furthermore, they are able to express other social skills, such as hugging, sharing, and helping. Because these are daily occurrences, teachers can promote a sense of community and show how people relate to one another within a community. Additionally, relationships that children develop with their teachers and friends impact social competence in later years (Howes, 2000; Marrison, 2007).

Preschoolers learn "from their hand to the head and not the other way around" (Wood 2007, p. 49). Understanding from the child's perspective allows teachers to help students begin to see outward instead of inward, encouraging them to think beyond their own single viewpoint (Piaget's preoperational stage) (Crain, 2005). Young children are egocentric, meaning they relate everything they initially learn to themselves. Personally interacting with their environment is precisely how they learn. To learn differently would require abstract thinking, which they simply do not have the ability to do yet (Piaget's concrete operational stage). Thus it is important to get them involved in activities that demonstrate community. Preschoolers can develop a sense of community through play in centers in the classroom. Preparing the environment by creating settings like a fire station, a grocery store, a post office, or some other "real life" center helps children develop vocabulary and verbal and relational skills. This also affords them the opportunity to explore roles as they understand them, to begin to see ways that people contribute to the greater good of the community. By taking on such roles, they interact with peers and materials in an authentic way.

Dramatic play provides an understanding of rules, roles, and boundaries. Preschool children begin learning to solve problems as conflicts arise. Teachers can also foster skills of compassion, cooperation, and compromise through hands-on activities that encourage problem-solving with objects through role-playing and using materials

Suzanne Clouzeau/Pearson

Children playing together.

like clay or Legos. They may also draw or make figures that represent the people they live with at home or use toy figures to represent people they know. This ability to use symbolic representation happens during what Piaget labeled the preoperational stage. Physically, the skill for creating figures using clay will improve as preschoolers grow older; a 5-year-old will demonstrate greater competence than a 3- or 4-year-old. Additional detail will be evident in whatever medium the child uses, along with a deeper understanding of what those details represent.

The following are suggestions for what the teacher can do to foster understanding of community and its importance in a developmentally appropriate way:

- Be warm and caring toward children.
- Know and build relationships with each child and his/her family.
- Work with children so they have positive relationships with other children.
- Encourage and support children's efforts to make friends by providing opportunities for children to play and work together.

Children solving problem.

David Kostelnik/Pearson

Kindergarten (5–6 years)

Kindergarten age children are able to relate and understand social relations better than preschoolers. At the kindergarten level, the teacher can use their ability to make friends, understand classroom rules and consequences, and problem solve to teach and create an understanding of how a community works. Also, children's abilities at this age enable the teacher to engage children in reflecting on their experiences, discussing them, and representing them by drawing, writing, or dictating to share, demonstrate, and learn community concepts. Further, they can provide opportunities for children to work and collaborate with others to develop skills that are used in the community. These are valuable skills, and children should not be led to believe they are wrong for having conflicts; instead, these authentic teachable moments are an opportunity to understand others, to develop a plan, and to learn to deal with feelings appropriately. Most children at this age still need a great deal of support and guidance in this process. Teachers must make the most of these learning moments.

Self-concept becomes better established in kindergarten. Involving children in discussing and expressing their emotions and attitudes about people and situations is important. Children talk about activities, such as, "We go to the library every day after school," as well as emotions and attitudes, such as, "I am so happy my grandpa is here."

Teachers need to include concepts of community in everyday situations and events in concrete, experiential ways, such as solving problems (conflict resolution) during morning meeting, listening to others' ideas and perspectives, and working together cooperatively on tasks.

Additionally, children can share their thoughts and feelings through visual arts. They can draw pictures to represent their understanding of objects they see and emotions they feel. Teachers are then able to gain insights about a child and their understanding of society, along with how they are developing within the community.

By their caring attitude, teachers can foster the understanding of community through developmentally appropriate practice for kindergarteners. They must encourage children to participate in various interactions with others and also get to know and interact with their families.

Primary (6–8 years)

Children of primary age begin to delve deeper into the understanding of community, which includes problem-solving together. The delicate balance between learning to stand one's ground and to compromise often needs guidance from adults. Adults must help children develop valued skills of the culture (Vygotsky, 1978; Weissbourd, 1996). Falk (2009) describes problems as opportunities to learn. This means that whether the problem involves trying to figure out how to build a balanced structure together or determining whose turn it is to play with a popular toy or tool, children can learn how to creatively and safely maneuver in the social world. Small group activities, projects, and dramatic play all provide an abundance of opportunities.

Primary age children have a better understanding of other people and their differences. They are able to work and play cooperatively and follow rules. Erikson (1963) described the conflict of industry vs. inferiority as a time when children at primary age, in order to develop a sense of industry, strive to acquire knowledge and skills expected of their culture.

Primary age children are better able to use their fine and gross motor skills. They are able to write and draw with more precision. For 6- to 8-year-olds, understanding community also takes on greater depth through literacy connections, mapping, and field trips. Working and playing as partners gives children a sense of personal contribution, essential to community.

Choices continue to be important, especially as self-expression and preferences take on greater significance for these children. Teachers, caregivers, and parents must consider the objective of any effort and allow children to choose ways to complete a project that achieve the desired outcome. An understanding of strengths, of ways to demonstrate one's knowledge and feel successful, is critical for all people. Children, especially, need to have opportunities that remind them of their capabilities. Their peers need to see, and learn to appreciate, varied ways to demonstrate ability.

To promote social and emotional development (valued skills of the culture), teachers should create an environment of cooperation and avoid competition. For example, involving students in rule-making is important for many reasons. The process allows children to see why rules are in place while also encouraging language development as the group discusses the best way to state the rule for all to understand. Children are more likely to follow a rule they helped create, as it is coupled with knowledge of the meaning behind the rule, and with it comes a sense of ownership in their **classroom community**. Providing opportunities for students to work cooperatively on projects can also promote social competence. At the primary stage, children need to be taught content using a variety of resources such as books, the Internet, and classroom visitors, with the opportunity to interview them or hold discussions with them.

ASPECTS OF COMMUNITY

Identity and Family

The young infant's primary need is for security. Mobile infants focus mainly on exploration, and toddlers are at the stage where they are forming their identity. Young children establish their identity through the use of "communication skills to indicate their desires and refuse what they do not want at the moment. As their social awareness expands, they pick up cultural messages about who they are and how they should be" (Copple & Bredekamp, 2009, p. 65). They use words such as *no, me, why, mine,* and *me too.* Teachers can nurture toddlers' individuality by giving them choices and introducing guidelines. Here is an example:

> *Ms. Chad asks her toddlers during free play which station or toys they want to play in or with. "Sherrie, what would you like to play with, the Legos or dolls?" Sherrie responds, "I want dolls. This is for me."*

In relation to their families, children come to school with ideas of how much their families value them and what place they occupy within the family, that is, how much of their parent's attention they usually have. At school it is, therefore, important for teachers to involve children in activities that help them see they are part of a family even if their family is different from those of the other children. Understanding that everyone has some form of family contributes to a child's seeing his/her place in the classroom and later in the world. Activities and discussions about families become increasingly important as children join the bigger community within their classroom. Kindergarteners may draw their family members and include themselves. Teachers should encourage them to point out who each family member is. Sharing families—talking about traditions and experiences and relationships— is the very foundation of broadening the sense of self. Below is an example of how a teacher can highlight families:

> *Ms. Baker, a kindergarten teacher, is excited to work with families. She asks them to bring family photos in. She also displays a "student of the week" bulletin board, which features a child in the center, surrounded by photos or pictures of family members, family cultural activities, hobbies, and so forth.*

The teacher must be aware that some children may be living in a variety of home situations, including foster care or homeless shelters, or may have an incarcerated family member. Planning for family engagement activities would need to be modified to meet these situations. Teachers must always be sensitive to how a child may feel uncomfortable about any family circumstance. It becomes the teacher's responsibility to help the child belong, and this may mean reassuring the child so he/she still feels valued and aiding him/her in participating. For example, in the description above, imagine that the child's family does not send in any photos or respond to the project in any way. Ms. Baker would need to take photos of the child to post on the bulletin board. Then Ms. Baker would work with the child one-on-one to develop a fun, appropriate bulletin board by, possibly, cutting out pictures from a magazine of favorite animals, activities, or foods. Hanging a favorite book on the display, drawing a family portrait, and writing a brief biography together would include the child in a meaningful way, while still valuing the family.

Building Community in Early Childhood Classrooms

The teacher can find ways to encourage the idea of community in the classroom. First, the teacher must ensure an optimal physical environment by preparing the classroom so that everyone feels welcome and can function comfortably. This can be accomplished in the following ways:

- Use children's names and photos on their own cubbies.
- Display photos from their families.
- Make sure there are clear pathways in the classroom.
- Set up choice boards or other means to select centers or stations.
- Use predictable methods to transition from one activity to another.
- Adhere to routines that are age-appropriate and involve singing, moving, and so on.
- Maintain an organized space that allows children to make choices without competing with other children for materials (have duplicates of popular items, for example).
- Set up clearly marked shelving that is easily accessible for young children.

A second way that teachers can foster the development of community thinking is by establishing certain routines and procedures, as listed below:

- Use **class meetings** to discuss problems or challenging behaviors.
- Use "peace tables" for children to work out differences using puppets or dolls.
- Establish interpersonal relationships with adults that involve listening, acceptance of feelings, and extended conversations.

Finally, the teacher can use activities to promote a sense of community. Daily stories in group times can include themes about living in communities, caring for others, and so on. The teacher can also regularly provide examples and interactions of ways that communities work together, such as the following:

- For pre-kindergarten: dramatic play with helpers as the theme
- For primary grades: role-playing themes of stories in which characters act out community helper story lines
- For third and fourth grades: creating solutions for problems in the school or community to be sent to the building principal

Classroom Community

The best way to teach community is to authentically come together as a community through the following: (1) planning and setting expectations, (2) scheduling class meetings on a daily basis and as needed, (3) promoting responsibility to each other, (4) including teamwork and mutual support activities, (5) establishing a **sense of belonging**, (6) involving community helpers, and (7) understanding and celebrating diversity. Developing these types of consistent classroom routines within a flexible framework allows students to feel creative and secure. Each step builds on the tone and success of the previous one. Establishing a plan is up to the teacher, and the wording and expectations are established before the children enter the room. Clarity is important, as these are behaviors that are expected from every member of the "community." Class meetings allow for further clarification, as necessary, for discussion and negotiations that come up periodically (Kreite, 2002). The sections that follow expand on the seven ways to enhance the teaching of community that are listed above.

Planning for and Setting Expectations

Securing a positive climate is something the teacher must be proactive about. Beginning with class "plans" or "promises" will set a more positive tone than a typical rule chart (Figure 3.1). The plans, written on individual squares of colorful cardstock, are up to the teacher but may include such statements as, We say something nice every day, We believe in ourselves, We believe in our friends, We share opinions,

Figure 3.1
A List of Rights and Responsibilities in the Classroom

Individual teachers work with children in their classes to create their own set of group expectations, whereas schools often design an overarching plan for the entire school.

It is important for school communities to come together when designing the framework. Mapping out the language of positive statements and having all stakeholders involved in the writing process, as well as their commitment to the ideals, are critical to its overall success. In her book **Teaching the Way Children Learn**, Falk (2009) highlights the Bill of Community Responsibilities and Rights at the Bronx New School as a commitment to respectful, equitable, and democratic relationships for all. Below are a list of rights and responsibilities that can be used the class.

Rights	Responsibilities
The right to	The Responsibility to
• Be in safe surroundings	• Behave in a safe manner
• Express emotions and view points	• Speak at the appropriate time and in an acceptable way
• Be heard by others	• Listen to others
• Be respected with regard to our differences	• Respect the cultures and traditions of everyone
• Have our property respected	• Have respect for the property belonging to the school and other people
• Learn	• Never hinder the learning of other people
• Learn from mistakes	• Accept accountability for my actions

We don't criticize, We ask for help when needed, We are kind to each other, We are a team, and so on. The actual sayings can vary greatly. There should not be more than about four sayings for a pre-kindergarten or kindergarten class, and the sayings should certainly be couched in language the children are able to understand. The idea is that the plans are the class expectations, and if everyone follows the plans to the best of his/her ability, then the class will not need rules such as, "no yelling" and "no hitting." The expectations become clearer through guidance; for instance, the teacher might clearly state that this is a positive classroom where everyone tries his/her best to treat others with kindness.

Scheduling Class Meetings on a Daily Basis and as Needed

The class meeting is an ideal way to establish an understanding of community. It is a microcosm of the larger community. Group collaboration and cooperation are the very first lessons in being part of a community. Class meetings help establish routines and expectations. They are most beneficial when held in the morning, in an effort to start the day and explain what lies ahead. Children like to know what to expect in the near future and come to rely on this information. ("What are we doing today?" and "Do we have library today?" are common kinds of questions that can be heard in morning meeting.) Meetings can be adjusted to satisfy all kinds of needs. Ideally, the teacher can allow at least 20 minutes of uninterrupted time just to focus on their ideas, thoughts, and concerns. Children are given practice at being polite listeners and good communicators. This heightens their understanding of being both polite and reciprocal. Outlining, discussing, and practicing expectations put the responsibility on the children, which becomes a positive way to hold them accountable. Practice, as with any other skill, is essential, and reminders are key, and it is explained that everyone (even adults!) sometimes needs reminders. Reminders give everyone an opportunity to refocus and stay on track. Avoiding any negative tone is critical. During group meetings, problems can be solved, children can be recognized for their contributions to the group, and explicit feedback can be given on how children are working together as a group (Seefeldt, 2005). The teacher encourages, just as he/she would with a math problem or a reading challenge. Learning social skills requires similar practice. The amount of time spent in the morning meeting is important. For most children, 15–20 minutes is enough time to engage in meaningful exchange with peers. Morning meetings tend to fall apart when children are expected to sit for much longer.

Some classes have started implementing an afternoon meeting, which offers another relatively short time for the class to come together as a group. Morning and afternoon meetings have also been referred to as previews and reviews. In the afternoon meeting, the class reflects on how the day has unfolded instead of discussing the day's upcoming schedule and plans. Afternoon meetings allow children to have some sense of closure in their day, to summarize the many activities they engaged in, and to discuss simple key reminders for tomorrow (e.g., "remember to wear your sneakers tomorrow because we have physical education" or "bring your library book" or "try to remember to return your permission slip for our field trip"). The idea is for children to relax a bit together and reflect rather than rushing out the door.

Promoting Responsibility to Others

The routines of any classroom help contribute to the organization of the community. Even when the parents of infants come into a center and hang their bag in a cubbie, talk to the caregiver about their child, and help get the child settled, the child has a sense of membership in a community. As toddlers and preschool children begin to follow this routine and take over some responsibility, they acquire a sense of ownership in their own community. These expectations carry over and increase for 6- to 8-year-olds as the expectations increase to include routines, behaviors, and contributions to the overall function of the classroom.

Responsibilities in the classroom can include jobs. Young children are excited about helping, and jobs add to the routine and consistency of a classroom community. Each job must be valued by the teacher. If children feel as though no one will care or notice whether or not they do their job, the sense of responsibility and contribution is lost.

Including Teamwork and Mutual Support Activities

Human interaction is critical to the development of social skills. Such development has also been referred to as social competence. Social competence refers to an array of abilities, behaviors, and responses directed toward other people that serve to build positive human relationships (Jalongo, 2006).

Teamwork provides a sense of belonging that is critical for children of all ages. To be included in daily work and play allows children to feel appreciated and valued within the group or community. As infants and toddlers are encouraged to perform actions like "roll the ball" or "hold my hand," they begin to understand accomplishment through teamwork. The encouragement of supportive caregivers gives way to mutual support among all children as they interact with their peers. Children imitate what they see in order to accomplish a certain goal. Preschool and children of primary age also experience teamwork through many facets of their day, such as dramatic play, organized games and activities, and tasks like preparing a snack together.

When pre-kindergarten and kindergarten children work together, teachers should acknowledge the effort with enthusiasm and recognition of their growing social skills. This positive environment will make children aware of the rewards and the value of their personal contribution. Supporting one another cannot be taught too early. As children see their peers working on something, they model adult behavior in cheering them on and saying encouraging words such as, "Good job, yay for you!!" or "Keep trying—you are almost there!" Children will imitate such responses. Through relationships they learn love, trust, caring, support, and empathy. These are the social-emotional competencies that become the foundation for learning and healthy development (Cohen, 2001).

Establishing a Sense of Belonging

A classroom community builds a sense of belonging. Teachers must be diligent about making sure all children are included and feel like valuable contributors to their classroom. The key words here are "their classroom." Every year the classroom is different. The activities may vary, the lessons follow the children's lead, and because the teacher provides the framework and lets the class guide the rest, the classroom develops with their own personal touch. All children in the classroom should feel a personal attachment to the room, and it should provide them with comfort, as they know what to expect and they feel safe. Any posters around the room should reflect a diverse group of learners. Pictures should be real photographs, not cartoons. The photographs on outdated calendars from organizations that are child-centered, such as the National Association for the Education of Young Children (NAEYC), are ideal for this purpose.

If their artwork is proudly displayed on the walls of their classroom, children may feel more connected. (Let them hang it wherever *they* want; allow children to get the tape and select a spot—little things like this contribute to their sense of belonging and ownership.) The most important idea is that the room belongs to this group of learners and should reflect their personal artwork, stories, and even photos. Even in infant and toddler rooms, photographs of the children and individual artwork should be displayed to reflect their classroom community.

Certain concepts are key to instruction in social skills/community building:

- Teachers must believe in the value of the classroom as a community and be committed to it.
- Teachers must make certain that instruction is embedded in the day and is consistent.
- Teachers must be consistent with expectations but understand each child's needs.
- Teachers must be compassionate and willing to sincerely talk with a child when problems arise.
- Teachers must be consistent with meeting times.
- Teachers must try to get the whole school involved; year-to-year consistency strengthens skills.
- Teachers must plan outings that allow children to explore the community they live in.

When carried out properly, this approach is time well spent. The tone it establishes can eliminate a large portion of the day-to-day conflict students face in the classroom. By investing this time, teachers have students who are better prepared to work on academics with a clear, more enthusiastic focus. Their playtime, which is often when social conflict arises, becomes more positive and actually allows for more productive learning in the long run.

Involving Community Helpers

With classroom community established, children are anxious to move on to the bigger picture and now have a foundation of understanding to build on. This prior knowledge is essential. A good way to broaden a child's sense of community is to talk about the people they see working in their community. Do they see police officers? Restaurant workers? Post Office workers? Who else? What kinds of things do these people do? Why do they do them? Young children often do not realize that people perform jobs to gain income. This discussion of people in the community and doing jobs to make money can lead into lessons on consumerism. Activities on this topic for pre-kindergarten and kindergarten students abound. Having a dress-up station for children to dress as community workers and stations for them to role-play jobs is not just fun for the children but builds inter-active language skills while reinforcing the idea of careers, responsi-bility, and work. Many of these jobs may also require the handling of money, and therefore children are further engaged in learning and can pretend to "charge" their customers a given amount and then "give change." This type of activity also presents an ideal opportunity to include families and learn about diversity with regard to family traditions and celebrations. Having family members visit to act as guest readers or to cook at a station develops the outreach necessary to foster a sense of the larger community (having a holiday cookie baking day allows family members to share a favorite recipe, cook with the children, and share a variety of cookies with everyone in the class). This kind of community-building helps children understand the people within a community. Discussions that focus on what jobs parents do can lead to inviting parents and other professionals into the classroom. The teacher should allow children to take roles in the classroom that will demonstrate they are also helpers in their class-room community. Children who take on this role are usually called teacher's helpers or classroom helpers.

The next step may be to help them understand the physical lo-cation part of community, and this can begin in their own neighbor-hoods. Young children love basic maps. They also love to pretend. (A large map, a phone, and some plastic firefighter hats can provide fun and invite engagement, whether teaching fire safety, the use of 911, or maps and directions, or just listening to the language development and verbal skills that take place at this type of center.)

Primary age children are at a stage in which they can understand community relations and activities at a more complex level. For ex-ample, they can develop treasure maps around the students' actual own community, and the teacher can take them out exploring and problem-solving as the area allows. Children can start by drawing a map of their own house and whatever surrounds it. They are able to build on the understanding of a neighborhood when they draw a neighbor's house in relation to their own. Directionality can be taught with regard to the placement of a driveway, parking lot, or street route to school. These maps, drawings, and posters should be hung around the room, prominently displayed for all to see. Children can share in peers' ideas, and families can readily see the latest topic of study in a meaningful way.

Understanding and Celebrating Diversity

In a diverse society like the United States, teachers must first learn the cultural norms of each student. This can be accomplished by finding out what is socially acceptable in their community by reading and by talking to colleagues, people who belong to that ethnic group, and even parents (Melendez et al., 2000). Children are a great source of information. Encourage them to share their culture. Such sharing can then be used to celebrate how we are different and similar. This allows children to honor and value each other as human beings first and foremost. Children who understand similarities among people are less likely to fear, distrust, and stereotype others (Seefeldt, 2005). Celebrating diversity includes encouraging families to share stories, traditions, and arts that honor culture and experiences. The teacher can provide opportunities for children to learn about others by singing songs, reading stories from various cultures, discussing gender, and inviting presentations from speakers or parents.

Activities such as these provide authentic learning experiences. For infants and toddlers, an activity as simple as painting hands and placing handprints on a large class page to complete a project can provide a feeling of celebrating differences. Children are often excited to point out their own handprints and view them as part of the larger picture. Student work may be displayed on the wall as a way to represent a variety of views on the same subject and at the same time recognize their presence in the classroom.

"Ensure that children with special needs or disability are included in the classroom socially and intellectually as well as physically" (Copple & Bredekamp, 2009, p. 290). The teacher should deal with specific questions about diversity, such as special needs, by giving simple and accurate responses. The teacher must respect the child he/she is speaking about by first having a very clear understanding of what the child feels comfortable answering and sharing. Figure 3.2 presents an example.

Seeing themselves as part of the group is an important balance of belonging and accountability. All children need to feel welcome, and, when they do, they are more likely to take on the responsibilities that come with group work. It is important to use team-building activities to start the year and continue to update changes along the way. This helps students understand that they belong to the classroom community and that they contribute to the whole group. The teacher should stress the importance of working as a group even if classmates are different in

Figure 3.2
Homes and Our Community Activity.

When a child with several disabilities, including being in a wheelchair, was spending time in an inclusive kindergarten classroom, the teacher first had a conversation with her parents and the special education teacher to understand the child's strengths and needs. The kindergarten teacher wanted to know if she could learn how to lift the child out of the wheelchair and prop her up in a beanbag chair or sit on the floor behind her, propping her up for support, so that she could truly be engaged with peers. She then spoke directly with the child to talk about questions the children might ask. She asked the child if it was okay for the children to touch the wheelchair and handle the different parts. She then asked if there were any questions the child would not want the kindergarteners to ask. The child replied, "I don't want them to ask how I go to the bathroom." This allowed the teacher to be prepared and to not put their new friend in an uncomfortable situation. This was critical in securing a positive transition for all. Mostly the children wanted to know if her legs hurt and if they would get better someday. They did want to see all of the moving parts of the wheelchair and understood that it was not for climbing and that they needed to ask before they pushed her anywhere. And, though the teacher was prepared to interrupt and remind the children that bathroom questions were personal, no one asked. They wanted to know if she could paint, if she could play in the dress-up center, and what her favorite color was. They wanted to know if she had any pets and if she wanted to hold the class guinea pig. Key to understanding that they were ready to accept her and were finished with questions, for now, someone said, "Can she be in my group?" When the teacher said, "Of course, and it sounds like we are ready to get started" there were groans from others, who said, "Why can't she be in my group?" and "Can she be in my group tomorrow?"

any way, such as color, language, or families. Sharing of different opinions should be encouraged so that each child can respect others for who they are. The teacher will need to guide children through these beginning stages of understanding the perspective of others.

Lesson Plans for Teaching Understanding of Others

A suitable team-building activity at the beginning of the school year may be a mural, with all children contributing a section to the large wall painting. The group can brainstorm a theme together, plan a location and design, and all work on it at the same time or in smaller groups in sections. When children see that the sections all fit together and complement one another, they feel a sense of teamwork and shared contribution. They find it interesting to look at what others drew or added and excitedly point out their part of the mural. The mural can be hung in the classroom, hallway, or lobby. The teacher can take a photo of it to send home so children can explain the activity to their families. Murals can be created by infants and toddlers with footprints, handprints, finger-paints, and colorful doodles.

Another team-building activity involves constructing homes. Figure 3.3 shows the specific steps involved in such an activity.

Figure 3.3
A Sample Activity for Understanding Communities.

Homes in My Community

(This activity can be adjusted to any age level keeping it simple for younger children and increasing complexity for elementary age children.)
Group Activity
Learning Objectives
Given pictures and various building materials (wood, block, logs), the children will be able to build a home together.

Procedure

Whole group:
Lead a discussion of the kinds of homes the children might know.
Read books about different kinds of homes.
Show pictures of homes and discuss the characteristics:
   - sizes and types of homes
   - types of materials homes are made of
Small group:
The children will complete the following steps:
Sit with a partner or small group.
Select a picture of any of the homes discussed as a class.
Select the type of building material desired.
Create the home in the picture.
Sample book: *House and Homes* by Ann Morris

Learning Centers: Neighborhood/Community Places Center

Learning centers can be used to great advantage in teaching about community.

1. Use blocks to represent models of real places (pre-kindergarten–8 years).

    Play area idea: Allow children the opportunity to use blocks to build real places. Encourage group collaboration to build a community using blocks. Discuss different things they can do by asking questions such as, Is the library close to your church? What can you do to make the road wider? Can these cars share the road without banging into each other? (Maxim, 1997, p. 207). Provide large sheets of paper, markers, crayons, and pencils, and encourage children to draw a map of their block community. Encourage them to label and add signage to their block town as well, labeling roads, business signs such as "Town Bank," "Sam's Store," "Gas Station," "Fire Station 65," stop signs, speed limit signs, traffic lights, and so on.

2. Set up a learning center based on a bank, restaurant, grocery store, or hospital.

    Include dress-up items and other items found in the chosen place, such as money in a bank, the bank building itself, and checks. Allow time for children to play at the center during dramatic play. Reference the center when talking about community and items found in the community. Reach out to the community for authentic materials to include in the center. Many are generous in giving supplies such as canvas bags, menus, boxes, stickers, and much more. For example, a local home improvement store may be willing to donate canvas aprons in children's sizes—it's always worth asking about. If a company does donate to the classroom, be sure to send a thank you note (work on writing it as a class, and have the children all sign it, or each child can write or draw his/her own) and send a picture of the children using the materials. This is a positive community outreach, and when the children go to the place of business and see their class note and picture, they are very excited! Of course, pay close attention to permission slips for photographs that parents should be asked to sign at the beginning of each school year.

HOME/SCHOOL CONNECTION

Home/school connection is extremely important in the development and learning of young children. The family is the first community experience that the child has before coming to a learning community. Thus, the relationship between these two communities is very important in terms of continuity and a nurturing experience for the child. It is therefore important that a supportive relationship exists between the two. This relationship begins with positive daily interactions between families and teachers. It is even more important for children to experience home and school community, working together as part of learning how to live in a community. First and foremost, teachers need to be attentive to families in order to understand differences and similarities and at the same time guide them to become involved in school activities and procedures.

To demonstrate community, welcome families to accompany children on field trips and into the classroom. Invite parents and other professionals to come to school and share their professions with the children. Engaging families in both general conversation and educational goals for the children enhances community. Also, reading stories and discussing topics related to any of the elements of community at home will enhance the relationship between children and the community.

Suzanne Clouzeau/Pearson

ACCOMMODATIONS FOR CHILDREN WITH DIVERSE NEEDS

In planning the curriculum that centers on child development, families, and communities, accommodations must be made for children with diverse needs. Teaching social studies to young children must incorporate adaptations for English language learners (ELL) (Figure 3.4) and adaptations for children with special needs (Figure 3.5).

Figure 3.4
Adaptations for ELL.

Adaptations for English Language Learners

When working with children who are English language learners (ELL), it is important to have some basic working knowledge of their culture as it relates to their community and family. As a teacher you will need to (and want to!) allow them to share information so that other children will understand the differences. Encourage children to share information and pictures if they have access to pictures from their ancestral home and cultural traditions. These can be compared with pictures from their present community. Be aware that some families may not feel comfortable sharing their stories; therefore, a conversation with families first is very important. This will help them feel welcome and secure in the classroom environment.

Other activities for supporting ELL and families in the classroom community are as follows:

1. Send home written letters in the home language to welcome the family. Should the home language be difficult to access, teachers can connect with the ESL teachers or the district ESL teacher, regional education center, or other language resources within the community.

2. During open houses make arrangements for welcoming. Examples of those who might welcome are school staff or community members who speak the home language. Use an app with a code-reader that families can use with their phones that describes the program, daily schedule, rooms in the school, and so on.

3. Create buddies to help the ELL transition to the classroom. (*Note*: Select students who are empathetic and willing to work with others.) Place signs around the room in both English and the child's home language.

Figure 3.5
Adaptations for Children with Special Needs.

Adaptations for Children with Special Needs.

All young children, including those with special needs, will benefit from handling items when learning. Tactile support enhances connections. Students with special needs must be included in every facet of the classroom community. This is important for all students in the class as they are learning to live as valued members of a community. Whatever it takes to include everyone in all daily activities, as well as walks and field trips, should be done. Understanding a child's learning requirements is especially important when teaching students faced with special needs. They may require additional tactile, fine or gross motor, visual, and auditory opportunities. Working with parents and other teachers to meet the child's needs is critical.

CONNECTIONS TO LITERACY

The following books help to reinforce the idea and value of community:

Community Helpers from A to Z (Alphabasics) by Bobbie Kalman

Celebrating with the Wennings by mrscanup

Clifford the Big Red Dog by Norman Bridwell

Paperboy by Dav Pilkey

See How They Go by DK Publishing

Dazzling Diggers (Amazing Machines) by Tony Mitton and Ant Parker

I Want to Be a Builder by Dan Liebman

A Day in the Life of a Construction . . . by Heather Adamson

I Want to Be a Police Officer by Dan Liebman

Rosie's Walk by Pat Hutchins

A Job for Wittilda by Caralyn Buehner

Bruno the Tailor by Lars Klinting

A Castle on Viola Street by DyAnne DiSalvo

Swimmy by Leo Lionni

The Enormous Potato by Aubrey Davis, illustrated by Dusan Petricic

Pumpkin Soup by Helen Cooper

With Love, Little Red Hen by Alma Flor Ada, illustrated by Leslie Tyron

SAMPLE ACTIVITIES

Various activities can be helpful in teaching children first-hand about the value and functions of community. These activities can focus on various aspects of community, as listed below.

Process

Involve children in processes such as the following:

1. Identify and describe examples of tensions between and among individuals and groups.
2. Observe how the school and their families interact.
3. Show children how various aspects of the community, such as schools and hospitals, work to meet their individual needs.

Community Activities

These activities involve visits to public places, such as those below:

1. Plan a trip to the public library. Create a simple map the children can follow as you travel there. Have each child obtain a library card and check out some books during the visit. Try to revisit the library often.
2. Go to the grocery store together. Have community helpers talk to the children about their jobs.
3. Map out and take a trip to a locally owned restaurant where the children can order from the menu. Again, have workers share the specifics of their job with the children.

Product

Children can demonstrate understanding through the following activities, which incorporate the concept of product:

1. Provide children with opportunities to demonstrate understanding of self by comparing their photos from the beginning of the year with the latest photo and describing how they have changed.
2. Make a list of physical differences and similarities.
3. Make "a collage of work roles in the community" (NCSS, 2010, p. 78).
4. Make "a graphic organizer of groups to which class members belong" (NCSS, 2010, p. 78).

5. Engage infants and toddlers in activities that encourage safe interactions and enjoyment. Infants will generally enjoy peek-a-boo or listening to a book read while sitting on a caregiver's lap. With toddlers, sing, do finger plays, and act out simple stories.

6. Engage in classroom activities that promote differences and similarities as a group.
   Sample activity: This activity focuses on each child as a member of the classroom community. Students discuss their differences and similarities. This can be done during class meetings or at another designated time during the day. Students make suggestions on how they are different and similar. Write them on the board for reference during the discussion. Bar charts can be used to represent the differences in family size, number of siblings, and so forth. This activity may lend itself well to showing cultural differences in language, food, and so on, demonstrating the core concept in social studies that we are all different and that we "bring [something] different but something special to our classroom community" and that we are "interdependent—that we have to work and learn together" (D'Addesio, Grob, Furman, Hayes, & David, 2005, pp. 50–57).

7. Show understanding of how individuals work together to achieve group goals.
   Job charts: Through the use of job charts, children learn how they can keep the classroom running smoothly, safely, and in a clean and fun manner (D'Addesio et al., 2005, p. 51). Each student gets a chance to experience being helpful and impacting the classroom community in a positive way.

8. Promote collaboration and friendships both at school and at home.

   Encourage friendship by having the children take turns and share; provide children with opportunities to work in groups, for example, "group collaboration making a map of the classroom, with different groups assigned a different portion of the room" (Mindes, 2005, p. 16).

9. Have children identify the people who live in their family
   Sample activity: In this activity children will explore what constitutes a family. After discussing the different make-up of families, have children draw the people they consider their family members. Allow children to share the number of family members they have and how they are related.

RESOURCES

In preparing lessons and activities about community, teachers have a world of information at their fingertips. The list below suggests some valuable online sites.

Beyond the Journal, Young children on the Web, September 2005: naeyc.org/yc/

Scholastic: Open a World of Possible: scholastic.com/teachers/ teaching-resources

ProTeacher Collection: proteacher.org/c/411_communities.html

Kindercare Learning Center blog: kindercare.com/blog/ teaching-young-children-about-community/

Assessing Learning Outcomes

- Discuss how you would measure students' awareness of their role as a member of a group, such as the family or the class.

- Describe why it is so important to help students become aware of their role as a member of a group, such as the family or the class.

- Explain how you would help children understand themselves in relation to their families.

- How would you help children work together to achieve group goals? How would you evaluate their level of understanding?

- Why is it important for children to be able to describe the characteristics of where they live and visit?

- How do you make sure you visit as many places in the neighborhood community as possible?

- Explain how you would help ELL students understand their neighborhood community.

- Describe how you would include students of diverse needs in your community of learners.

References

Cohen, J. (Ed.). (2001). *Caring classrooms/intelligent schools.* New York, NY: Teachers College Press.

Copple, C., & Bredekamp, S. (2009). *Developmentally appropriate practice* (3rd ed.). Washington, DC: National Association for the Education of Young Children (NAEYC).

Crain, W. (2005). *Theories of development: Concepts and applications.* Upper Saddle River, NJ: Merrill Prentice Hall.

D'Addesio, J., Grob, B., Furman, L., Hayes, K., & David, J. (2005). Learning about the world around us. *Young Children, 60*(5), 50–57.

Erikson, E. (1963). *Childhood and society.* New York, NY: W. W. Norton.

Falk, B. (2009). *Teaching the way children learn.* New York, NY: Teachers College Press.

Howes, C. (2000). Social-emotional classroom climate in child care, child-teacher relationships and children's second grade peer relations. *Social Development, 38,* 113–132.

Jalongo, M. (2006). Professional development: Social skills and young children. *Early Childhood Today. 20*(7), 8–9.

Kreite, R. (2002). *The morning meeting book.* Greenfield, MA: Northeast Foundation for Children.

Marrison, F. J. (2007, March 20–April 1). *Contemporary perspectives on children's engagement in learning.* Symposium presented at the biennial meeting of the Society of Research in Child Development, Boston, MA.

Maxim, G. W. (1997). Childhood education: Infancy through early adolescence. *Journal of the Association for Childhood Education International, 73*(4), 206–211.

Melendez, R. W, Beck, V., & Fletcher, M. (2000). *Teaching social studies in early education.* Albany, NY: Delmar Thomson Learning.

Mindes, G. (2005). Social studies in today's early childhood curricula. *Young Children, 60*(5), 12–17.

National Association for the Education of Young Children (NAEYC). (2005). *Beyond the Journal, Young children on the web.* Retrieved from www.journal.naeyc.org/btj/200509.

National Council for the Social Studies (NCSS). (1988). *Social studies for early childhood and elementary school children preparing for the 21st century. A report from NCSS task force on early childhood/elementary social studies.* Retrieved from www.socialstudies.org/positions/elementary. Update.

National Council for the Social Studies (NCSS). (2005). *Curriculum standards for social studies.* Upper Saddle River, NJ: Merrill Prentice Hall.

National Council for the Social Studies (NCSS). (2010). *National curriculum standards for social studies: A framework for teaching, learning, and assessment.* Silver Spring, MD: NCSS.

Seefeldt, C. (2005). *Social studies for the preschool/primary child.* Upper Saddle River, NJ: Merrill Prentice Hall.

Vygotsky, L. (1978). *Mind in society: The development of higher psychological processes.* Cambridge, MA: Harvard University Press.

Weissbourd, R. (1996, August 19 and 26). The feel-good trap. *The New Republic,* pp. 12–14.

Wood, C. (2007). *Yardsticks: Children in the classroom, ages 4–14* (3rd ed.). Turner Falls, MA: Northeast Foundation for Children.

4 Using Age-Appropriate Methods and Strategies for Teaching History to Young Children

Learning Outcomes

After reading this chapter you should be able to:

- Discuss everyday concepts for teaching children about past, present, and future.
- Discuss how to engage families in language opportunities that enhance understanding of past, present, and future for their children.
- Explain various teaching strategies to build depth in understanding.
- Outline themes that further support the concepts and that can be used throughout the year for children at different ages.

Big Ideas for Chapter 4: Teaching History	Classroom Application	Standards Met
Developmentally appropriate practice when teaching social studies concept of past, present, and future	Integration of DAP thinking as the teacher plans, implements, and assesses	Time, continuity, and change (NCSS 2)
Accuracy in historical facts and details	Research events and details to ensure accuracy and avoid inaccuracies	Time, continuity, and change (NCSS 2)
Scaffold understanding of past, present, and future	Pay close attention to various levels of understanding in an effort to maximize historical understanding for all learners	Time, continuity, and change (NCSS 2)

HISTORICAL THINKING

Before delving into the specifics of historical thinking with regard to young children, it might prove helpful to bear in mind the National Council for the Social Studies (NCSS) standard for teaching history. In this chapter, the second of the 10 NCSS themes—**time**, **continuity**, and **change**—is most pertinent. This theme states that through the study of the past and its legacy, learners examine the institutions, values, and beliefs of people in the past, acquire skills in historical inquiry and interpretation, and gain an understanding of how important historical events and developments have shaped the modern world. This theme appears in courses in history, as well as in other social studies courses for which knowledge of the past is important.

As children learn to locate themselves in time and space through learning the concepts of past, present, and future, they also gain a sense of order and time (NCSS, 2010). Furthermore, "the use of stories about the past can help children develop their understanding of ethical and moral issues . . . they begin to understand that stories can be told in different ways" (NCSS, 2010, p. 15). History is a story. The story begins with the child and then extends to members of the family, and finally to other people (Schoenfeldt, 2001). Children love to talk about themselves, so this should be an interesting place to start. Then move on to talk about the people of history through the use of historical artifacts, field trips, and historical fiction.

Early childhood teachers must provide opportunities for children to develop historical thinking through the following five ways (National Center for History in the Schools, UCLA, 2014):

1. Chronological thinking
2. Historical comprehension
3. Historical analysis and interpretation
4. Historical research
5. Historical issues

Chronological Thinking

The ability to think chronologically is rooted in understanding a **sequence** of events. In the patterns of their days, children begin to recognize past, present, and future through connecting events and **routines**. As teachers incorporate language associated with chronology, children are able to see both connections and times of occurrences (Figure 4.1).

Teachers must present and adapt each component to the developmental needs of the group they are working with, as necessary, to meet the learning needs and abilities of their students.

Developmental Basis for Teaching Children Past, Present, and Future

Historical learning for young children must begin with foundational opportunities that develop historical understanding. **Historical understanding** begins with a sense of past, present, and future. A child's perspective on time, events, people, and cultural awareness is also rooted in historical understanding. Therefore, historical learning

Figure 4.1
Chronological Thinking Outcomes.

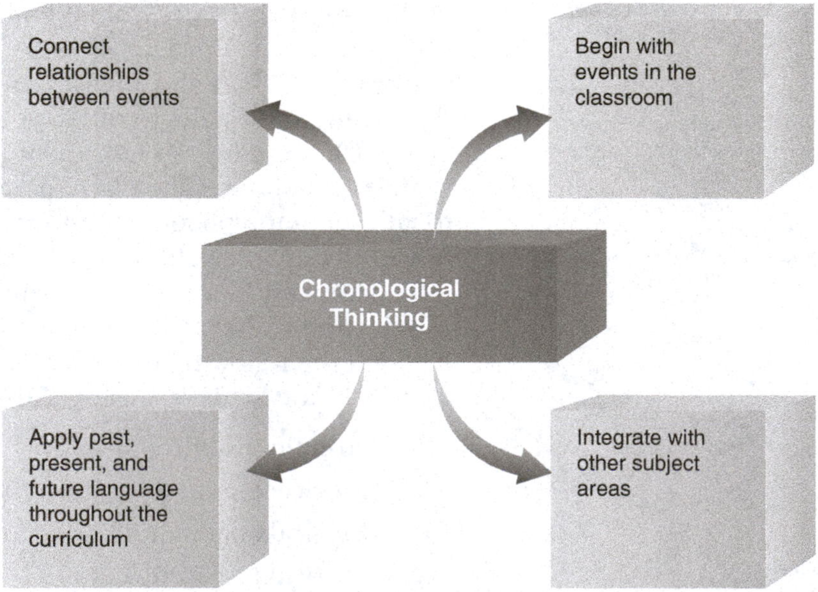

Connect relationships between events

Begin with events in the classroom

Chronological Thinking

Apply past, present, and future language throughout the curriculum

Integrate with other subject areas

Source: Adapted from National Center for History in the Schools, UCLA, 2014.

must provide opportunities to be exposed to such chronological and cultural topics. To that end, teaching for historical learning must be intentional and meaningful.

Understanding past, present, and future allows children to feel a sense of security in routines and expectations. We know that children depend on adults to help them feel safe in their day-to-day world. Positive predictability is an important way for children to have a sense of being comfortable, knowing what they will be doing, where they will be going, and who they will be with.

For infants this sense of routine begins during Erickson's trust versus mistrust stage, in which the infant learns whether or not to expect that his/her needs will be met. The first routine would be the feeding cycle. For an infant who is consistently fed every 2 hours, there is a sense of security in the trust built between him/her and a caring adult. As children grow and a greater sense of independence blossoms, more emphasis is placed on learning routines, such as bedtimes, dressing, and other self-care responsibilities. Families who are mindful of developmental expectations provide support and encouragement in this growing independence. Expecting too much of children when they simply are not developmentally ready undermines the trust and initiative, respectively, of Erickson's trust versus mistrust and initiative versus guilt stages.

As children grow in the handling of routines and the sense of security, they are aware of cycles. A cycle of getting up in the morning, having breakfast, getting dressed, washing one's face, brushing teeth, combing hair, and preparing a backpack for the day is a morning routine for many. When they arrive at preschool or school, they are faced with another routine, which may include free play, morning meeting time, snack, centers, recess, lunch, quiet time, centers, clean-up, and preparation to go home. Although heading home means a variety of different routines, it is, again, most likely a cycle children grow to depend on. The routine may proceed this way: arrive home, hang up the backpack, have a snack, play with siblings and neighbors, have dinner with family, clear the table, take a bath, read a story, lay clothes out for the next day, and get ready for bed. That routine may be in place for a few days a week or for 5 or more days. Some children quickly learn the change in routine on weekends when bedtimes or other details may change. And, so the cycle goes. The cycle provides children with the beginnings of a sense of past, present, and future. When something is the same, there is a way to attach it to the past and the future. If tumbling class is always on Tuesdays, children can begin to recall the last time they had tumbling and the next time they will have it. If it is only for four weeks and today is the last day, they can begin to conceptualize that next Tuesday they will not have tumbling.

This sense of past, present, and future is necessary for people to follow due dates, appointments, and work schedules, and to be in the general flow of society. It is a way to plan and organize our lives.

The language of past, present, and future is key. "Before" and "after" are the essentials for teaching young children about past, present, and future. As they begin to take part in the kinds of routines outlined above, they are able to place experiences into elements of time. To hear that the child has a haircut appointment after breakfast gives a sense of when it will occur—it will be in the near future. To hear that the last time the child went to this same hair salon she got a lollipop connects her to a past experience; at the same time it builds on the sense of trust because it is an experience she already had, and so she can be assured it will be positive again. To say, "After you get your haircut we will meet Aunt Carol for lunch" gives additional perspective, building on the perception of future. As this child recalls her day, she is likely to be able to reflect on it this way: "First I had breakfast, then I got my haircut, then we went to see Aunt Carol." As this sense is developed, it becomes a natural transition to express yesterday, today, and tomorrow. Again, conversation reinforces this understanding when, the next day, the child is reminded that she got her hair cut yesterday. Through the course of everyday life events and supportive dialogue, families and teachers build important understandings of this concept.

The Tools for Learning Past, Present, and Future

- Certain tools and practices enhance the learning of time sequences, allowing children to visualize the passage of time. Keep in mind that active language in authentic experiences is key to building a sense of past, present, and future.

  As with most concepts children are beginning to master, it is most effective to address the topic according to how it relates to the child himself: The sense of what he will be doing before and after a part of his routine and what he did yesterday and will be doing today and tomorrow is most relevant and meaningful to him. Additional experiences and more complex understandings come with further development and maturity.

- Avoid confusion with calendar dates and other abstract concepts. Providing hands-on measures of time is more meaningful to children.

Although looking forward to an upcoming event, such as a cooking activity tomorrow, and reflecting on a recent experience, such as a field trip last week, are both concrete ways to develop an understanding of time, it is unrealistic to expect young children to understand last Thursday, this Thursday, and next Thursday simply because they exist. Children construct knowledge through meaning; if no meaning is connected to the lessons, it is doubtful that children will connect to the concept.

- Remember that most children have a different concept of time than adults.

    Young children are very active in experiencing their surroundings. Past can mean 10 minutes ago, and future can be defined by the very next thing they will be doing. Helping them organize and broaden their understanding should include opportunities to discuss the segments of their days. Essentially working from the child's world outward will provide **concrete** connections that enable foundational understandings leading to the more **abstract**.

Timelines and the Concept of Continuity

Teaching history through past, present, and future lessons is a matter of using opportunities to highlight all that is going on in a child's world. There are matters within the schedule of the day as well as events in the child's own life that lend themselves nicely to discussions about past, present, and future. **Timelines** can also offer a way for children to understand time and events. The visual of the timeline will help those who are developmentally ready to "see" this sense of time. Building on a timeline can foster deeper understanding as well. In her article "Everything Flows and Nothing Stays," Frances Blow (2011) highlights the importance to children of learning that connections from past to present are directly linked, rather than being individual events. Change is essentially progress, from one advancement to another, and could not happen without each step connecting past to present. Teachers need to create lessons that allow children to see these connections.

This understanding of continuity is an important component in learning about past, present, and future and our place in time. If children can begin to see their place in time, their connection to the past, and their role in the future, they will have a deeper connection to their social world. Initially, for children, this sense of continuity can be a generational study. In comparing and relating their own experiences to those of older relatives, children begin to see the connections of time. This fosters an authentic understanding, rather than isolated views of the past, the present, and the future.

Engaging families in the active learning process is most beneficial, as it broadens the opportunities for children. In the following timeline activity, families are an integral part of personalizing the activity for children and making important personal connections.

Sample timeline activity: (This activity would be suitable for kindergarten and first and second grades. Teachers should establish the criteria according to the abilities of the children.) Create a basic timeline of events in the classroom. Along the line highlight specific points, such as the first day of school, and events, such as a fall festival, Labor Day, and so on. This will allow children to visualize the timeline. Keeping it fairly short is important; this practice allows children to see the timeline and experience creating it but confines it to a relatively short period. If the teacher tries to map out an entire school year, children will lose interest. Longer time spans can be used only when children are fully able to conceptualize them.

Have an open-ended discussion with the class about a variety of timelines, sharing thoughts about timelines in their own lives, as well as some basic examples. This will also help the teacher gauge their level of understanding. To start, the teacher may ask, Do you remember when you were a baby? (When were you born? is a question that is entirely too abstract for young children.) Do you remember when you crawled before you were able to walk? (Again, When did you first crawl or When did you first walk? would require a numerical answer that young children are not able to recall.) These discussion points can lead to more specific times/dates, such as the following: Did you go to preschool? At what age did you begin? When did you get your first tooth? Haircut? Design a basic template to share with families that will allow them to choose several highlights to be placed on the timeline by their child (these choices can be communicated through notes or email, whichever may be most convenient for families). In the classroom, large wall-size timelines promote greater understanding of the topic being studied. Alleman and Brophy (2003) describe using timelines as teaching tools that encourage children to engage with materials, artifacts, photos, and drawings and thereby allow them to visualize the way things were in an effort to better understand why change occurred.

Take a photograph of each child to put above his/her timeline. Give each child squares of paper. The children can either use the timeline they created with their families or decide which events to use on their own. Using their lists, they should determine which event to write or draw about first. As they record all of their events and place them in chronological order, the teacher reinforces past and present language. Children are given a larger piece of paper with a heading of "Future"; they may choose to write what they would like to do tomorrow or even within the next year (e.g., I want to take swimming lessons this summer), or they may write about what they would like to do when they grow up. The concept of future is broad and can be addressed accordingly. Children then add an illustration and hang the last page at the end of the timeline.

We remind the teacher to be sensitive to children's circumstances; for example, if a child is in foster care, the foster family may not have any of this type of information. It would be important for the teacher to talk with the family members and decide how best to complete their own timeline, whether that be using approximations or creating a timeline that encompasses the time they have been together. There are several situations that may require adjustments to projects, and teachers must be both flexible and compassionate.

Historical Comprehension

To help children understand the time period they are studying, they need exposure to artifacts that will allow them to form ideas about that point in history (Figure 4.2). What was it like for people then? What were their experiences, their thoughts, their beliefs? This approach helps children gain a perspective from that time and not look at the period in a present-tense context. Historical maps of the geographic location, including natural and man-made features, further enhance understanding of the event.

Teachers must present and adapt each component to the developmental needs of the group they are working with, as necessary, to meet the learning needs and abilities of their students.

Historical Analysis and Interpretation

Comparing perspectives, situations, beliefs, motives, and stories allows learners to deeply analyze the situation being studied (Figure 4.3). The comparison of events and outcomes to how the situation actually unfolded is important. Whether an organized or accidental event, the outcome may have been different, so the question of What if...? adds an extra element to the analysis. Connecting past outcomes to current

Figure 4.2
Historical Comprehension Outcomes.

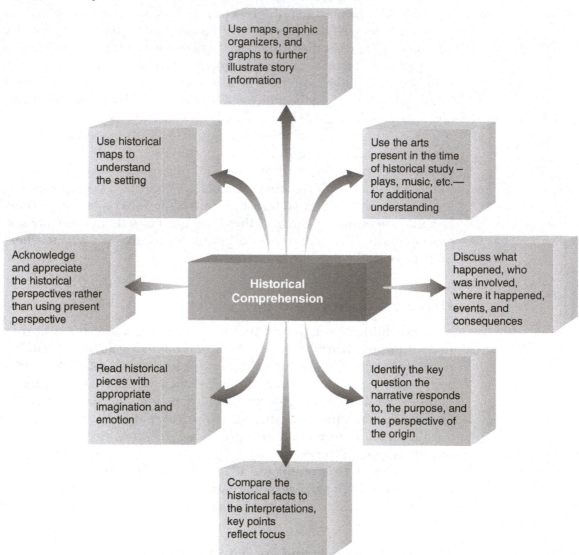

Source: Adapted from National Center for History in the Schools, UCLA, 2014.

influences helps children see the importance of studying and understanding history.

Teachers must present and adapt each component to the developmental needs of the group they are working with, as necessary, to meet the learning needs and abilities of their students.

Figure 4.3
Historical Analysis and Interpretation Outcomes.

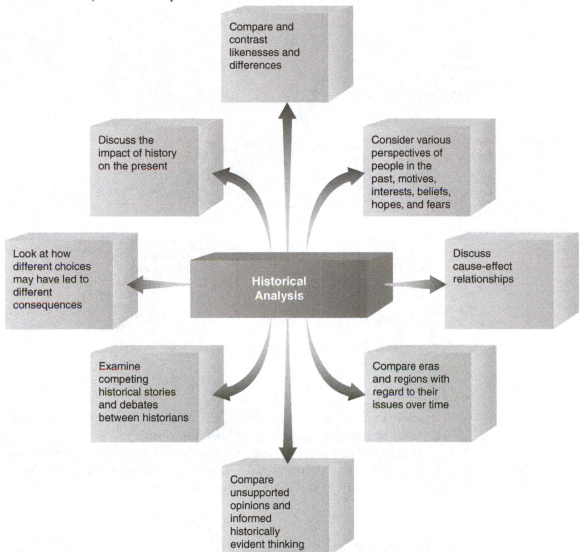

Source: Adapted from National Center for History in the Schools, UCLA, 2014.

Historical Research

Students need to access data from multiple sources in an effort to weigh authenticity, biases, and completeness (Figure 4.4). Examining data, including demographic information, will allow for greater

Figure 4.4
Historical Research Outcomes.

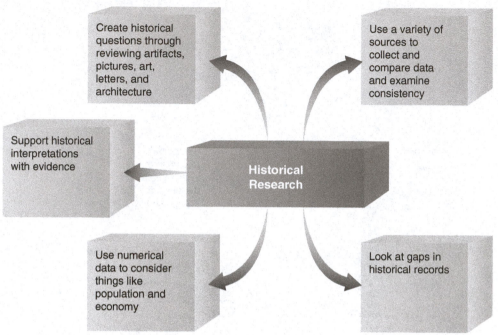

Source: Adapted from National Center for History in the Schools, UCLA, 2014.

understanding of the context in which the event occurred and inter-pretations of reasoned points as opposed to opinions.

Teachers must present and adapt each component to the develop-mental needs of the group they are working with, as necessary, to meet the learning needs and abilities of their students.

Historical Issues

Being able to identify issues and problems of the past and to con-sider other possible informed solutions and consequences in the long and short run helps students see how decision-making pro-cesses work (Figure 4.5). Evaluating the overall results of decisions and how all people were impacted allows for evaluative reflection by students.

Figure 4.5
Historical Issues—Analysis and Decision-Making Outcomes.

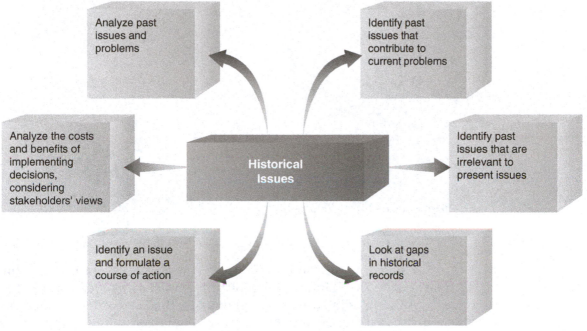

Analyze past issues and problems

Identify past issues that contribute to current problems

Analyze the costs and benefits of implementing decisions, considering stakeholders' views

Historical Issues

Identify past issues that are irrelevant to present issues

Identify an issue and formulate a course of action

Look at gaps in historical records

Source: Adapted from National Center for History in the Schools, UCLA, 2014.

Teachers must present and adapt each component to the developmental needs of the group they are working with, as necessary, to meet the learning needs and abilities of their students.

GOALS AND LEARNING OBJECTIVES

First, the teacher must identify the standards for the particular age group with whom she/he is working. Using the objective, the teacher next maps out the goals for the children within the standards identified. The design of the lessons will lead into the appropriate assessment for the concept of past, present, and future. Determining children's prior understanding of concepts is also important in knowing how to present a lesson. A teacher-guided activity with picture sequence cards can indicate children's understandings of the order in which events may occur.

Eucabeth Odhiambo

Sequence picture – Plant

Using a set of three or four cards with simple illustrations, the teacher asks the children which picture happens first, next, and last.

Although similar to seriation in math, this is an ordering of events rather than a sequencing of objects, and because multiple experiences in exploration are needed, this is an additional way to help children practice sequencing. Children begin to demonstrate some understanding of this concept at age 3 or 4, but it often takes them until age 8 or 9 to fully grasp it (Henniger, 2009).

With countless scenarios children can organize pictures and talk about what happens first, next, and last. These experiences should also include a discussion—in the scenario shown in the photo, for example—about the time it takes for a plant to sprout and grow tall; this sequence takes a long time. Another card set may show someone looking at a recipe card, cracking an egg into a bowl, and putting icing on a cake. This sequence can be done in a relatively short time. These activities help to build on the variety of scenarios and the kinds of time frames they reflect. Actually completing a simple activity would further enhance children's understanding and allow them to reflect on what they did first, next, and in the end. At the beginning of, say, a cooking activity, a teacher might use future words or word groups like "next," "soon," or "ready to start." During the activity, word groups like "now we," "it is time for," or "we need to" would reflect what is going on in the present. As the activity comes to a conclusion, the teacher would choose word groups like "we *did* it," "we are all *finished*," or "that *was* tricky/easy/fun/messy," highlighting past terms.

YEARLY, WEEKLY, AND LESSON PLANNING

While planning the overarching goals of understanding past, present, and future, the teacher should map out opportunities throughout the year that allow for use of the language and include activities that tie in well with such events. Counting down to picture day or a field trip can be done using paper chain links as visuals whereby one is removed each day until the big day arrives! Connecting the lesson concept to the children's lives in meaningful ways helps them understand when and where events happen with regard to their place in history. A compare and contrast picture chart can be created to show differences between items earlier in history and the same types of items now. Comparisons could include land phones versus cell phones, records versus CDs, and typewriters versus computers. This chart can be an ongoing project in the classroom that children are invited to add to and that families are encouraged to think about as well.

Marking events that are important to children is an easy way to incorporate this concept. Children's birthdays, community events, and even days for special classes such as music, art, gym, and library allow for discussions of past, present, and future. To plan for integrating subject areas, the teacher should also look at the yearly plan for teaching historical concepts.

(Note that teaching children social studies requires integrating the children's needs, interests, and abilities with the curriculum goals and objectives. The goal is to make social studies child-centered in an effort to spark meaning for the learner. By planning an overarching set of goals and objectives, teachers are more likely to be prepared to make important connections for children as the weeks approach. The main idea of the planning has been completed, allowing time and focus to be specifically tailored for individual groups of children.)

Yearly

What are the key concepts required within the curriculum for the grade level of each teacher? Each concept must be mapped out initially so that the instructor can teach at a pace that is measured and not rushed. Learning about times when certain animals became extinct, when settlers traveled to new lands, and when rights were made laws presents significant opportunities for children to gain historical knowledge.

Unit and Lesson Plans

Following the standards within the curriculum for the district provides a necessary framework.

The teacher should consider the following:

1. National, state, and district standards: is this concept required by these standards?
2. Objectives: what the student needs to know and do (including higher level thinking).
3. Product/assessment: how will students demonstrate what they know?
4. Prior knowledge: what do the students already know?
5. Lesson presentation through differentiation: ways of presenting this lesson in a developmentally appropriate way and including every student's learning needs.
6. Process: materials and activities to be used in teaching and practicing the skills required.
7. Lesson sequence: considering the timeline and instructional sequence, critical to students' abilities to make connections.
8. Culturally responsive teaching considerations: making sure the lesson addresses diversity, equity, collaboration, diverse voices, cultures, and families. (It is necessary to approach all lessons with anti-bias significance. Anti-bias teaching is addressed in Chapter 8.)

ENGAGING FAMILIES IN PLANNING

Families can help make lessons richer. The connections they can share with their children add strength to learning new concepts. When families know what the teaching components are, they will often increase opportunities for their children to learn. Personalizing information makes a connection for children, which adds depth to their understanding. When thinking about past, present, and future, families are able to connect this concept to experiences outside the classroom. Some schools invite family members in to talk about their childhood, to compare differences in the world between that time and now. An example of one such difference took place in a kindergarten classroom. Children brought in baby pictures to create a bulletin board, and the teacher also brought in a baby picture. The teacher's photo was black and white, and the children noticed. This generated a discussion of the fact that when she was a baby most film was black and white. She explained that this was true of television as well. Such learning opportunities broaden levels of understanding time and changes over time.

INTEGRATING HISTORICAL THINKING INTO OTHER CURRICULUM AREAS

Using historical concepts in other curriculum areas can further aid children's understanding. By using authentic stories in reading, examining dates and timelines in math, and looking at various inventions in science, children are able to "see" history in their daily lives.

Appropriate Teaching Strategies

Often the reading curriculum lends itself very well to tying in with social studies. When examining books that will be used throughout the year, it is important to look for the strands and domains of social studies for opportunities to teach history as a concept.

Following are steps the teacher can take for a successful thematic unit outcome:

1. **Choose a theme:** Once the core reading standards are outlined and the lesson is planned, it is important to then match the theme with the appropriate social studies standards. Creating two strong approaches is important; the social studies component cannot be simply an afterthought.

2. **Break down the topics:** By separating topics addressed in the storyline, teachers can maximize strategies, clarify possibilities, and elicit interest from children. Through conversations and introductory questions, teachers can determine students' prior knowledge. Finding what children are most interested in will ensure motivation and engagement throughout.

3. **Plan for resources:** Using a variety of resources not only helps make learning more meaningful and interesting but also helps

Lisa Cline

to reach a range of learning styles. Games, songs, art supplies, literature rich in historical theme, technology, time spent researching in the library, dramatic play centers, and creating a reflective classroom environment all lend themselves to more interesting learning opportunities when balanced and presented appropriately for different age groups. Lessons well planned and prepared ahead of time provide opportunities for the teacher to be fully engaged in the learning moment with the children while maximizing scaffolding in all areas.

4. **Assessment:** Depending on the resources used and strategies implemented, assessment can be directly applied to the activity the child participates in. For example, the child who chooses to create a clay representation of the story can explain the components and particular details of the project to the teacher. The child who chooses to find out more information through use of technology or the library can create his/her own documentation to be shared with others. Children engaged in a dramatic play center reflective of the study at hand can be overheard in their play, and the teacher can document assessment information through anecdotal records, becoming part of the play and asking appropriate questions in the context of the play, or even recording via video. This performance

approach allows children to demonstrate their understanding in a way that is interesting to them. Teachers are further able to differentiate teaching by varying opportunities of performance.

Pre-kindergarten

In the preschool years children's historical understanding is rooted in their routines. This lends itself well to forming the basis for understanding the historical time of past, present, and future. Social interactions are significant for the development of preschoolers, and as teachers support social interactions they weave important language into conversations. The language a teacher chooses to reinforce is aligned specifically with the concept, in this case past, present, and future. Words like *before, next, after,* and *later* set the stage for this initial learning. Helping children to understand the concept of these terms must be embedded in the language of their routines—for example, "we will play with water right *after* lunch" or "Let's wash our hands *before* we have a snack."

Kindergarten

In the kindergarten years, understandings increase to include greater spans of time, though they are still abstract and it can feel like "forever" until recess comes. This increasing ability allows children to recall when they were smaller and to know that, over time, they will grow bigger and get older. This expands the foundation of historical understanding. The continued use of language that defines past, present, and future is important. Introducing the names of days and months through songs and themes is appropriate, while expecting a kindergarten child to know that today is Tuesday, June 10, 2014, and to understand what that means chronologically, is not. While continuing to **scaffold** the abstract to the concrete, it is necessary to build the concept and allow children to eventually apply concrete meaning to the abstract idea. When teachers scaffold for their students, they aid learning by dividing concepts into small parts and guiding children through an understanding of each section, eventually building full meaning (McMillan, 2011).

This approach allows the teacher to specifically build skills based on a child's current and individual level of understanding.

Primary

Incorporating a variety of themes during the primary years fosters historical understanding. Although children still gather tremendous meaning by connecting historical learning to their own place in time, they are increasingly able to "study" history from an events perspective. When the material is presented in engaging ways, they may find people in history quite interesting, they may find events quite amazing, and they certainly find inventions to be fascinating. Most kindergarten children are very interested in dinosaurs and understand that they no longer exist, but it is not until later in the primary years that they can begin to map out different eras during which dinosaurs lived and to discuss theories of why they became extinct. At this age, children become fascinated by nonfiction, which fosters further engagement in the topic of history.

Project Approach

In 1994, Lillian Katz defined a project this way:

> A project is an in-depth investigation of a topic worth learning more about. The investigation is usually undertaken by a small group of children within a class, sometimes by a whole class, and occasionally by an individual child. The key feature of a project is that it is a research effort deliberately focused on finding answers to questions about a topic posed either by the children, the teacher, or the teacher working with the children. (Helm & Beneke, 2003).

The projects children can create to demonstrate historical events are endless. One of the best features of the project approach is that projects are self-differentiated, meaning children can apply as much understanding to the project as they have. The project approach can also extend beyond just building something to include creating clothing or other items of a certain era or related to an historical figure of study. The idea is to translate the objective to something tangible and reflective of the key concept of the learning goal. Projects can include a diorama, a clay sculpture, a block structure, a skit, a period costume, a student-illustrated book, a mural, and so on. The possibilities are limitless, reflecting the imaginations of the children and the encouragement of the teacher.

Second grade Fairy Tale Villages

Play/Learning Centers/Centers of Interest

Because children make meaning through play and especially through symbolic play, it is important they be allowed to explore the concepts through centers. Centers should be hands-on experiences that include concept-related materials and social engagement. Centers can be open-ended exploration or designed with an end goal in mind. Materials can, again, include costumes and other items of historical significance. For example, an older original style of phone with a bell receiver, a rotary style phone, a push button phone of various shapes with cords and without, and then the original bag-style cell phone, along with several of the various versions developed over the years, would provide children with hands-on examples they could manipulate and engage with. Because it may be difficult to gather all styles, teachers can use what they have and provide photos of others. Children could engage in a project of making a phone of recycled materials that reflects a certain time period with particular features from that era. This leads into arts and creative expression.

Arts and Creative Expression

Arts and creative expression tap into children's memories and leave a lasting imprint of an experience. Allowing children to express knowledge and understanding through individual expression is an important teaching strategy that cannot be taken out of the learning process if children are expected to be engaged and enthusiastic about learning. Singing songs or writing songs, viewing art or creating art, and observing or participating in dance are just some of the ways we can help children have a sensory experience while learning. Using materials reflective of an historical time to create an art project is of high interest for children; whether they use charcoal to create a drawing or crush berries to make a dye, they are learning about what others have done in the past out of necessity and finding joy in exploring with it today. Making a class or school museum to share with families is a wonderful culmination of a unit and encourages children to become the teachers/experts through writing and being tour guides.

Technology in the Classroom

Children are very interested in exploring with technology. The Internet provides them with opportunities to see reenactments of historical events and to research more as they are developmentally ready. This also provides teachers with the chance to "bring to life" many historical figures. The visual connection is important for many learners and can capture the authenticity of an event. The position statement of NAEYC and the Fred Rogers Center states, in part, the need to make informed decisions regarding the intentional use of technology and interactive media in ways that support children's learning and development; early childhood teachers and staff need information and resources on the nature of these tools and the implications of their use with children (NAEYC, 2012).

This position statement reminds teachers of the need for the careful and purposeful use of technology while paying close attention to the developmental needs of all learners.

Role-Playing

Allowing children to act as a character, to reenact an event, or to create a skit helps them understand the character, the era of time, and the significance of the event on a different level. This can be an open-ended dramatic play center geared toward a time in history or a reenactment of a particular event or historical person's life. A dramatic play center can be created by turning a table and chairs into a covered wagon or ship, using large rolls of paper, logs with yellow and red paper depicting a campfire, and dress-up clothing for children to put on. Books should always be placed in dramatic play centers for children to refer to. (*Sarah Morton: A Day in the Life of a Pilgrim Girl* and *Samuel Eaton: A Day in the Life of a Pilgrim Boy*, both by Kate Waters, are beautiful books that use photographs, by Russ

Eucabeth Odhiambo

Child's drawing of Sarah Morton

Kendall, to show what children wore during the 1600s and what they did during the day in the early English settlements of Plimouth Plantation in Plymouth, Massachusetts. The children speak throughout the book, adding authentic language and vocabulary to the study as well.)

Games

Playing games that were played by children in a different era also gives children greater understanding of the time being studied. Children who make marbles of mud and then learn to play the game outside on a flat surface or use a stick to manipulate a large hoop on a path begin to see what games played in an earlier time were like. They see the activity as fun and sometimes challenging. Teachers see it as experiential learning.

Group Discussions

Group discussions always give teachers insight into what the children are understanding. Because the teacher is able to ask questions directly tied to the learning, children are able to hear different ideas. By considering others' thoughts, they weigh their own, and this more complex thinking grows developmentally, always at different levels for different children. During group discussions, teachers can intentionally plan to have students share their newly found information. For example, the child who has recently examined the clothing of children in the 1600s can share that clothing did not have zippers and socks were called stockings.

Field Trips

Field trips give children an additional experience in learning authentic information. Field trips can be expensive, so sometimes teachers have to use the Internet for virtual field trips. Whenever possible, and if developmentally appropriate, museums are a wonderful experience for children. Several hands-on museums offer especially interesting and exciting exhibits for young children.

The strategies discussed above keep a classroom alive with curiosity and wonder. If teachers do not use a variety of teaching strategies, they struggle with maintaining the motivation and interest of learners. When Helm (2003) expresses concern about growing pressures and the focus on drill and skill, she sees an additional worry that this trend furthers limits children's learning by taking up time that should be spent exploring and investigating, which would foster more creative and higher level thinking.

LEARNING PREFERENCES AND DIFFERENTIATION

Learning Preferences

Understanding learning preferences is important for reaching all children. In a relatively short time together, a teacher can recognize a child's preference in learning. Is the child an active learner, engaged more deeply when there is movement involved? Is the child more inclined to work individually, pursuing information and creating solutions on his/her own? Does the child gravitate toward learning alongside others? Some children benefit from the confidence they gain in sharing ideas with others. In most classrooms, it is unlikely that children can learn according to their preference for every lesson; therefore, it is critical that teachers pay attention to preferences and offer a balance that allows the child to stay engaged and grow and that minimizes frustrations. If children do not feel comfortable in the learning environment, they will be less likely to find success. Understanding Howard Gardner's theory of multiple intelligences is another key consideration when examining learning preferences; images representing this theory can be found online. Pre-service teachers must research these varied learning styles to be best prepared to plan for, teach and understand young learners.

Differentiation

Understanding preferences must be accompanied by knowing children's strengths and needs. Differentiation allows the learner to process material in a way that makes sense and in which she/he is able to find meaning. For the child in need of support, material must be adapted according to the need. For example, a child who struggles with severe fine motor difficulties may be allowed to dictate a story to a scribe. A child with more general fine motor difficulties may be expected to write, but to write less. It is up to the teacher, and the objective at hand, to determine what content is most important for the child to write. For a child in need of enrichment, the teacher must look for opportunities for deeper learning along the same content lines. Doing independent research and creating a project aligned with the lesson are two ways to provide enrichment. Being able to work ahead in a textbook and continually being asked to help a classmate who is struggling are not models of differentiation, as they do not allow the child to grow in a meaningful way and do little more than keep the child busy. In an effort to meet the different ways that students learn, differentiated instruction meets the many levels of readiness, strengths, and interests that children bring to the classroom. This purposeful and flexible approach maximizes learning opportunities for all students (McMillan, 2011).

HOME/SCHOOL CONNECTION

Home/school connections are always important for positive relationships between families and teachers, which lead to heightened learning opportunities. It is important to always be aware of what families prefer as a line of communication. Often schools will ask that question on the initial enrollment paperwork completed each year. This allows for updating information while also respecting that not all families have computers. Knowing the family's communication preference is key.

When considering including families in classroom projects and activities (such as the timeline idea in this chapter), all must be afforded the opportunity to participate and can do so only when the information reaches them in a timely way. Teachers need to be sensitive to families when asking them to participate in a lesson. For example, if a goal is to allow a child to share information about her family, or complete a questionnaire, questions should be based on what each member is interested in, special hobbies, etc. To ask what each family member does for a living may leave those with family who are unemployed, incarcerated, or even absent feeling uncomfortable. Always analyze home involvement projects to make sure all family members can participate and feel positive and valued for their contribution.

In their article, "MAKESHOP: Family Engagement in Exploration, Creativity, and Innovation," Werner and Brahms (2012) highlight their belief that when children and their family members are engaged in learning together, the adults rekindle a love of learning which spreads this co-learning to other learning opportunities, strengthening both their relationship and the level of engagement for both. When adults are no longer simply supervising the children, they engage in meaningful creativity together.

ACCOMMODATIONS FOR CHILDREN WITH DIVERSE NEEDS

Teaching of the history curriculum must incorporate accommodations for children with diverse needs: both for those who are English language learners (ELL) (Figure 4.6) and for those with special needs (Figure 4.7).

Figure 4.6
Adaptations for ELL.

Adaptations for English Language Learners

Pictures offer a clear, visual connection as the teacher and student can find common ground in the language that each uses to express what the picture is about. Positioning the pictures in an **ordinal** fashion conveys the meaning of sequence when teaching past, present, and future ideas. This leads to the greater understanding of history. Helping children to understand the concepts and ideas they are focusing on within the content

Figure 4.6
(*continued*)

allows them to, first, identify the new terminology, and second, begin to apply the terminology in an authentic way. Therefore, children beginning to learn about the topic of history will first be introduced to words like *past, present, future, time, change, old, modern,* and so on. Learning past and future begins with understanding before and after, while identifying now as the present. This shift into thinking through history can be generated through sorting activities, timelines, and stories.

Figure 4.7
Adaptations for Children with Special Needs.

Adaptations for Children with Special Needs

- *Diverse learners* can use sequence cards to begin understanding first, then, and next; the visual experience can be key. Hands-on activities provide for the kinesthetic learner, songs and fingerplays for the active musical connection. This diverse approach is beneficial to all learners and meets a variety of styles but is particularly important for diverse learners. Pictures reflective of classroom events allow for yesterday, today, and tomorrow. Photos of historical events help make important connections for all learners. Young children faced with a learning disability that challenges their ability to read may also benefit from visual cues appropriately modified for the lesson. Adaptations for children with physical disabilities require understanding the disability and knowing the goals of each individualized educational plan (IEP). For example, raised cue points (letters, shapes, pictures) may be used for children with a visual impairment.

- *Sensory connections* are also important for all learners, especially diverse learners. When children dress up as an historical figure, build a project reflective of an event, or play a game from another time, they are given sensory experiences important to memory.

CURRENT EVENTS

Using current events in the community helps children tune in to a broader world around them. More significantly, world events can be a teaching opportunity as children hear adults discussing the importance of particular situations. Children are interested in learning and understanding the bigger world. Events such as the Olympics are an ideal springboard to lessons about the world and other cultures. Tragic events like 9/11 bring a daunting task to teachers as they struggle with how to explain what is going on in a developmentally appropriate way. Having open communication with parents during such discussions is critical to honor and acknowledge each other's needs during difficult times. Sharing newspaper articles with children encourages a broader understanding of life beyond their own.

SAMPLE ACTIVITIES

Observe several early childhood classrooms and look for ways in which teachers incorporate the concept of past, present, and future. Create a list for each age group, and write down every word used by both the children and the teacher that is reflective of the passing of time.

(Possible follow-up) Afterwards, review the list and, using the information gathered, create a mini-lesson that uses some of your examples in a purposeful way. Include in the mini-lesson the objective, materials, center set-up, and goals for the children. Also, consider how you would gather the information that allows you to examine the children's different levels of understanding (assessment).

RESOURCES

Books are ideal resources when teaching particular themes. The following are some children's books with a history theme (from *Beyond the Journal, Young Children on the Web*, September 2005):

The Flyers by Allan Drummond

George Washington's Teeth by Deborah Chandra and Madeleine Comora

The Great Expedition of Lewis and Clark by Private Reubin Field, Member of the Corps of Discovery by Judith Edwards

Sky Dancers by Connie Ann Kirk

Stars and Stripes: The Story of the American Flag by Sarah L. Thomson

Summer Sun Risin by W. Nikola-Lisa

Sweet Music in Harlem by Debbie A. Taylor

Watch the Stars Come Out by Riki Levinson

Assessing Learning Outcomes

- Explain key strategies in teaching the concept of past, present, and future.

- Explain integrating social studies with other content areas (math, reading, and science) and provide an example.

- Discuss a possible social studies activity that allows families to participate.

- List four social studies themes and one way that each theme can be introduced to young learners taking into consideration varied learning preferences.

References

Alleman, J., & Brophy, J. (2003). History is alive: Teaching young children about changes over time. *Social Studies, 00377996, 20030501, 94*(3).

Blow, F. (2011). "Everything flows and nothing stays"; how students make sense of the historical concepts of change, continuity and development. *Teaching History, 145,* 47–55.

Helm, J. H., & Beneke, S. (Eds.). (2003). *The power of projects: Meeting contemporary challenges in early childhood classrooms—strategies & solutions.* New York, NY: Teachers College Press.

Henniger, M. (2009). *Teaching young children: An introduction.* (4th ed.). Upper Saddle River, NJ: Pearson.

McMillan, J. H. (2011). *Classroom assessment: Principles and practice for effective standards-based instruction.* Boston, MA: Pearson.

Multiple intelligences, diagram. (2012). Retrieved from http://dsaathoff.edublogs .org/files/2012/09/Multiple-Intelligences-t1ie9f.png

National Association for the Education of Young Children (NAEYC). (2005). *Beyond the Journal. Young Children on the Web.* Exploring Social Studies Through Children's Books. Retrieved from http://www.naeyc.org/files/yc/file/200509/ SocialStudiesBooksBTJ905.pdf

National Association for the Education of Young Children (NAEYC). (2012). Technology and Interactive Media as Tools in Early Childhood Programs Serving Children from Birth through Age 8. Joint statement adopted 2012. Retrieved from http://www.naeyc.org/files/naeyc/file/positions/PS_technology_WEB2.pdf

National Center for History in the Schools, UCLA. (2014). Historical Thinking Standards. Introduction to Standards in Historical Thinking. Retrieved from http:// www.nchs.ucla.edu/history-standards/historical-thinking-standards/overview

National Council for the Social Studies (NCSS). (2010). *A framework for teaching, learning and assessment.* Bulletin 111. Silver Spring, MD: Author.

Schoenfeldt, M. K. (2001). Geographic literacy and young learners. *Educational Forum, 66,* 26–31.

Waters, K. (1993). *Samuel Eaton's day: A day in the life of a pilgrim boy.* New York: Scholastic.

Waters, K. (2008). *Sarah Morton's day: A day in the life of a pilgrim girl.* New York: Scholastic.

Werner, J., & Brahms, L. (2012). MAKESHOP: Family engagement in exploration, creativity, and innovation. *Family Involvement Network of Educators (FINE) Newsletter, IV*(2). Retrieved from http://www.hfrp.org/publications-resources/browse-our-publications/makeshop-family-engagement-in-exploration-creativity-and-innovation

5

Practicing Civics, Government, and Citizenship in Early Childhood Classrooms

Learning Outcomes

After reading this chapter you should be able to:

- Explain daily activities conducive to practicing civics, government, and citizenship.
- Explain the process and routine of giving children a voice in the classroom, developing skills that demonstrate children's understandings of democracy.
- Discuss the ways children can understand democracy at different levels.
- Outline dispositions for citizenship and leadership.
- Understand the significance of connections between families and the community to extend the definition of community for children.

Big Ideas for Chapter 5: Practicing Civics, Government, and Citizenship	Classroom Application	Standards Met
Understanding Community	Teaching community begins by being a community in the classroom, working together, and caring for one another	Individual development and identity (NCSS 4)
		Individuals, groups, and institutions (NCSS 5)
		Civic ideals and practices (NCSS 10)
Building civic practices	Children are able to understand serving the greater good through discussions and practices that support valuing their voices	Civic ideals and practices (NCSS 10)
Being democratic	Classrooms can and should reflect democracy, where children are guided by their teacher/leader through problem-solving and respecting one another's rights and responsibilities	Individual development and identity (NCSS 4)
		Individuals, groups, and institutions (NCSS 5)
		Power, authority, and governance (NCSS 6)
		Civic ideals and practices (NCSS 10)

NCSS Standards

The National Council for the Social Studies (NCSS) has organized social studies into 10 broad interrelated holistic themes. Those addressed in this chapter are in bold:

1. Culture
2. Time, continuity, and change
3. People, places, and environments
4. **Individual development and identity**
5. **Individuals, groups, and institutions**
6. **Power, authority, and governance**
7. Production, distribution, and consumption
8. Science, technology, and society
9. Global connections
10. **Civic ideals and practices**
    (NCSS, 2010)

NAEYC Standards

The following NAEYC Standards for Professional Preparation Programs are addressed in this chapter:

Standard 4. Using Developmentally Effective Approaches to Connect with Children and Families

4b: Knowing and understanding effective strategies and tools for early education

4c: Using a broad repertoire of developmentally appropriate teaching/learning approaches

Source: NAEYC Standards for Early Childhood Professional Preparation, http://www.naeyc.org/files/naeyc/files/2009%20Professional%20Prep%20stdsRevised%204_12.pdf

DEVELOPMENTAL BASIS FOR TEACHING CHILDREN ABOUT CIVICS, GOVERNMENT, AND CITIZENSHIP

What does it mean to be a citizen? What is government? How do we practice civics? The foundation for answers to all of these questions is rooted in opportunities to belong to a **community**. Additionally, such a foundation allows us to understand roles and opportunities within our community, whatever that community may be. These beginnings demonstrate, for children, the ideals of and need for rights, responsibilities, fairness, dignity, and goals of the greater good. As children grow in these foundational concepts, their security becomes a springboard to greater learning potential and a stronger sense of self. It is key that children know what to expect in the classroom; this includes routines, the daily schedule, consistent expectations, and a caring teacher. The routine allows children to feel comfort in knowing what will happen throughout their day. The daily schedule, which must include picture cues, puts them at ease, as they can easily view when different events will occur and, most importantly, what will be happening next. Consistent expectations make up the second layer of the routine; they may be defined as how the teacher will likely respond to the children's actions throughout the day. If consistency is not maintained, the comfort of the routine is undermined and the child is left confused and hesitant. Essential to all community classrooms is a caring teacher, one who will listen when a child is frustrated or struggling, one who will explain to students when, and why, a change in routine will occur, and one who will reassure them that everything will still be alright.

Looking for ways to minimize changes and talk about them when they do need to happen is important to community. For example, if library is canceled today because the librarian is ill, a caring teacher will explain that to the children and then may add, "So I will be taking you to the library today. I will read you a story and we can look at books, but we won't be able to check books out because only the librarian can do that for us." Or, the teacher may say, "So we will be having library time in the classroom today. Maybe we can set up a library station and take turns being a librarian." This caring flexibility models for students a relaxed response to change in routines and a sense of ease in modifying routines in a positive way.

Changes like assemblies or fire drills, when known ahead of time, can also provide a learning opportunity. When an assembly is scheduled, the teacher may state, "We won't be having music class today but we have a wonderful opportunity to listen to a band at our assembly. We will be able to see many kinds of instruments and musicians at the assembly." Or, in the case of a fire drill, the teacher may say, "At 10:00 this morning, when we are in our reading circle we will be having a fire drill. That means we will need to stop what we are doing and pay careful attention to this important practice for emergencies." In this case, it is essential for the teacher to walk the children through what they will need to do. ("When the alarm rings you will put your book down, stand up, and walk quickly toward the door. We should get into a quiet line. I will stand right here in front of you and we will walk to this door, and we won't do any talking until we are outside.") The teacher should have the children actually walk through the steps for practice, reminding them that the alarm will be loud, that their teacher will be right there with them, and that this drill is just for practice so that everyone can safely leave the building and knows where to go. After the actual fire drill, the children will need to talk, for just a few minutes, about the experience; the teacher will reinforce why such a drill is so important, find out what made them nervous, praise them for what they did well, and so on. This brief example shows that children can learn how to be civil during an important event, how to pay attention to a leader who is safely guiding them, and how to be a helpful citizen within their classroom community.

Additionally, language is important in developing citizenship. When teachers use words and word groups like *we, together, caring about each other, helping one another, cooperating, working together, sharing ideas,* and *discussing solutions,* they send the message that being a positive citizen is important and is done collaboratively.

A caring teacher is in tune with his students; he knows them well enough to spot inconsistencies in their actions and responds by checking in with them, making sure that they are okay and know he is available to them. A caring teacher understands the developmental needs of his students and balances the day accordingly. His sense of connection with them is essential to their success within their classroom community. Also, his expectations and increments of independence reinforce a sense of expectations for the community as a whole. When a student is given the freedom to work in all areas within the room, to go to the bathroom when the need arises, or to share ideas with a classmate, the message is clear about the need to be productive and efficient with a goal of respecting all involved. This behavior, of course, must be specifically discussed, taught, modeled, and refined over time. A community is always developing, and its members' needs are often changing; therefore, each participant improves the community by being more attuned to each facet of the group. The teacher leads this effort with positivity, purpose, sensitivity, and a sense of humor!

Taking the concept of citizenship to a broader sense, *global citizenship,* is a big step for young children. Teachers may start the dialogue by asking, "How can we show we care about people we don't know? Are there things we can do to help people we have never met?" By posing these kinds of questions, teachers are opening a view for children to consider situations they may not be exposed to in their own lives.

Figure 5.1 shows an example of children beginning to think on a more global level. The concept is outside their personal lives, and it is still a bit abstract for them, but they find themselves interested in trying to understand it.

Figure 5.1
Developing Concept of Citizenship Scenario.

> Mr. Dane overhears three of his kindergarten students talking while they are eating their snack. Bri says to two other girls, "My mom's getting her hair all cut tonight. She's giving it to Locks of Love." Marissa asks, "Why is she giving her hair to someone?" Bri replies, "They will give it to people who are sick and need hair." A. J. looks at Bri and says, "But who?" Their teacher continues to listen while allowing the discussion to go on but remains in proximity should the girls need some help in understanding this concept.

Developmental Basis for Teaching the Concept of Community as it Relates to Civics, Government, and Citizenship

The Infant Years

A caring, responsive environment provides infants with a sense of citizenship; they are able to feel that they belong and that others care about their needs. Being able to interact, to be engaged in a reciprocal relationship (for infants, this would be the beginning conversation of cooing, and for toddlers, it might be negotiating), provides the security of being heard, having thoughts and opinions, and connecting to others.

The responsive environment must also provide empathy and supportive gestures of hugs and consoling others, which models empathy and caring for all community members. Learning to negotiate peacefully is a key opportunity at this age, when children can often understand only their own wants and needs, and when dealing with strong emotions is especially difficult. Providing acceptable choices empowers toddlers while also allowing the community to be a more controlled, safe environment.

Preschool

As children's social circles and sense of community broaden, so, too, does the complexity of understanding their roles in these settings. Preschoolers may begin to see themselves as part of a community within their immediate family, extended family, classroom, and many others. What does it mean to be a citizen within these groups? Do children have more of a say in one group than another? What kind of voice, opinion, and control do they have in each? It can be challenging to understand the expectations in each group and how they may change depending on which "community" the child is part of in the moment. For their teacher, opportunities arise throughout the day to teach concepts of civics, government, and citizenship.

Civics takes root in civil interactions, the beginnings of understanding that one has a voice and others do as well. Preschool teachers teach civics when they listen to preschoolers and help them reach satisfying conclusions that are fair to all. Preschoolers begin to understand government when they are able to regard their teacher as a leader, someone who will guide them and help them by making the best decisions for the group as a whole, while also keeping them safe.

For preschoolers, leadership and decision-making are the cornerstones of learning about government. Understanding citizenship carries with it the responsibilities one has within the group: that of treating others with respect and kindness and that of recognizing what each individual contributes to the group. When a teacher sees each child's strengths within a group, she is identifying contributions. When a teacher outlines group expectations, she is identifying expected contributions. These lead to a child's comprehension of what it means to be a citizen and what each individual can offer to the overall function of the group.

Kindergarten

As children move on to kindergarten, another layer of community is added. Once again, they must figure out their role in this community. How do they express themselves, and just what are the expectations? As they continue to develop, they are better equipped to understand the perspective of others and that circumstances for others may be quite different from their own. They also bring their prior experiences in being a member of a community. Some will have quite a bit of experience, others very little. This is a time of transition. During the kindergarten year, teachers must use their knowledge of child development to guide children through social relationships. Children learn from observing other people, getting ideas of how to incorporate new kinds of behavior and using these ideas to guide their actions (Bandura, 1977).

Children will need opportunities to practice and learn new behaviors in group settings. Social skills such as taking turns speaking, listening, and sitting without disturbing peers are important. Teachers will need to discuss and practice these skills with children, who must be afforded sufficient time to practice them before they can be expected to successfully manage them (Henniger, 2009).

Careful and purposeful guidance will allow children to truly be a part of the classroom community and thereby understand civics on the small scale. As teachers **model** kindness, understanding, fair negotiation, and clarity in boundaries, children live and experience democracy.

Dan Gartrell, in his book *The Power of Guidance* (2004), identifies democratic life skills as those that children need to acquire in order to become productive citizens and healthy individuals. He outlines these abilities for children as both being able to see themselves as capable members of the group as well as worthy individuals in their own right. This also includes being able to express strong emotions in non-hurting ways and solving problems ethically and intelligently. The ability to be understanding of the feelings and viewpoints of others along with working cooperatively in groups while accepting human differences among all members further defines these democratic life skills (Gartrell, 2004, p. 69).

Any time children are expected to develop particular skills, it is essential that the skills are modeled for them. It is also critical that children have many chances to practice skills in an authentic way. For example, if children are rarely allowed to socially interact with their peers throughout the school day, how can teachers expect them to work successfully in pairs or groups? There must be purpose in teaching community skills. Opportunities to practice being part of a community and being civic minded must be woven into the lessons and learning of the day. Meeting times bring rich, authentic opportunities to discuss classroom issues, to revisit expectations, and to examine, together, viable solutions.

Class meetings offer a time to reinforce community within the classroom. Gartrell (2004) notes that circle gatherings have historical roots in Native American and other cultures, with the purpose of coming together for public deliberation in the spirit of equality.

Class Meeting.

Suzanne Clouzeau/Pearson

The skills learned and practiced during meetings enhance the child's understanding of community and strengthen the community itself as a result. Although morning meetings are key to instilling a sense of belonging in children and in giving them practice in the necessary skills of attention, listening, expression, and cooperation, they are also important all day long and in every lesson, every transition, every upset and conflict, every day and all year long (Kriete, 2002).

The meeting provides a sense of coming together for the greater good. When discussing classroom events and circumstances, the children are invested in situations that are real to their day. They can see how their ideas impact the flow of the classroom and the actions of their peers. They are able to observe what actually works and what does not. The school setting is an ongoing social experiment much like events in everyday society. Their classroom is a tiny microcosm of a much larger, more complex world, but it is theirs nonetheless, and the importance is real and the lessons deep in meaning. The best lessons about civics and citizenship arise from impromptu occurrences in the classroom. This is not to say that purposeful planning and design are not critical; to the contrary, it means much has to be in place to allow for these occurrences to arise and to play out in meaningful ways.

Primary

In the primary years, community becomes increasingly complex. Children build peer relationships and may face new experiences both socially and academically. They continue to benefit from class meetings as they grow in their understanding of others' perspectives, thoughts, and opinions. The ongoing support from their teacher and the need for a classroom environment that provides a safe place within which they can take learning risks remains critical to their personal success and the positivity of the group as a whole. Teachers need to plan with a growing concept of community in mind. Children should be afforded the opportunity to understand that, while we do not have to all be close friends, we do all need to learn to compromise at times, to be able to work together, and to respect one another. The idea of not leaving anyone out of the community is especially important for this age group. Helping those who may be struggling, reaching out to someone who is sad, and supporting a classmate who needs a helping hand are all modeled by the teacher and incorporated into the culture of the classroom. This is essential in the day-to-day experiences of the children.

LESSON PLANNING

Learning about Civics, Government, and Citizenship through Stories and Activities

When examining the topics of this chapter, government stands out as an area of specific curriculum planning. Civics also lends itself well to lessons and areas of focus, whereas citizenship is best modeled for young children on a routine basis, allowing them to experience what it is like to be a citizen within a community.

Citizenship can be taught through partner and group pairings, meeting times, and allowing children a voice in debates that naturally come up during the day. Debates in an early childhood classroom can weigh whether a dog is a better pet than a cat, carrots a better snack than grapes, or whether or not recycling should be required by law. Children have different levels of exposure to current events and often have fairly strong opinions as well. Thinking about their own opinions and realizing that others may have differing thoughts are both important considerations. For some children, being asked their opinion is a new experience and being asked to support an opinion, a new task. Allowing others to voice and explain their opinions is a new experience for many children.

As the classroom leader, the teacher must guide children through this process so there is a respectful discussion format that does not deteriorate into arguing. Current events are a good springboard to these kinds of conversations. Local happenings, such as events at a fair, a concert series, or an art contest, and national or worldwide events, such as an election or a debate, are examples of possible topics that children could discuss, expressing their thoughts about the event, raising points to consider, and offering ways in which people might help each other.

Yearly

Teachers must always organize the year by first looking at the standards and the curriculum from an overall perspective before they begin to break down the concepts expected to be covered. What do the standards directly refer to with regard to government, civics, and citizenship? What does it mean to live in a democracy? How does voting impact decision-making? What does citizenship mean to a 4-year-old? Giving children opportunities to be contributing members of their town communities is important for both the children and the adults within that community. Collecting items for families in need, or canned goods for a local food bank, and contributing artwork to the town library and banks are fairly common ways that children can give to their community. In a project called Places to Play in Providence, authors Mardell and Carpenter (2012) created a book in which children touted the best places to play in their community. This project was essentially a visitor's guide to their town, in which 3- and 4-year-olds expressed their perspectives on Providence's best places to play, their area of expertise to be sure. A key part of this project was that children's ideas were the focus; great care was taken to make sure the book reflected their ideas and contributions. The end result was a deeper understanding, for both the children and the adults, of their community and their relationship to it.

Teachers need to help children really connect to their neighborhoods, to be able to express ideas and to be heard by adults within the community. From a curriculum perspective, this takes learners on a more meaningful journey, where their ideas are valued and their contributions tangible. It also reminds adults that children are important stakeholders in the community. They are, in fact, the future of the community.

Therefore, it may be an overarching goal, within the course of the school year, for teachers to plan one such project that allows for the visibility and thoughts of the children to be highlighted within their own community. Broadening from the community of the classroom to the towns and neighborhoods in which they live is a significant scaffold for children. Community gardens, health fairs, and the building of a bike path around a town park would all be possible longer term projects to which children can contribute, see their efforts unfold, and ultimately share in the results. Along the way, lessons would surely include learning about civics and local government processes, further enhancing this authentic learning.

Weekly

The routines of the classroom continue skill-building and knowledge for this chapter topic. Children begin to notice a variety of jobs, see the need for their completion, understand what happens when the jobs are not done, and experience the sense of accomplishment in doing something for the greater good.

Classroom jobs enable children to contribute as citizens of their class community. It is essential that teachers select jobs that are meaningful to the flow and environment in the classroom. It is also important that if a job is not completed, teachers offer a gentle reminder of the need. Children notice very quickly if a job is not valued and their contribution not really important. The job of "substitute" becomes a valuable job, similar to real life, so when someone is absent the flow is maintained.

Class meetings foster an understanding of civics and government, and the leadership and guidance of a caring teacher allow children to experience democracy. As children learn about the basics of government, leaders making decisions, and citizens voting, they can also experience this knowledge firsthand during class meetings.

Unit and Lesson Plans

The unit and lesson plans require thoughtful preparation and consideration of certain key elements. Figure 5.2 presents a sample lesson plan format.

Figure 5.2
Sample Plan Format/Key Elements.

Unit and Lesson Plans

Understanding Lesson Plan Formats requires an understanding of the concept of the language. Therefore, any of the following terms (or others with a shared conceptual definition) may routinely be used in lesson plan formats/structures:

- Standards: National standards, state standards, district standards, common core standards, standard links, early learning standards
- Objectives, goal statements, learning outcomes, performance terms, instructional objectives, goal description
- Identify prior knowledge, connected knowledge, prior understandings, basis building
- Materials, resources, supplies, activity details
- Activating strategy, anticipatory set, gain attention, lesson 'hook', pique interest
- Lesson presentation, procedure, key concepts, steps
- Lesson sequence, guided and independent practices, lesson timeline, instructional sequence
- Assessment, product/process assessment, suggested assessment activities, progress information, skill demonstration
- Closure, retention activities, recall, retain and transfer
- Adaptations, support/challenge, for diverse abilities, responsive teaching

(see Chapter 4 Unit and Lesson Plans, framework)

INTEGRATING GOVERNMENT, CIVICS, AND CITIZENSHIP INTO OTHER CURRICULUM AREAS

Using the strands associated with government, civics, and citizenship can bring greater richness to lessons already incorporated into the overall curriculum. Helping children understand the history of government is an important foundation. They may start by learning leadership roles. They may also begin to see how policies affect them. In learning about traffic signals, for example, and the design of safety for drivers, children come to grasp the ebb and flow of the movement of society and its members. This can lead to an understanding of the foundation underlying, and reasons behind, civic decisions.

Appropriate Teaching Strategies

The teacher can use the steps given in Chapter 4 for designing a lesson with a successful cross-curricular focus.

- Choose a theme
- Break down the topics
- Plan for resources
- Assessment

The key to the success will be developing a lesson that has a meaningful approach to all content areas. Content areas that are added merely for the purpose of coverage will not allow for thoughtful learning. Also critical is the variety of activities provided; meeting many learning styles and interests will generate engagement that fosters deeper connections for the learner. For example, the teacher might design a lesson about voting (often linked to an authentic national or local election that has stirred some interest in the children). Children first need to understand the concept of voting. What does it mean "to vote"? Can you vote only once? How do you decide for whom (or what) to vote? How is your vote cast? As children develop additional understanding, they can become more knowledgeable voting members by creating a voter's card, comparing information about that which they will be voting on, and helping to tally votes. In classrooms with young children, it is important for them to vote on topics or for fictitious characters rather than actually "running" against one another, which can cause hurt feelings for those deemed unsuccessful. From a civil service perspective, there are always enough roles and jobs for every member of the classroom to find a valuable way to contribute and that also speaks to their interests and strengths. Very young children can be voters when the teacher hangs a T chart on a wall and puts two large pictures at the top as voting choices. The possibilities for topics are endless—foods, animals, colors, storybooks, and so on. To "vote," the children could use sticky notes on which their pictures have been placed; they would then hang the notes in the appropriate spot on the chart. The related NCSS social studies theme is power, authority, and governance, as well as **civic ideals** and practices:

- **Theme 6—power, authority, and governance** (goals, in part): Learners will develop an understanding of the principles, processes, structures, and institutions of government, and examine how power and authority are or have been obtained in various forms of government. They will learn how people in democratic nations organize in groups and attempt to cooperate and resolve conflicts for purposes such as establishing order and security, and seeking social justice.

- **Theme 10—civic ideals and practices** (connecting to the greater good, in part): An understanding of civic ideals and practices is a fundamental goal of education for citizenship in a democratic society. Basic freedoms and rights, and the institutions and practices that support shared democratic principles, are foundations of a democratic republic. In some instances, civic practices and their consequences are becoming more congruent with ideals, while in other cases, the gap is wide and calls for continued civic action by individuals and groups to sustain and improve the society. Learning how to apply civic ideals to inform civic action is essential to participation in a democracy and support for the common good.

Lesson Planning

An early approach to understanding leadership can also be presented through stories. For example, using the book *Duck for President* by Doreen Cronin (2004), children begin to differentiate between leader (farmer) and constituents (animals) and to understand how their needs and wants may differ. They follow Duck as he runs for various offices, votes are counted, and he comes to find out how much work each job entails. It is a lighthearted introduction to "running for office" and elements of democracy, as well as the concepts of "more than" and "less than" with regard to votes. This math connection would provide many opportunities for voting on countless topics of interest to the children, counting and comparing tally marks, and even graphing results.

As children grow a little older, they are able to become increasingly complex in their thinking about government and their role as citizens. *Grace for President* by Kelly DiPucchio and LeUyen Pham (2008) provides children with information about electoral votes as well as demonstrates how candidates can show a commitment to service. This book would cross over well with a math curriculum, including adding combinations of states to come up with a total of electoral votes, comparing subsets, and calculating differences.

Resources may include a variety of data collection materials, such as:

Clipboards

Paper for tally charts

Chalk and chalkboards

Dry erase boards and markers

Sticky notes

Markers, pens, pencils

Ballot boxes

Large paper for T chart

Children could create campaign slogans and signs. Those able to perform complex writing tasks can use a variety of ways to present persuasive arguments:

- Write and publish through the editing process.
- Write and then script for a skit or oral presentation.
- Write as a commercial to be completed via audio and/or videotape.
- Write as a song or rap.
- Write and then transpose into an artistic mural.
- Write and then script for a cartoon rendition.

This kind of creativity can also help children see and understand the impact of marketing (another curricular aspect is available in this regard: helping children learn to be more savvy consumers—NCSS theme 7, production, distribution, and consumption). Technology also opens up endless possibilities for children to tap into their creative sides and be more engaged in the task overall. Choices about working on their own, with a partner, or in small groups can give children added motivation and confidence.

Assessment must be focused on the objective for each content area. Objectives set forth in the beginning of the lesson planning process will shape the assessment. Therefore, when guiding students toward the activity, teachers must clearly connect to the objectives; for example, children are able to use a very simple checklist (with picture cues) in completing a task.

Project Approach

Recall from Chapter 4 that the project approach (according to Katz, 1994) is a thorough approach to a meaningful topic (as cited in Helm & Beneke, 2003). The teacher can therefore also consider possibilities for projects pertaining to government, civics, and citizenship. A simple project may involve children creating illustrations of different community helpers, first having a discussion and making a list or concept map of what the illustration would need to include to be an authentic representation, and then creating a class book that can be shared with families. In the same vein, children could instead dress up as certain community helpers and be individually photographed for a class book. The book could then include their writing or dictated contributions, fulfilling their role as author. The project approach would encompass the stages of rough drafts, editing, publishing, and the actual construction of the book.

The same format could be used with government leaders. Those whom the children see as leaders could be the topic of an interesting discussion in and of itself. Similarly, a class mural, with contributions from each student, could grace a classroom or school wall, the theme to be decided during a class meeting. Taking the project level further, and as children are developmentally ready, the teacher would center on examining children's thoughts and knowledge about a particular community event, landmark, or business. Creating a concept map to display understandings keeps a visual for all to refer to throughout the project. Visiting the point of interest would be a great opportunity for children to see important details. If a visit is not feasible, a virtual tour or expert visitor are possible alternatives. Children can then be encouraged to create their own representation with specific objectives outlined by the teacher. The teacher may also want to give the children an authentic experience that connects to the point of study—for example, cooking and setting up a dining area if a restaurant is their focus. Studying and re-creating local landmarks constitute a great way for children to connect with the history of their own communities. A town statue, or the

Suzanne Clouzeau/Pearson

Community/Helpers.

large clock or fountain outside town hall, would be exciting to find out more about and re-create. The more they learn about their community, the more likely they are to care about it. Projects need not be costly; using cardboard boxes, tape, clay, and string, children are able to create many interesting things. The vocabulary, signage, and writings that accompany their projects reflect important connections to their understandings.

Play/Learning Centers/Centers of Interest

Dramatic play centers frequently offer children opportunities to dress up as community helpers. Firefighters, postal workers, bakers, and restaurant workers are all common characters in dramatic play. They allow children to engage in pretend play while exploring real jobs in the community.

Mapping is another center of high interest. Beginning maps can include the classroom itself or the pathway students follow out of the room during a fire drill, on their way to lunch, and so on. Children enjoy drawing maps, noting points of interest between home and school, and also looking at real maps with keys identifying, for instance, water, forests, parks, and highways. Local maps would be another community connection.

Arts and Creative Expression

Allowing children to be creative, constructive learners both builds motivation and makes for more authentic learning opportunities. In being creative, children use their individual strengths while connecting to the material in a way that makes sense to them. An architectural lesson about the historic buildings in the community might require children to draw their renditions of a particular structure or re-create it using a three-dimensional form. A comparison of new structures with older buildings within the community would also give children additional insight into the changing landscape of their town.

Technology in the Classroom

Using technology to research historical facts about the community as well as demographic data would provide even more information to children. Using websites, the children can learn about their community leaders, find current topics for discussion, and even write to officials with ideas and opinions.

Children in second, third, and fourth grades could create a community website and share artwork, favorite places, and interesting facts. The teacher might also develop a blog that would allow the class to interact with community members and find out what others did in the community when they were the same age as the children. Multigenerational opportunities enhance connections in the community.

Role-Playing

Most children enjoy role-playing. The opportunity to interact with tools and uniforms as they "perform" the jobs of community helpers is an ideal way for young children to learn about the people who live and work in their town. Older children can act out the roles of community leaders, writing about and presenting topics that are important within their community.

Games

Children can create board games that are based on their own town and make their own cards and maps to direct players across town to certain points of interest.

For older children, third or fourth grade through high school, a website like icivics.org, founded and led by retired Supreme Court Justice Sandra Day O'Connor, is a fun, interactive way for children to learn about civics and government. There are games, such as Branches of Power, Cast Your Vote, Counties Work, and many more, in which children can earn "badges" and "impact points" that they can then apply toward real world service projects.

Several classic board games for younger children present an opportunity for finding landmarks while also using locations on the board for the players to travel through. This may include games for varied age groups such as CandyLand for very young children or one of the many city versions of Monopoly, using landmarks unique to the city, for older children. This, coupled with a basic map outlay, gives children a broad view of a town or place. Also, for young children, many versions of Old Maid have cards depicting community helpers, such as a firefighter, doctor, or baker. Such games provide conversational opportunities for building language and understanding community.

Group Discussions

Whether a follow-up discussion after a story, a class meeting, or a lead-in to a lesson, group discussions give teachers tremendous insight into children's levels of understanding pertaining to concept development. They also allow teachers to introduce new vocabulary and allow children to experiment with and practice using new language. Discussions about how and why ordinances and laws are made help children to understand the reasons behind such decisions and the processes followed to implement such actions. For example, the teacher or children may ask, Why do we have stop signs? How do we decide where to put them? Who makes those decisions? Who pays for the sign? Who installs the sign? What if we thought there should be one near our school— what must we do to try to make that happen? Simple topics can become increasingly complex, depending on the developmental levels of the students.

Field Trips

Local field trips are an ideal way to teach children about their own community. Visiting town halls, community centers, and voting locations allows children to see government in action. A variety of leaders can show children what they do and where they work, giving an important introduction to real world community activities.

LEARNING PREFERENCES AND DIFFERENTIATION

Learning Preferences

The ways that children can learn about government, civics, and community are as varied as their many learning preferences. Those who enjoy writing and researching, and documenting facts and figures, have countless opportunities to dig into history, to examine current events and topics, and to formulate needs and plans for the future. Those who prefer to actively engage in events can create an action plan based on community needs. Those with interpersonal strengths may choose to interview community leaders. It is key that young children have many hands-on learning opportunities and are able to be socially engaged in the process.

Differentiation

A teacher must present information according to children's needs in a variety of ways, allowing learners to connect with the material in a manner that enables them to build meaning. For children who need support, pictures can provide important cues. For example, when learning about leadership, a student-created matrix that includes pictures of people in different roles can help students visualize and remember each one. Those ready for advanced work could examine an issue faced by local leaders and write a persuasive speech to publish or present. The key is developing their personal level of understanding and continuing to build on that.

EFFECTIVE TEACHING APPROACHES FOR ALL STUDENTS

Meeting the needs of all learners is no small task, and yet it is a responsibility all teachers face. *Diverse learners* may benefit from role-playing historical figures, examining the time within which their figure lived and what their individual contributions were to government and civics. Taking on a role gives the learner a different sense of perspective. Whether young children dress up as famous leaders or older children research conflicts and take sides in a debate, role-playing can be beneficial for diverse learners. A teacher's understanding of how the learner best acquires understanding is critical to meeting his/her needs. Hands-on activities, multiple resources, and the use of technology will provide children with several opportunities to examine a concept. By offering choices and allowing children to gravitate toward the option that is most intriguing to them, teachers will be able to have a clearer understanding of what the children are learning. Children are more likely to engage and sustain that engagement when they have some level of choice. This can lead to greater motivation to pursue a task because they have been able to choose their approach to learning. Hyson (2004) refers to "emotionally relevant activities" as those that involve cause and effect. In other words, how the child interacts with the material will have a direct impact on the outcome. Such activities spark curiosity in children and invite their participation. Providing activities in which children maintain engagement and purpose in their exploration yields cognitive, academic, and emotional benefits (Hyson, 2004).

Sensory connections can be made by examining what makes a community unique. If children can recognize the smell of the local bakery, the sounds of traffic, pictures of local landmarks, and even the taste of specialty cuisine, they can appreciate what is different about their community and further compare it with others. Teachers need to provide such experiences for children in order to help them identify these special sensory characteristics.

HOME/SCHOOL CONNECTION

Sharing topics with families is always helpful because they may be able to support learning in their own creative ways at home. For example, family members can perhaps vote on what they would like to have for dinner on Friday night, where they would like to go, or which movie they would select for movie night. Highlighting, for children, the ways they contribute to the community of their family demonstrates for them their role, the impact of their efforts, their contributions, and their responsibilities.

Current events for a family would include special dates like a reunion, a birthday, or a family trip. Broadening the current events to the community may include a parade or a town festival. As children see this common, shared event, they begin to formulate the concept of community events, reaching beyond their families and celebrating wider themes.

Learning about community helpers is a common lesson in early childhood classrooms. Many books are geared toward this theme. It presents a wonderful opportunity to invite family members into the classroom to share what they do in their jobs. When children are given the experience of hands-on learning, handling equipment, seeing uniforms, and hearing from those with expertise, this generates both a new and renewed interest in the experience. Additionally, local field trips allow children to see settings within the community they may not typically see and behind the scenes of the places they may frequent regularly with their families. Imagine their interest in being behind the counter of the Post Office or in the kitchen section of a local pizza shop.

Home and school connections for this chapter are twofold. First, including families in teaching the topics of government, civics, and community allows for more learning opportunities. Second, it also supports the idea of community when schools and families work together. Children may hear their families talk about government decisions, they may see officials speaking on television, and they may go with family members to the voting booth. These are all potential learning opportunities, and when families know the children are learning about these topics they can more purposefully contribute to their learning through discussions with the children that broaden their understandings. Seeing how their families interact within the community can help children realize how members support and care about one another. Whether donating money, sharing used clothing, donating to food banks, or performing simple, genuine acts of kindness, families are powerful role models for children. Families that are able to receive needed items within their community demonstrate to their children that it is acceptable to have a need and that others will likely help out during such times. These kinds of actions go far in teaching children about civics and community.

ACCOMMODATIONS FOR CHILDREN WITH DIVERSE NEEDS

In teaching civics, government, and citizenship, appropriate adaptations for children with diverse needs must be made. Such adaptations for English language learners (ELL) are presented in Figure 5.3; those for children with special needs are explained in Figure 5.4.

Figure 5.3
Adaptations for ELL.

Adaptations for English Language Learners

Pictures are always helpful. Having picture cues for classroom titles and tools helps children feel included. For children whose primary language is not English, consistently being included and welcomed into the group helps them experience community. The classroom community engenders their core sense of working together, caring for one another, and building skills together. These qualities can translate to the broader community. When the teacher models the caring effort of this inclusion, support in learning, and even the challenges of communication, all children take note. Children then, typically, mirror the teacher's efforts and realize that an outstretched hand, a smile, sharing of materials, and helpful gestures are all ways to extend community to one another.

For children learning concepts in civics, government, and citizenship, teachers must, again, look for opportunities to cue learners into thinking from this perspective through engaging in the language of the topic. Defining community, civic practices, and democracy together through brainstorming allows children to attach personal meaning to the terms. Creating authentic recognition of the terms in action through classroom experiences further clarifies these terms. When the children come together as a class to share, they are representing a community; when they problem solve and discuss action plans, they are practicing democracy; and when they participate in supporting others, they are practicing civics. When a teacher labels actions as such, and documents them (class books, posters, and so on), the children can reflect on the experience and the terms with better understanding.

Figure 5.4
Adaptations for Children with Special Needs.

Adaptations for Children with Special Needs

In helping young children understand civics, government, and community, it is imperative that those with special needs are authentically included in all classroom activities. Therefore, the physical environment must allow for maneuverability of equipment, such as wider paths for wheelchair accessibility, and room for children to sit side by side, to encourage peer support and social connections. Helping all children recognize the different abilities of their peers with special needs alleviates fears, fosters understanding, and encourages creative problem-solving. Teachers must feel comfortable in discussing abilities with children while modeling strategies that maximize involvement for all children. A community level of inclusion would allow a child in a wheelchair to, possibly, sit in a beanbag chair during meeting and story times. A book with enlarged print and pictures, held by a child with a visual impairment, allows the child to follow the story with more connections. Use of assistive technology enables a nonverbal child to voice an opinion or vote on a class topic. Even a slant board can help a child with fine motor difficulties find greater success in writing and drawing. All of these adaptations make it possible for children with special needs to truly be members of their classroom community, actively engaged with their peers.

CURRENT EVENTS

In her article, "Social Studies in Today's Early Childhood Curricula," Gayle Mindes (2005) points out that solving issues within the classroom and examining neighborhood and community concerns supports the growth of social studies understanding, civic awareness, and invokes a sense of pride.

Taking the time to look for local community events and to help children be a part of them will connect students in a way that benefits the event as well as the children. A store grand opening, an art show, and a festival in a local park could all provide connections for involving a classroom of children. Whether making welcome signs, contributing artwork, or taking a field trip to the park, children would be active members in a community event. When these events stem from community outreach, children begin to learn that even they can make a difference when they can help others. How teachers provide this experience for children might be different in every circumstance. Some schools sponsor food drives, and some take donations of clothing, toys, and school supplies. Teachers must exercise caution; at any given time, families being asked to participate may be some of the very same families in need of such items. Schools need to provide families with information on how to access such resources in their own communities, and offer help in doing so, while always being sensitive to their situations.

National events are topics of discussion in many households. Children are likely to be curious about the event and may bring ideas and questions to the classroom. For young children, presidential elections offer a glimpse at a national current event. Hearing thoughts from children brings a view from that child's perspective, which can then guide a teacher in explaining the event in ways that children can comprehend. Helping them understand the voting process and how people choose leaders are also important beginnings in their understanding of democracy.

Government, civics, and community are interwoven in such a way that as children learn about one, their understanding of the others deepens. Leadership is key to each area, and with their teacher as their leader, children can continually learn these concepts on increasingly complex levels.

SAMPLE ACTIVITIES

Two sample activities for teaching civics, government, and citizenship are described below.

- Observe in an early childhood classroom. List four ways that children are able to experience concepts of community and civics.
- Create a mini-lesson in which children have the opportunity to vote. Based on the developmental level of the group for which you design your lesson, describe how you will teach them to cast their vote and include the materials that you will provide.

RESOURCES

The following books may be helpful in teaching children about government, civics, and citizenship (from *Beyond the Journal, Young Children on the Web*, September 2005):

Beautiful Blackbird by Ashley Bryan

Castles, Caves and Honeycombs by Linda Ashman

Coming to America: A Muslim Family's Story by Bernard Wolf

The Country Noisy Book by Margaret Wise Brown

Everybody Bakes Bread by Norah Dooley

Everybody Works by Shelly Rotner

George Washington's Teeth by Deborah Chandra and Madeleine Comora

I Read Signs by Tana Hoban

Lots of Grandparents by Shelly Rotner and Sheila Kelly

Rainy Day by Emma Haughton

Recycle Every Day! by Nancy Elizabeth Wallace

Send It! by Don Carter

Sky Dancers by Connie Ann Kirk

Smokejumpers One to Ten by Chris Demarest

Summer Sun Risin by W. Nikola-Lisa

Sweet Music in Harlem by Debbie A. Taylor

Assessing Learning Outcomes

- Explain how children in a classroom are able to experience being members of a community.

- Explain how 4- and 5-year-olds can learn about the concept of voting, and provide one example.

- Share two ways that children can develop their understanding of government.

- Describe one way a classroom of first-graders can demonstrate civic engagement.

- Discuss a community event that could connect families and the school.

References

Bandura, A. (1977). *Social learning theory*. Englewood Cliffs, NJ: Prentice Hall.

Gartrell, D. (2004). *The power of guidance: Teaching social-emotional skills in early childhood classrooms*. Washington, DC: Thomson Delmar Learning.

Helm, J. H., & Beneke, S. (Eds.). (2003). *The power of projects: Meeting contemporary challenges in early childhood classrooms—strategies & solutions*. New York, NY: Teachers College Press.

Henniger, M. (2009). *Teaching young children: An introduction*. Upper Saddle River, NJ: Pearson.

Hyson, M. (2004). *The emotional development of young children: Building an emotion centered classroom*. New York, NY: Teachers College Press.

Kriete, R. (2002). *The morning meeting book*. Turners Falls, MA: Northeast Foundation for Children.

Mardell, B., & Carpenter, B. (2012). Places to play in Providence: Valuing preschool children as citizens. *Young Children, 67*(5), 76–78.

Mindes, G. (2005). Social studies in today's early childhood curricula. *Beyond the Journal. Young Children on the Web*. (September): 1–8.

National Association for the Education of Young Children (NAEYC). (2005). *Beyond the Journal. Young Children on the Web*. Exploring Social Studies Through Children's Books. Retrieved from http://www.naeyc.org/files/yc/file/200509/SocialStudiesBooksBTJ905.pdf

6

Helping Young Children Understand Economics and Social Issues

Learning Outcomes

After reading this chapter you should be able to:

- Explain the developmental basis for teaching economics and social issues to young children.
- Outline the key economic concepts for young children.
- Use a variety of strategies that support economic learning.
- Create a simulated classroom economic system.

Big Ideas for Chapter 6: Economics	Classroom Application	Standards Met
Developmentally appropriate understanding of economics	Involving children in day-to-day economic activities that are developmentally appropriate, such as making center choices or selecting snacks	Social studies teachers should have the knowledge and skills to lead children into various day-to-day experiences in production, distribution, and consumption (NCSS 7)
Economic institutions, individuals, people: aspects of economics that directly impact children	Involving children in understanding how they are impacted by and how they influence aspects of economics, such as advertisement, visiting banks or stores, production of goods and services, class store	Social studies teachers should possess the knowledge and skill to involve children in aspects of economics that impact them directly or indirectly (NCSS 5 and 7)
Economic institutions and practices as they relate to children	Involving children in economic experiences such as classroom/school jobs and services, naming businesses that are in the community to build on local understandings first	Social studies teachers should have the knowledge and skill to involve children in economic experiences and skills (NCSS 5 and 7)

Standards Addressed
in this Chapter

NCSS Standards

The National Council for the Social Studies (NCSS) has organized social studies into 10 broad interrelated holistic themes. Those addressed in this chapter are in bold:

1. Culture
2. Time, continuity, and change
3. People, places, and environments
4. Individual development and identity
5. **Individuals, groups, and institutions**
6. Power, authority, and governance
7. **Production, distribution, and consumption**
8. Science, technology, and society
9. Global connections
10. Civic ideals and practices (NCSS, 2010)

NAEYC Standards

The following NAEYC Standards for Professional Preparation Programs are addressed in this chapter:

Standard 1: Promoting Child Development and Learning

   1b. Knowing and understanding the multiple influences on development and learning

   1c. Using developmental knowledge to create healthy, respectful, supportive, and challenging learning environments

4. Using Developmentally Effective Approaches to Connect With Children and Families

   4b. Knowing and understanding effective strategies and tools for early education

   4c. Using a broad repertoire of developmentally appropriate teaching/learning approaches

   4d. Reflecting on their own practice to promote positive outcomes for each child

(continued)

DEFINING ECONOMICS

Economics is the study of the distribution of goods and services. Young children experience economic interactions on a daily basis both at school and at home. During these interactions many parents or caregivers do not necessarily teach children about goods, services, money, production, or distribution; however, they talk about these concepts constantly. Every day, children have to make decisions about whether they need to spend money, make choices of one thing over another, and interpret the message of commercials on TV. Recently, more young children have experienced the effects of unemployment and inflation on their families. Thus, when children come to the classroom they have economic ideas and experiences. They may also have misconceptions or limited understanding. As such, it is the role of the teacher to clarify those misconceptions and help them make sense of their economic world.

As with all concepts, children need to build their knowledge of economics through meaningful, active, and memorable experiences starting from simple to complex concepts and using authentic interactions with both people and materials. According to NCSS (2010), "social studies programs should include experiences that provide for the study of how people organize for the production, distribution, and consumption of goods and services" (p. 82).

DEVELOPMENTAL BASIS FOR TEACHING THE CONCEPT OF ECONOMICS TO YOUNG CHILDREN

Children have the ability to learn economic concepts when they are taught in developmentally appropriate ways (Sosin, Dick, & Reiser, 1997). Young children are motivated to learn concepts that are practical, relevant, and presented in hands-on ways—especially in the field of economics, where the concepts are experienced day to day.

5. Using Content Knowledge to Build Meaningful Curriculum

5a. Understanding content knowledge and resources in academic disciplines

5b. Knowing and using the central concepts, inquiry tools, and structures of content areas or academic disciplines

5c. Using their own knowledge, appropriate early learning standards, and other resources to design, implement, and evaluate meaningful, challenging curricula for each child

Source: NAEYC Standards for Early Childhood Professional Preparation, http://www.naeyc.org/files/naeyc/files/2009%20Professional%20Prep%20stdsRevised%204_12.pdf

The Infant Years (0–3 years)

Piaget's theory ties in with economic understanding at the sensorimotor stage, moving into the preoperational stage, during which children learn through their senses (Piaget & Inhelder, 1969). This means that teachers involve children with physical objects or processes at ages 0 through 2. At the preoperational stage, toddlers (2–3 years) are involved in accomplishing tasks such as asking for what they need and providing explanations for utilizing something else. The dramatic center is important in teaching economic concepts such as purchasing goods and using pretend money. Talking about where parents work, asking what jobs they would like, and reading books are other ways of teaching this along with other economic concepts.

Benjamin LaFramboise/Pearson

Three-year-olds do not understand the concept of something being worth more or less; however, they can distinguish between money and other objects. Some 3-year-olds mimic the process of buying by exchanging money for goods, yet they are not aware that money is needed to purchase goods from the store in real life. It is difficult for them to understand how parents work in exchange for money.

Preschool–Kindergarten (3–5 years)

At this stage it is important to take advantage of children's curiosity and interest in their surroundings. Children learn through their prior experience and knowledge. Each child has a unique learning style and unique abilities and experiences, all of which support further learning. During the preschool years, children ages 3 through 5 continue to develop complex perceptions of the world around them. At this stage they are investigating their environment and are highly curious.

Money is an example of an economic concept that children deal with regularly. At the preoperational stage older preschool children understand that money has to be used to purchase things, but they do not know the value of money. They view the value based on coin size: The bigger the coin, the more value is assigned to it (Seefeldt & Galper, 2006). Children in kindergarten and the early elementary grades have the basic understanding of what money can do. They can see that money is needed to purchase goods, that the value of denominations varies, and that denominations with higher value will buy more things. They have some understanding of paid occupations and can mention vocations such as mail carrier, nurse, and teacher. They are able to expand their understandings to include systems and how those systems operate. The teacher should involve children in activities that include store and restaurant centers; reading literature with simple economic concepts; and making choices for themselves and with the group.

Primary (6–8 years)

Primary age children are at Piaget's preoperational stage, moving on to the concrete operational stage, and they have a plethora of abilities that will aid them in the learning of economics (Piaget & Inhelder, 1969). They are able to see the world through mental images and at age 7 and 8 are able to think hypothetically and reason about hypothetical situations.

At this age they are able to:

- Regulate their thought processes and attention.
- Plan and organize in series or steps.

- Classify and sort into groups or categories.
- Recall past events due to improved short- and long-term memory.

Subject integration, authentic assessment, and child- and teacher-guided activities are important in teaching economics, as they are in teaching other subjects. Examples of these methods include talking about advertising that is meant to influence children's choices, examining currencies from other countries, and using money to buy items in the classroom. Integration with other subject areas should be emphasized in order to consistently teach children that social studies encompasses everyday events. Visual aids are useful; graphic organizers such as T charts can show needs and wants, and flow charts can represent things they use (their consumptions). Discussing reasons why they decided to buy one item rather than another is very relevant. State social studies curricula provide detailed lists of the economics topics relevant for specific grades.

ESSENTIAL ECONOMIC CONCEPTS

Teaching economic concepts helps to clarify ideas, identify myths, and dispel misconceptions. Because economics plays an important role at all local, national, and international levels, understanding of economic concepts will ensure that children succeed in an interdependent world. The Council for Economic Education (CEE) works with organizations at the national, state, and local levels to promote economic and financial literacy education in order to build better and stronger economic and financial literacy in schools. The policy and advocacy section of the CEE website (councilforeconed.org) provides tools to use with young children.

The teacher's goal should be to allow students not only to ask questions but also to share stories, which will give the teacher an opportunity to clarify information. It is also important that the teacher gain an understanding of students' prior knowledge on the subject at the beginning of economics units or at the beginning of each lesson; in this way the teacher is able to concentrate on new topics based on student knowledge. Lessons organized in thematic units can include economic concepts that students have a chance to practice at centers.

According to NCSS standard 7 (2010), "social studies programs should include experiences that provide for the study of how people organize for the production, distribution, and consumption of goods and services" (p. 82).

Questions to explore in the early grades include the following:

- What questions are important to ask about wants, needs, goods, and services?

- Why can't people have everything they want?
- How are goods made, delivered, and used?
- How do people decide what to produce and what services to provide?
- How do we make choices about scarce resources?
- How does the availability of resources influence economic decisions?

Figure 6.1 sets forth what children in the early grades should know regarding NCSS standard 7.

Figure 6.1
Understanding Production, Distribution, and Consumption.

Children should know (Understand)	Children should be able to (Process)	Children should demonstrate understanding by (Product)
How people and communities deal with scarcity of resources.	Ask and find answers to questions about the production, distribution, and consumption of goods and services in the school and community.	Participating in a simulated classroom economic system.
The difference between needs and wants.	Analyze the difference between wants and needs.	Developing a visual that illustrates strategies for distributing scarce resources in the classroom, school, or community.
What people and communities gain and give up when they make a decision.	Evaluate how the decisions that people make are influenced by the trade-offs of different options.	Inventing a new product and organizing a classroom or individual business that markets that product to classmates or the community.
How economic incentives affect people's behavior.	Examine and evaluate different methods for allocating scarce goods and services in the school and community.	Designing and using a classroom currency, demonstrating the functions of money.
The characteristics and functions of money and its uses.	Assess how consumers will react to rising and falling prices for goods and services.	Increase the price of a classroom product.
Various organizations that help people achieve their individual economic goals (banks, businesses, labor unions).	Examine how communities help individuals in achieving their goals.	Engage in games and activities that allow for role-playing of people in the community.
The characteristics of a market economy.	Identify the use of advertisement to create "wants."	Conduct and analyze (through charts, graphs, and so on) marketing effects through the use of class/school surveys.
The goods and services produced in the market and those produced by the government.	Research where goods and services come from, including those produced by the government.	Visit community sites that produce and sell goods and provide services; discuss process. Include family members that work in these sites.

Source: Adapted from NCSS standard 7 (2010).

Figure 6.2
Children's Literature for Economics (K–5).

National Council for the Social Studies Notable Economics Trade Books for Young Children

Irena Sendler and the Children of the Warsaw Ghetto by Susan Goldman Rubin.

Dear America: Like the Willow Tree by Lois Lowry

Megan's Year: An Irish Traveler's Story by Gloria Whelan

Here Comes the Garbage Barge! by Jonah Winter

The Life of Rice: From Seedling to Supper by Richard Sobol

The Firehouse Light by Janet Nolan

The Hallelujah Flight by Phil Bildner

Waiting for the Owl's Call by Gloria Whelan

Give a Goat by Jan West Schrock

Show Me the Money: How to Make Cents of Economics by Alvin Hall

---

Source: Based on NCSS Trade Books for Young People, www.nccss.org/resources

The value of reading material in supporting the teaching of economic concepts and in illustrating how economics works in the everyday world cannot be overestimated. Figure 6.2 lists some of the books regarded as notable by the NCSS.

Scarcity and Decision-Making

Wants, Needs, and Choices

Wants, needs, and choices are basic economic concepts that young children are capable of identifying. Throughout the day, children have to make choices between needs and wants. Through classroom activities, the teacher can help children learn to distinguish between needs and wants. The goal should be to help young children develop an understanding of scarcity, thereby setting the stage for economic decision-making.

Needs are things we need. **Wants** are things we would like to have. Examples of needs are shelter, food, affection, and safety. Examples of wants are cars and toys. Basic needs are culturally universal and so can be used to extend children's knowledge and understanding of others.

- Ask the children to name the things their families need and explain why. Sort answers into needs and wants. Discuss what constitutes a need and what constitutes a want. After the discussion, children can draw their families' needs and wants. Older children can write about them.

- Children can have fun cutting out pictures from magazines of their needs and wants and placing them on a T chart. Integrate such an activity by labeling different items and having children do a word sort.

- Using the classroom store, give children tokens that they can use to purchase whatever they want. Make sure the prices are large and visible and easy to count. This activity can help teach the math concepts of money, counting, and returning change, as well as limitations and choice.

Scarcity: Limited Resources

Children need to understand that there are limited amounts of some resources. Thus, being able to make decisions is an integral part of the study of scarcity. The teacher must explain the concept of enough/not enough. She can talk about what the class needs and what is available in small amounts. With infants and toddlers, the teacher can combine words with actions in getting across the idea that there are no more materials or snacks. When children ask for more or when they let the teacher know supplies or other materials need to be replenished, the teacher can expand their understanding by suggesting something else to do and redirecting when a specific item has been used up. This is a good time to talk with children about how they can share something that is limited. Activities can be made meaningful to 4- and 5-year-olds, for example, by scaffolding understanding with language, photos, and learning center activities to show limited resources, and pointing out whenever children share something during activities like painting, water play, and playground times. Reading age-appropriate books about scarcity also boosts understanding of this concept. Older children can assess limited resources in the school and community and provide solutions for how those needs can be met.

Supply and Demand

In addition to learning about production, children need to understand the meanings of **supply** and **demand** and how they relate to small business. Supply is how much of something is available, whereas demand is how much of something one wants. Therefore, products (**goods**) are made depending on the need or wants of the **consumers** (people). Supply and demand leads to the concept of scarcity and needs and wants. Examples of small businesses that supply needs in the community are a great resource for primary age children. What happens when resources are limited? With younger children, an effective exercise is to find solutions for what could be done if only a few pieces of paper can be found in the classroom. Solutions might include cutting up the pieces of paper and sharing, keeping the scraps for later, or using slates or dry erase boards instead. When replenishing classroom resources or when no more resources are to be had, bring this to their attention, and discuss possible solutions for obtaining more resources. Involving children in economic real life situations in the classroom improves their economic awareness and skills.

Production and Consumption: Production, Consumers, Goods, and Services

The concept of production closely connects to consumption because **production** is an attempt to meet the wants of consumers. **Distribution** is the way goods reach the consumer. The concept of exchange of money is related to production in that money is used by consumers to purchase goods and services. Through active exploration, children can begin to develop an understanding of consumption, production, distribution, money, goods, and services.

The teacher should develop the idea of who a consumer is and then discuss advertising and its goals; choices that are made based on advertising and the variety of goods available; and factors that influence the choices we make, such as cost, value of a product, personal preferences, and advertisement.

Consumption

Who is a consumer? Everyone is a consumer. Children become consumers as soon as they are born. They consume goods and services, express needs and wants, and later make choices about what they want. As children grow older, they become better at choosing what they want. The teacher's function is to help children understand that they are consumers and to help them learn how to make responsible choices as consumers. Children need to understand their role in consumption and the part they play in making decisions about consumption within their families. Being informed about goods and services contributes to personal efficacy, that is, being able to make wise choices (Alleman & Brophy, 2003). When children make purchases, they are consumers. They need to understand that money is required to pay for goods and services.

The teacher needs to explain the relationship between consumers and producers. At the same time he/she should discuss how producers compete to persuade consumers to buy their goods and services. Children can role-play how to convince other students to buy or choose their product. This will lead to discussion regarding advertisement and how students should be educated consumers. To help children understand the consumption process, a store can be set up in the classroom so that children can buy and make choices during purposeful play.

The teacher can use scenarios in which children identify what they like and dislike, such as stories, games, and foods. A good strategy is to provide opportunities for children to make choices about purchases from the class store center. This way, they are able to practice making choices and clarifying their likes and dislikes. As purchasers, they will play the part of a consumer; as clerks they will be producers.

The concept of reuse should be introduced when discussing production and consumption. The teacher should point out items that people reuse at home and highlight those that are reused in class. Here, the recycling process can be integrated with geography; as the teacher talks about making our environment a better place, he/she can discuss the ideas of saving money and not wasting resources, especially considering that many resources are scarce and must be protected.

Advertising Influence on Decision-Making

Children are targets of TV advertising. With this in mind, the teacher can show examples of TV advertisements geared toward children. Discussion can focus on whether the children believe they really need those items and whether they think they are getting a good-quality product. The teacher should talk about the words used in the advertisement. Are the claims true? Can a particular item really bring "endless joy"? The teacher can explain that advertisements encourage consumers to make decisions without thinking through what they are buying. Children can then begin to understand how to make informed decisions by assessing the truth of the information they hear. Below are some ideas for activities to reinforce the teaching of these ideas.

- For young children, discuss Arthur's choice (found on "Arthur's TV Trouble" at pbskids.org) and their experience in making choices in the classroom during center time and in other activities. Such an activity might involve choosing between saving money and purchasing candy. Ask the child, "Will you enjoy the candy for a long time? Might it be better to save money for a while first?" Also, choices about completing an activity on time as opposed to putting it off until later could help children begin to see how to prioritize and organize through making appropriate choices. Sharing whether or not they think options are good choices, or drawing pictures of good choices and putting a line through choices that may not be best, may foster additional discussions.

- Children in early primary grades can do activities like making their own advertisement; other activities on this website would also be appropriate.

Production and Distribution of Goods and Services

This concept covers jobs that people have, as well as the production of different goods. Production involves producing goods to meet the needs and wants of consumers. Production also pertains to products that a country sells to other countries, leading to global distribution. The most practical aspects of production that children can understand are jobs their families do and community jobs. People with community jobs are producers of services. Other people produce goods. The teacher can bring the concept of production alive in the classroom by, for example, having children make a card for their principal or a painting for a sick classmate. The teacher expands understanding of this concept by allowing children to list the tools they need, where they come from, and how much they cost.

It is important to help children understand where goods come from. Young children may think that goods are produced in the marketplace or just simply appear on the shelf. Children can investigate product sources and the various ways they reach the marketplace. For instance, children can research where their desks come from. Examples of production can include actual goods produced (pizza, bakery cupcakes) or services provided (students' chores at home, family members' chores, classroom chores, students' parents' jobs). Excellent places for field trips would be a pizza shop, a bakery, farmer's markets, and a candy factory, to mention a few.

Jobs and Careers

Developing the understanding that jobs are a way to earn money is an important topic. The goal is for children to grasp the idea that jobs are both a service and a source of income. Children may not have much choice as to how they can earn money. However, they can get involved in money-making activities in the school. Through these projects children are able to apply the concepts related to money. Other opportunities for children to have jobs can include classroom responsibilities and tasks. Teachers can share with students different career options that are important to their lives, as well as gender representation in jobs often mostly associated with one gender or the other, such as female construction workers, doctors, and scientists, and male nurses, teachers, and cooks. When talking about gender representation, teachers need to carefully choose their words to be gender inclusive, using "police officer" instead of "policeman," "mail carrier" instead of "mailman," "firefighter" instead of "fireman," and so forth. Another way that teachers can enhance understanding is to allow opportunities for children to dress up and talk about the profession they like. The dramatic play area can be stocked with items from different professions. Finally, family members and different professionals can be invited into the classroom to share aspects of their jobs in a developmentally appropriate way.

Money

Children need to understand and appreciate the reasons for using money—as a medium of exchange to obtain our needs and wants. Additionally, they need to understand related concepts, such as supply and demand, scarcity, and profit. A money unit would include income and the various ways one can make an income.

Money Is Used for Acquiring Products and for Trading at Community and National Levels

At an early age, children have limited ideas about money and the value of money. They often think that everybody can get money from the bank anytime she/he wants to, and that goods are sold for whatever price they were bought. They think economics is more of a benevolent system than a business (Byrnes, 1996). Thus children need to understand where money comes from, where it is used, and by whom. The following are some basic areas the teacher needs to address when discussing money:

1. Purpose of money—used as an exchange medium
2. History of money and exchange—barter trade, early forms of money
3. Advantages of money—used as an exchange and storage convenience
4. Features of American coins and paper money
5. How and where money is manufactured
6. Banks—their importance, concepts of checks, credit cards, money machines, and so on

Purpose of money: The teacher should incorporate literature that discusses the history of money and mediums of exchange. Books about money can be used for studying the history of currency, the U.S. Mint where money is printed, the historical figures and pictures on money, the serial numbers on bills, and much more.

Financial institutions: Young children need to understand how banks work. Banks are money centers. Basic concepts about banks can be taught to young children. Visiting a bank can be the first step in demystifying banks as "a place where money comes from." A discussion about checks, debit cards, and ATMs as ways of drawing on the money the bank keeps for its customers helps clarify the limitations adults have on money (Alleman & Brophy, 2003). Information about deposits, loans, interest, and how they are related is usually acquired at ages 9 to 10, although it can be taught earlier (Berti & Monaci, 1998).

Teaching Economic Concepts to Children in Various Age Groups

Techniques and approaches should be tailored to the different age groups:

- *Infants and toddlers* can be introduced to concepts about supplies, resources, and giving and taking by playing sensory-motor games of hide-and-seek, peek-a-boo, and the like. Providing consistent, stable relationships for infants and toddlers lays the foundation for later conceptual understandings. Creating routines that meet their needs establishes the kind of social and mental processes that are critical to later cognitive development and the ability to comprehend concepts about the economy.

- *Pre-kindergarten, kindergarten:* Reinforce the idea that people work and earn money and that money earned is used to buy things. Use a variety of dramatic play centers, such as banks, restaurants, and stores, to give children experience in buying and selling.

- *First grade:* In addition to the above, talk about savings and community helpers; also, visiting a financial institution will further reinforce the concept of money and earnings.

- *Second grade:* In addition to the above, talk about means of payments and prices.

- *Third and fourth grades:* At this level, students will define economic terms, identify examples, and explain the concept. Additionally, they will discuss economic institutions, the function of government in the economic system, markets, income, profit, and wealth.

USING SOCIAL ISSUES TO TEACH ECONOMICS

Social issues are events that happen around the community where children live. Children often become aware of social issues through the media. Questions and topics will come up in the classroom that the teacher needs to clarify and discuss. Some of the issues may be beyond the children's level of understanding. However, children are affected by some of these issues, such as homelessness and safety. Social issues can be taught in other subject areas, such as current events with geographic, cultural, and other themes. Coverage of social issues can focus on specific aspects, such as safety and violence in the social environment and matters of civic responsibility.

Students must learn that people cannot obtain goods and services if they do not have money. Money is earned, but sometimes jobs are not available for various reasons, such as lack of required skills, too few jobs, and so on. As questions arise, the principle of developmental appropriateness is pertinent. The following topics are related to economics and should be discussed in the context of lack of goods and services (scarcity).

Current Events

Current events happen around us on a daily basis, making them a necessary part of the social studies curriculum. Good teachers look out for what they can bring into the classroom that is both current and relevant. "Essentially children benefit when the curriculum fosters the development of a sense about what happens in the community and in other places . . . provides a sense about reality and strengthens individual identification with society" (Melendez, Beck, & Fletcher, 2000, p. 263). Discussions of current events should be made part of classroom activities, such as sharing news during circle time, allowing the chance for students to ask questions about any kind of news, including something they may have seen on TV. Some educators are not comfortable discussing such topics because of the belief that the topics are too complicated for children to understand. However, it is better to discuss these topics and dispel myths and misconceptions than not discuss them. The teacher should listen to what children have to say about things that interest them while allowing them to discuss issues as they understand them. There are opportunities for teachable moments during such discussions.

Current events may pertain to geography and the environment: for example, extreme weather such as a tsunami, or a volcanic eruption; historic events such as the launching of a space shuttle; national holidays; and local and special elections. Holidays bring up the concepts of making choices, celebrating cultures, and purchasing gifts. The election of President Barack Obama was historic and worthy of class current events coverage and discussion.

Social Justice Issues

Social justice issues are also important current event topics. These include concepts such as poverty, homelessness, diseases, violence, and family struggles that arise regularly in the community. They need to be addressed because children and families are impacted by poverty, disease, and so on. The most nonthreatening way to bring up a discussion in class can be through reading stories and children asking questions. Such discussions are important to children's sense of belonging and self-worth by providing them with understanding and a voice. See the Connections to Literacy section.

Safety

Safety for children is a minute-by-minute event. Teaching about safety is an integral part of classroom management. Furthermore, children often express concern regarding their safety. The goal is to reassure children that they are safe and to educate them about safety. Safety issues include traffic safety, fire safety, and stranger danger and are often part of the early childhood curriculum. Field trips to the firehouse or in-class demonstrations by firefighters, police, or any relevant organization can be arranged. This kind of activity can also be connected to learning about community roles, jobs, and services.

Poverty, Homelessness, Disease, and Violence

Poverty, homelessness, disease, and violence are a reality for many children. Other children are impacted indirectly, meaning that teachers have to talk about these issues. Just by listening to children's conversations, teachers are able to get a sense of how these issues affect children in their classrooms.

Poverty impacts the well-being of a child. According to the Population Reference Bureau and the U.S. Census Bureau, 26 percent of children ages 1 through 5 and 21 percent of those ages 6 through 17 in the United States are considered poor (The Annie E. Casey Foundation, 2008). According to the Income, Poverty, and Health Insurance Coverage in the United States report, 44 percent of children lived in low-income families in 2011. Of the 44 percent, 10 percent were considered very poor (Bureau of the Census, 2011). There is a great need to prepare children to deal with these issues effectively.

Homelessness has become more evident in these difficult economic times here in the United States. "The Department of Education reports that nearly 1,065,794 children were identified as homeless over the course of the 2010–2011 school year by public schools" (United States Interagency Council of Homelessness, 2013). Homelessness must be addressed in the classroom. Listening to children's views about homelessness is a great way for the teacher to know who is affected and to help children understand what it means to be homeless. Use literature to initiate such discussions.

Violence is another topic that must be addressed in the classroom. Children can't help but hear violence talked about (or see it acted out) on TV. Many children live in areas where violent behavior is a fact of life. Furthermore, the media are full of news about violent behavior. Unfortunately, media constitute one variable that might put children at risk of aggressive behavior (Gentile, 2007).

"Although high-quality early childhood programs are *not* an inoculation against the destructive effects of violence, positive early school experiences and warm, nurturing relationships with teachers are known to be critical contributors to children's ability to cope with stress and trauma" (NAEYC, 1994, p. 4). Thus early childhood educators must deal with violence through "advocating for public policy actions; partnerships with parents; early childhood programs and curriculum; and professional preparation, development, and support" (NAEYC, 1994, pp. 2–3). See the Resources section for tips on how to talk to children about these issues.

INTEGRATING ECONOMICS INTO OTHER CURRICULUM AREAS

As discussed in various chapters in this book, social studies concepts should not be taught in isolation. Therefore economics can be taught in the context of a variety of other subject areas and concepts: for example, money in math, reuse in geography, and social issues in geography. Reading and listening to economics-related stories integrates with language arts. Through reading, children learn new vocabulary and how to write sentences, thereby interacting with literature in ways that can be used to teach language arts. Art is always applicable to economics as well as other areas in social studies; drawing, coloring, and making signs and posters all contribute to effective activities. When producer and consumer behavior is taught, children learn how to view themselves and their relationships with other people. They get to make choices, discuss their needs and wants, and also engage in interrelationships in the production of goods and services—and experience how they and others serve. These concepts encourage positive behavior as children take on a multitude of roles.

PLANNING FOR ECONOMICS

Daily/Weekly Planning

The foundation of social studies for children is their personal experiences and their understanding of themselves in relation to their families, school, and community. The key topics related to economics that are discussed in this chapter, which include needs, wants, choices, scarcity, production, consumption, distribution, goods, services, and money, are meant to be taught in developmentally appropriate ways.

Infants and Toddlers

Planning for infants and toddlers is based on the teacher's understanding of the kinds of economic activities that children are involved in throughout the day. Daily and weekly planning for this age group hinges on the teacher's ability to facilitate hands-on experiences that build knowledge and comprehension. Teachers should plan to interact with children, "asking open-ended questions to scaffold children's thinking and problem solving skills" (PA Keys, 2009). Planning will entail choosing topics as outlined in the standards and curriculum. Teachers should read books, talk about concepts the children are learning, place play items in the dramatic play area, and schedule outside activities such as playing games and creating gardens.

Pre-kindergarten and Kindergarten Children

Planning for pre-kindergarten and kindergarten children will involve some formal instruction. Such instruction might include inviting a speaker to come to school to talk about jobs, taking field trips to community institutions, and discussing facts with children during which they are asked questions and given time to think through ideas.

Primary Age Children

Much of the planning for this age group includes formal instruction as well as experiences facilitated by the teacher. The curriculum is more structured, and developmentally these children are ready for more formally organized learning.

As has been mentioned in other chapters, planning involves children in the process. The teacher first finds out what they would like to learn and then goes further by asking what they already know about the topic and what they would like to know. This method aids the teacher in focusing on topics or aspects of a topic about which children have very little knowledge.

General Guidelines for Planning Economics

The following are steps teachers should consider when planning to teach economics, or any topic, to young children:

- Identify the topic for the week.
- Outline the skills to be learned and what to look for in the children's actions and responses.
- Observe children's actions.
- Ask open-ended questions.
- Acknowledge and reinforce their action as it relates to the concept.
- Talk about the concept.
- Read about the concept.
- Provide play items relevant to the concept planned.
- Plan an activity emphasizing the concept.
- Assess knowledge by observing children in action, understanding through their behavior.

Different topics can take different amounts of time. The teacher should remember to regularly revisit skills that children are working on even when other topics are taking center stage at a given time.

Yearly

Yearly planning must be organized by first looking at the standards and the curriculum from an overall perspective before breaking down the concepts expected to be covered. What do the standards directly refer to with regard to economics? Yearly planning is important especially for project planning and thematic units. These are teaching styles that require a large amount of time to plan and execute. Also, other factors have to be considered, such as whether a more suitable time of year is preferred. Yearly planning (long-term planning) gives the teacher an opportunity to look at curriculum requirements in order to budget for materials and any other needs. It also helps the teacher to plan for cross-curricular integration. It is impossible to plan integration on the spur of the moment. Some experiences, such as working with the community, involve both school and community cooperation. Yearly planning before the year begins also ensures quality teaching and that whatever needs to be taught is on the calendar. For example, in planning a thematic unit on money, the teacher must consider when the topic of money is being taught in math. Reading and other activities can easily reflect this theme.

Learning Centers

Centers of interest such as stores, offices, and factories are appropriate for very young children to practice economic concepts. The teacher should be sure to place a variety of props such as cash registers, play money, receipts, empty food boxes, bags, and small carts in the centers, as well as clothes for various jobs in the dress-up section.

Props with Economic Themes

Listed below are some props associated with specific places that reflect economic themes:

Grocery store: plastic fruits and vegetables, empty boxes of sample groceries, cash register, calculator, brown paper bag

Bank: old checkbook covers, computer-made checks, date and other stamps, calculator, play money

Bakery: baking molds, flour, mixing bowls, rolling pins, measuring cups, bread trays, aprons, empty cookie boxes, bread bags, brown paper bags

Pizza place: flour, rolling pin, pizza boxes, plastic pizzas, paper plates, plastic pizza cutter, price markers, order forms

HOME/SCHOOL CONNECTION

Parents and guardians are assets for economic literacy. Parents and children experience economics together in a variety of ways and places, such as at department stores, restaurants, gas stations, supermarkets, and jobs. Encourage parents to discuss economic concepts with their children (Seefeldt & Galper, 2006). At the same time, parents can encourage children to participate in economics activities, such as making choices between toys they can or cannot afford to buy, or making purchases with the parent's money and help. Send information home through assignments, projects, or a letter letting parents know exactly how you want them to help.

ACCOMMODATIONS FOR CHILDREN WITH DIVERSE NEEDS

Effective and equitable teaching of economics must ensure that accommodations are made for children with diverse needs, including those who are English language learners (ELL) (Figure 6.3) and those with special needs (Figure 6.4).

Figure 6.3
Adaptations for ELL.

Adaptations for English Language Learners

To meet the needs of ELL students, use diverse materials, resources, and strategies, such as picture books, one-on-one help from teachers' assistants, and allowing children with differences to share their personal experiences about some of the following topics:

- Cost of things that they want (e.g., games, toys, food) with which they are familiar

- Phrases that their families say to them about spending or requests

- Discussion of ATMs, going to the bank, waiting for pay days

- Planning impulse control, choices and decision-making, and delay of gratification activities throughout the year (transitioning, waiting skills, turn-taking, projects, holiday celebrations).

- Using books such as *The Berenstain Bears' Trouble with Money* may help ELL students make economic connections beyond any personal experiences.

These strategies are not only for diverse learners but for all students, as well; however, using them increases success for students who are ELL.

Emphasize academic language by creating a section on the wall for economic words. Have pictures next to those words. Involve ELL students along with the rest of the class in activities in which they have to use those words, such as completing a T chart with needs on one side and words on another; think-pair-share what their wants and needs are.

Figure 6.4
Adaptations for Children with Special Needs.

Adaptations for Children with Special Needs

Students with learning disabilities can, at times, have difficulty understanding abstract concepts. Therefore, using authentic materials and
natural resources helps with comprehension. This is also useful for
ELL students. Use large and durable objects with students who have
limited motor skills. Encourage children with low vision to smell and
touch items. Make sure they are safe (Melber & Hunter, 2010).

CONNECTIONS TO LITERACY

As with other areas of social studies, books offer a rich source of
materials for learning and teaching. The following books are based
on NCSS Notable Economics Trade Books for Young Children
(ncss.org/notable).

Farm by Elisha Cooper

Hard Hat Area by Susan L. Roth

The Hard-Times Jar by Ethel Footman Smothers

Lawn Boy by Gary Paulsen

Lunch Money by Andrew Clements

Send It! by Don Carter

Money Books

The Berenstain Bears' Trouble with Money by Stan Berenstain and Jan Berenstain

The Big Buck Adventure by Shelley Gill and Deborah Tabola

Buying a Pet from Ms. Chavez by Alice K. Flanagan

Choosing Eyeglasses with Mrs. Koutris by Alice K. Flanagan

Market! by Ted Lewin

Money by Joe Cribb

Money Sense for Kids by Hollis Page Harman

Mr. Santiago's Tasty Treats by Alice K. Flanagan

Mr. Yee Fixes Cars by Alice K. Flanagan

Our Money by Karen Bornemann Spies

Round and Round the Money Goes by Melvin Berger and Gilda Berger

The Story of Money by Betsy Maestro and Giulio Maestro

Ultimate Kids' Money Book by Neale S. Godfrey

Earning Money/Service

Bea and Mr. Jones by Amy Schwarz

Ben Goes into Business by Marilyn Hirsch

A Job for Jenny Archer by Ellen Conford

A Quarter from the Tooth Fairy by Caren Holtzman

Tom and Annie Go Shopping by Barry Smith

Money Concepts: Decision Making, Recognizing Resources, and Recognizing Success

How the Second Grade Got $8,205.50 to Visit the Statue of Liberty by Nathan Zimelman Whitman

Jerome the Babysitter by Eileen Christelow

Just Shopping with Mom by Mercer Mayer

Ox-Cart Man by Donald Hall

Paddy's Pay Day by Alexandra Day

Buying and Selling

Coins and Bills by Ted Lewin

Our Money by Karen Bornemann Spies

Round and Round the Money Goes by Melvin Berger and Gilda Berger

The Story of Money by Betsy Maestro and Giulio Maestro

Ultimate Kids' Money Book by Neale S. Godfrey

Safety and Jobs

A Castle on Viola Street by DyAnne DiSalvo

The Goat Lady by Jane Bregoli

Officer Brown Keeps Neighborhoods Safe by Alice Flanagan

Si, Se Puede! Yes, We Can! Janitor Strike in L. A. by Diana Cohn

A Trip to the Firehouse by Wendy Cheyette Lewison

Uncle Willie and the Soup Kitchen by DyAnne DiSalvo-Ryan

You and Me and Home Sweet Home by George Ella Lyon

Homelessness

Changing Places: A Kid's View of Shelter Living by Margie Chalofsky, Glen Finland, and Judy Wallace

December by Eve Bunting

Fly Away Home by Eve Bunting

Home Is Where We Live: Life at a Shelter through a Young Girl's Eyes by Bonnie Lee Groth

Homeless by Bernard Wolf

The Lady in the Box by Ann McGovern

Lives Turned Upside Down: Homeless Children in Their Own Words and Photographs by Jim Hubbard

Mr. Bow Tie by Karen Barbour

Rosie the Shopping Cart Lady by Chia Martin

Sélavi, That is Life: A Haitian Story of Hope by Youme Landowne

Shelter Folks by Virginia L. Kroll

A Shelter in Our Car by Monica Gunning

Someplace to Go by Maria Testa

SAMPLE ACTIVITIES

Activities abound for teaching economic concepts. The activities listed below are arranged by topic.

Needs, Wants, Choices, and Money (Exchange)

Establish a dramatic play area:

- Set up a restaurant and have children create and illustrate a menu with the cost of various foods on it. You can also use menus from a real restaurant; local restaurants are often willing to share their menus and other consumable items in an effort to advertise. Children often recognize the logos and materials provided. Use play money and have children make choices based on the amount of money they have and the cost of the food. Primary age children can group the foods in three or four food groups and then make choices toward a balanced meal, that is, fruits, vegetables, meat, and dessert.

- Set up a store using bins to hold merchandise, a cash register, play money, play receipts or pads, and so on. To meet the needs of language diverse learners, label merchandise bins in all the languages represented in the class.

- Take your class to a restaurant that serves food from another culture as an opportunity to learn about and eat food from another culture. Parents can give their children enough money to buy something; however, children should view the menu beforehand (download the menu from the Web or pick up a copy from the restaurant) so they have time to think about and choose what they want to eat.

Production and Consumption

- Take a trip to visit a parent at work. Have children prepare questions beforehand that they will ask. Arrange for hands-on experience. Choose from a variety of places to visit, such as a bakery, a restaurant, or a library.

- Take a field trip around the school. Have children prepare questions in advance. Interview the principal, a teacher, a janitor, or a cook.

- Have children, together with their parents, make a list of items they consume at home. Have them make a collage with wrappers, labels, and/or magazine picture cut-outs.

- In the classroom, keep an assortment of clothing and uniforms and other items that are associated with various types of work. During discussions, have children dress up to reflect jobs being discussed.

Money

- Take a trip to the local bank. Have children prepare questions that they will ask at the bank. Introduce the unit by talking about what the bank does and defining vocabulary such as bank teller and checks. Prior to the day of the visit, write your own check and withdraw money as students observe. Have the teller explain the process so that children understand that a person does not just write a check and "get money."

Environment

- Start a recycling project. Label two bins where children can sort the papers and cans for recycling.

- Visit a recycling plant with primary age children.

RESOURCES

The list below features Internet sources for material relating to economic concepts; social justice issues; and help for children with regard to trauma, crises, and distress.

- National Council of Social Studies website: NCSS.org

- Poverty: socialstudies.esmartweb.com. See the annotated biographies link, then select economics.

- PBS.com: Assessing children's learning; assessing and evaluating children's economic concepts should be a continuous group and/or activity using the following:
  - Observations
  - Small- and large-group discussions or activities
  - Portfolios of children's work, such as collages

- • Games
- • Parental feedback

- Children and Money. Institute of Consumer Financial Education: financial-education-icfe.org. See the Children and Money section.

- Managing money: Needs vs. wants. PBS Kids: pbskids.org/itsmylife/money/managing (accessed July 7, 2013)

- McKinnon, S. 2004. Allow an allowance. Consumer Economics Update. University of Missouri Extension: extension.missouri.edu/ceupdate (accessed July 7, 2013)

- Social Studies for Kids. n.d. Want vs. need: Basic economics: socialstudiesforkids.com/articles/economics (accessed July 7, 2013)

- Council for Economic Education: councilforeconed.org (accessed July 14, 2013)
  - • Alleman, J., & Brophy, J. (2003). *Social studies excursions, K–3. Book three. Powerful units on childhood, money, and government.* Portsmouth, NH: Heinemann.

- Poverty and schools: wholechildeducation.org/podcast

- Coping with traumatic events: families.naeyc.org

  - • The National Child Traumatic Stress Network: Tips for talking to children about the shooting. See more at: families.naeyc.org
  - • The National Education Association School Crisis Guide. See more at: families.naeyc.org
  - • American Academy of Pediatrics : Talking to Children. See more at: families.naeyc.org
  - • Child Care Aware: Helping Families and Children Cope. See more at: families.naeyc.org
  - • American Psychological Association: Helping Your Children Manage Distress. See more at: families.naeyc.org

Technology Resources

Technology resources are plentiful and available for download. Some are listed below.

Preschool

- ABC ZooBorns

Kindergarten

- Britannica Kids: Volcanoes

First Grade

- Barefoot World Atlas
- Khan Academy

Second Grade

- Barefoot World Atlas
- Geocashing

Third and Fourth Grades

- The Magic of Reality
- Khan Academy

Assessing Learning Outcomes

- Explain how children's literature can be used to support the learning of economics.
- Describe the types of adaptations that can be planned for learners with special needs that might help them acquire social studies concepts.
- Use economic concepts such as supply, demand, and price to help explain events in the community and nation.
- Explain how activities and field trips can be used to support the learning of economics.

References

Alleman, J., & Brophy, J. (2003). *Social studies excursions, K–3. Book three. Powerful units on childhood, money, and government.* Portsmouth, NH: Heinemann.

Annie E. Casey Foundation. (2008). Kids count data center: A project of the Annie E. Casey Foundation. Retrieved from http://datacenter.kidscount.org

Berti, A., & Monaci, M. (1998). Third graders' acquisition of knowledge of banking: Restructuring or accretion? *British Journal of Educational Psychology, 68*, 357–371.

Bureau of the Census (2011). *Income, poverty, and health insurance coverage in the United States: 2010.* Retrieved from http://www.census.gov/prod/2011pubs/p60-239.pdf

Byrnes, J. (1996). *Cognitive development and learning in instructional context.* Boston, MA: Allyn & Bacon.

Gentile, D. A. (2007). Public policy and the effects of media violence on children. *Social Issues and Policy Review, 1*(1) 15–61.

Melber, L. M., & Hunter, A. (2010). *Integrating language arts and social studies.* Los Angeles, CA: Sage.

Melendez, W. R., Beck, V., & Fletcher, M. (2000). *Teaching social studies in early education.* Albany, NY: Delmar Thomson Learning.

National Association for the Education of Young Children (NAEYC). (1994). *Violence in the Lives of Children.* Position Paper. Washington, DC. Retrieved from http://www .naeyc.org/files/naeyc/file/positions/PSVIOL98.PDF

National Association for the Education of Young Children (NAEYC). (2010). *NAEYC Standards for Early Childhood Professional Preparation.* Retrieved from http://www .naeyc.org/ncate/standards

National Council for the Social Studies (NCSS). (2010). *National curriculum standards for social studies: A framework for teaching, learning, and assessment.* Silver Spring, MD: Author.

PA Keys. (2009) Pennsylvania learning standard for early childhood: Early learning standards. Retrieved from http://www.pakeys.org

Piaget, J., & Inhelder, B. (1969). *The psychology of the child.* New York, NY: Basic Books.

Seefeldt, C., & Galper, A. (2006). *Active experience for active children: Social studies.* Upper Saddle River, NJ: Merrill Prentice Hall.

Sosin, K., Dick, J., & Reiser, M. (1997). Determinants of achievement of economics concepts by elementary school students. *Journal of Economic Education, 28*(2), 100–121.

United States Interagency Council of Homelessness. (2013). *Families with children: Population trends and characteristics.* Retrieved from http://usich.gov

7

Age-Appropriate Understanding of Geography

Learning Outcomes

After reading this chapter you should be able to:

- Define and describe geography.
- Explain the relevance of teaching geography to young children.
- Give examples of how geography can be incorporated into the everyday curriculum of the early childhood classroom.
- Identify geographic tools each age level should learn.
- Design a lesson based on any relevant geography concept.

Big Ideas for Chapter 7: Geography	Classroom Application	Standards Met
Culture: understanding similarities and differences	Explore world cultures, especially those represented in the school or classroom	Social studies teachers should possess the knowledge, capabilities, and disposition to provide instruction and experiences that allow for the study of culture and cultural diversity (NCSS 1)
Relationships between people, places, and things: understanding the physical world and how people interact with places and things	Use children's experiences in the immediate environment—physical and human—to help them understand those relationships and interactions	Social studies teachers should possess the knowledge, capabilities, and disposition to provide instruction and experiences that allow for the study of people, places, and environments (NCSS 3)
Technology and society: recognizing the importance of technology and the changes it has gone through	Use a variety of technology Explore technology's impact on individuals, others, and society Explore various media	Social studies teachers should possess the knowledge, capabilities, and disposition to provide instruction and experiences that allow for the study of relationships among science, technology, and society (NCSS 8)
Global connections: understanding the interconnectedness of the world and its people	Interact with information and artifacts from other places through actual artifacts, books, and media	Social studies teachers should possess the knowledge, capabilities, and disposition to provide instruction and experiences that allow for the study of global connections and interdependence (NCSS 9)

NCSS Standards

The National Council for the Social Studies (NCSS) has organized social studies into 10 broad interrelated holistic themes. Those addressed in this chapter are in bold:

1. **Culture**
2. Time, continuity, and change
3. **People, places, and environments**
4. Individual development and identity
5. Individuals, groups, and institutions
6. Power, authority, and governance
7. Production, distribution, and consumption
8. **Science, technology, and society**
9. **Global connections**
10. Civic ideals and practices (NCSS, 2010)

NAEYC Standards

The following NAEYC Standards for Professional Preparation Programs are addressed in this chapter:

Standard 1: Promoting Child Development and Learning

   1b. Knowing and understanding the multiple influences on development and learning

   1c. Using developmental knowledge to create healthy, respectful, supportive, and challenging learning environments

4. Using Developmentally Effective Approaches to Connect With Children and Families

   4b. Knowing and understanding effective strategies and tools for early education

   4c. Using a broad repertoire of developmentally appropriate teaching/learning approaches

   4d. Reflecting on their own practice to promote positive outcomes for each child

(continued)

THE VALUE OF GEOGRAPHY FOR YOUNG CHILDREN

The study of **geography** can be very interesting to young children if it is brought to life and made relevant to their experiences. More so, it can be easily integrated into all subject areas. Geography is "the study of people, **places**, and the environments and the relationships among them" (National Geographic Joint Committee, 1994, p. 1). According to the Expanding Communities Model, learning begins with children's personal experiences and their initial understanding of themselves in relation to their families and homes. Gradually, as their perception grows, children expand their understanding to include their schools, neighborhoods, communities, and the larger world. Furthermore, children learn geography throughout the day inside and outside the classroom. Children begin to comprehend the nature of their world and their place in it as they observe and experience their surroundings (Schoenfeldt, 2001). Through the study of geography, children are able to develop understanding of the "relationships between human populations and physical world"; they learn about "spatial perspectives and examine changes in the relationship between people, places, and environments" (NCSS, 2010, p. 16).

DEVELOPMENTAL BASIS FOR TEACHING GEOGRAPHY

Infant Years (0–3 years)

Children at this age learn about their environment through exploration. Therefore their environment needs to encourage exploration by providing sensory materials, natural surroundings (Seefeldt & Galper, 2006), and proper access. During the infant and toddler years, children have not developed a complex perception of the world around them. Because play is the way in which they build knowledge, children must be given opportunities to develop skills through hands-on

5. Using Content Knowledge to Build Meaningful Curriculum

5a. Understanding content knowledge and resources in academic disciplines

5b. Knowing and using the central concepts, inquiry tools, and structures of content areas or academic disciplines

5c. Using their own knowledge, appropriate early learning standards, and other resources to design, implement, and evaluate meaningful, challenging curricula for each child

Source: NAEYC Standards for Early Childhood Professional Preparation, http://www.naeyc .org/files/naeyc/files/2009%20Professional%20 Prep%20stdsRevised%204_12.pdf

activities that stress exploration. Their interpretive ability does not extend to spatial objects, distance, and so on. However, children in this age group are developmentally able to understand relationships at the level of self and the people around them, especially as they move toward 2 years of age. As they discover new things, they begin to see their environment as an interesting place to be. A few guidelines will make the environment enriching and safe. First, the organization of their environment needs to encourage exploration from one area of interest to another. Second, play areas should include objects they can climb easily and carpeted floors they can fall on or jump down on safely. Outside areas must have soft grass or other materials that children can fall onto without harm. Third, centers should have familiar items. For example, the kitchen center will include plates and sippy cups that are similar to what they use at home. As children grow older, the teacher can start to point out and comment on what they see—how high places are, how deep, how wide around, and how far away.

Preschool (3–5 years)

Children learn through prior experience and knowledge. Each child has a unique learning style, abilities, and experiences, all of which support further learning. During the preschool years, children ages 3 through 5 continue to develop a complex perception of the world around them. At this stage they are investigating their environment and are highly curious. They are developmentally ready to understand basic geographic concepts, such as developing an understanding of themselves within a community and movement.

Preschool children are ready to learn the following geographic skills and concepts (Pennsylvania Department of Education, 2014, p. 48–49):

• Identify similarities and differences of personal characteristics.

- Demonstrate an appreciation of one's own characteristics and those of others, as well as others' cultures.
- Display an awareness of his/her role as a member of a group, such as the family or the class.
- Show understanding of how individuals work together to achieve group goals.
- Recognize how things are spatially related to one another.
- Describe the characteristics of where she/he lives and visits.
- Identify location and direction.
- Develop a beginning understanding of maps as representations of actual places.

Kindergarten (5–6 years)

Kindergarten age children experience a change that Whiting and Edwards (1988, p. 188) defined as the age of reason. Children are more able to focus on learning and to stay engaged. Additionally, they are highly curious (Hyson, 2008). "Kindergarten social studies curriculum is organized into broad integrated topics of study. The content connects to children's lives, and study is integrated with other learning domains" (Copple & Bredekamp, 2009, p. 243). In kindergarten, children learn key skills of literacy, numeracy, and social problem-solving. They are able to develop their understanding of the world and how it relates to them by interacting with materials, other children, and their teacher. Thus, concepts that connect to basic geography literacy are relevant: These include geographic tools, such as maps; physical characteristics of people and places, such as land forms; and interactions between people and places, such as those associated with farming, housing, and so forth.

Primary (6–8 years)

During the primary years, children are able to learn more complex ideas. As in the younger years, social studies should be integrated and should include authentic assessment. Children should be engaged in learning that is meaningful, complex, and memorable, yet interesting and engaging, such as role-playing (Hyson 2008; Sylvester, 1995).

There is continual need for learning through experiential and hands-on activities that are both engaging and challenging. "Children younger than 8 or 9 are still learning in uneven and episodic ways and cannot always perform on demand . . . while they may demonstrate

David Kostelnik/Pearson

Building with Blocks.

Benjamin LaFramboise/Pearson

Building with blocks – understanding scale.

new knowledge or a new skill one day, they may not be able to show it on demand the next day" (Copple & Bredekamp, 2009, p. 258). At the primary level, the content of the social studies curriculum should connect to children's lives and other learning domains, as with younger ages. Key learning takes place through "projects and activities involving use of library resources, visits to interesting sites, visitors' interviews, discussions, and relevant use of language, writing, and reading skills" (Copple & Bredekamp, 2009, p. 316).

GEOGRAPHY IN THE EARLY CHILDHOOD CURRICULUM

The Relevance of Teaching Geography to Young Children

As previously indicated, young children are naturally curious about their environment. The enthusiasm they have for discovery is a characteristic that suits learning anything very well, including the concepts of geography. Through geography children can investigate their environment at levels relevant to their development and understanding. Teachers have the opportunity through geography to guide children toward developmentally appropriate exploration and symbolic representation of their world.

Brophy (1990) suggests that learning geography requires the following:

- Using sensory-motor experiences (e.g., climbing, running, jumping) to develop abstract concepts of direction and space—physical movement in space.

- Incorporating sensitive interactions with adults who give children verbal labels, thus extending their knowledge.

- Introducing and using words that describe the physical characteristics of objects to help children learn the different aspects of the earth's surface—hard, soft, rough, smooth, sandy.

Figure 7.1 lists language that may be introduced to preschoolers in order to foster the understanding of geography according to early learning standards.

Furthermore, it is important to answer the question, Where do I live in the world? Geography includes everything children do on a daily basis, such as going to school, visiting the grocery store, and visiting their friends' and relatives' homes (movement, distance). Their bedroom is full of geography—under the bed (under), next to the bed (next); so is their classroom—up in the cupboard (up), sliding on the slide (down), **location** of items in the classroom (across the room, beside, near, and far). One of

Figure 7.1
Words to Describe Geographic Terms.

Space: up, down, over, under

Physical objects: hard, soft, rough, smooth

Earth surfaces: ground, sky, water

Direction: direction-giving sign, such as exit here sign

Environmental print: trash sign, recycle signs, road signs

Source: Adapted from Neuman, Roskos, Tanya, & Lenhart, 2007.

the first maps children can draw is that showing the area from the class to the playground (Neuman, Roskos, Tanya, & Lenhart, 2007).

Through play children experience and use geographic skills and concepts. For example, as they dig in the sand box and pour water into containers, they are interacting with the physical world. They are able to feel the materials their surroundings are made of. The teacher must provide opportunities for children to actively explore their physical world through the physical characteristics of objects (Neuman et al., 2007). Piaget (1969) noted that children understand the world through first-hand experiences. Therefore, both first-hand experiences and concrete materials foster understanding of complex concepts such as mapping. For young children, the use of blocks is a way to represent the world around them. As they play with blocks, children gain spatial learning and a sense of scale. Beginning map-making can take place through using blocks, as well.

Elementary school age children are in the concrete operational stage of thinking (Piaget, 1969). They understand the world by engaging in it both physically (Piaget, 1969) and socially, as expressed by Vygotsky (Vygotsky, 1978). This underscores the importance of social interaction and working together to solve problems. During play, words such as *fast* and *slow* can be used. Such words introduce geographic concepts to very young children.

According to the National Geographic Joint Committee (1994), in Melendez, Beck, & Fletcher, 2000, the following reasons (numbers 1–5 in the list below) support geography education in the early years:

1. An understanding of space provides the foundation for well-informed individual decisions later in life.

2. A person who is aware of spatial relationships acquires a sense of personal control over the environment.

3. Knowledge about geographic space fosters in children an appreciation and sense of places and things, near and far away.

4. Geography education also promotes a sense of responsibility toward the environment.

5. Children will come to understand the connections among human, animal, and plant life along with other elements of the environment.

   Two additional reasons have been suggested:

6. Geography helps children know where they are, where they are going, and where they are from, which is true for all of us—a sense of self-orientation in relation to space (Parker, 2005, p. 127).

7. Geography helps people understand the wants and needs of other people, as well as the daily events in their lives (NCSS, 2010, standard 9).

GEOGRAPHIC THEMES

As discussed above, exposing young children to geographic experiences forms the foundation for learning the following seven geographic themes and skills. The *seven geography key themes* discussed in this chapter represent concepts that children commonly interact with and that form the foundation of geographic knowledge. Five were created by the National Council for Geographic Education and the Association of American Geographers in Natoli, Boehm, et. al (1984) to facilitate and organize the teaching of geography in the kindergarten through 12th-grade classroom. The NCSS 2010 framework for teaching, learning, and assessing social studies themes related to geography includes technology and society, and global connections (Figure 7.2). These concepts ensure that children's learning goes beyond the traditional approach of human-environment relationships.

1. **Location and Direction: Location** pertains to positions of people, places, and things on earth. **Direction** is the lateral movement of an object or the body.

   Related concepts: Location includes one's exact position and place on earth, estimating distance, using maps, constructing maps; relative position—start by talking about where the child is in the classroom as compared to something else.

Figure 7.2
Geographic Concepts Children Should Know Based on NCSS Standards (2010).

Strand 1

Culture; similarities; differences; beliefs; values; cohesion; diversity; cultural and value development

Strand 3

People; places; environments; location; direction; distance; scale; physical and human characteristics of the school, community, state, region; people's interaction with environment; human settlement; land; water; seasons; climate/weather; migration; customs; making a living; discovery and use of resources; similarities; differences; tools—maps, globes, geospatial technologies

Strand 8

Use of media and technology; influence of media and technology; science and technology in transportation and communication; impacts of media and technology

Strand 9

Cultural exchange; travel; meeting cultural needs; global connections

Direction: Children build directional orientation through body movement. Earlier on they become familiar with words such as *left-right, up-down,* and *front-back. Rosie's Walk* and *Going on a Bear Hunt* are good books to use. Play games in which children locate items pointed out by the teacher ("find something under the table"). A good movement program will address the exploration of movement. Movements include rolling, wriggling, scooting, crawling, walking, running, skipping, galloping, sliding, leaping, hopping, and jumping. Movement associated with speed would be slow, medium, and fast. Also, movement of any body part—such as head, arms, legs, feet, and neck—contributes to the understanding of direction. Use songs and verbal commands in order to assess children's level of clarity. In the lower grades, focus on children's understanding of these movements. For example, have the children show how fast they can move, and different ways they can move (Pica, 2013; Seefeldt, Castle, & Falconer, 2014). Use books such as *Bringing Rain to Kapiti Plain* by Verna Aardema or *The Legend of the Indian Paintbrush* by Tomie dePaola.

Cardinal directions can be taught informally through experiential learning, such as sunset and sunrise. For example, have the children watch the sunset over and over again and emphasize the sun's rising in the east and setting in the west, a method used by Howe (1969). Illustrate direction by drawing a story map using books such as *Rosie's Walk* or *Going on a Bear Hunt.*

Location: Geography literacy begins with understanding where we are in relationship to others and being able to answer questions such as, Where am I? To be geographically literate, children have to interpret information about the environment. Talk about the location of different things in the classroom, using words such as *left, right, up,* and *down.* Involve them in illustrating location, direction, and distance through drawing a signpost showing where things are in relation to where they are sitting. For example, ask them to draw a circle on the center of a page and label it ME. Next indicate classmates' positions in the room by pasting their pictures or writing their names on the page. Then draw an arrow from the word ME to each person or object, demonstrating the distance between the child and the person or object.

2. **Place:** The concept of place encompasses the physical and human characteristics of a place, including where we live.

   Related concepts: land and water forms, vegetation, animal life, climate, language, culture, settlement patterns, transportation, communication, and human activities.

   > Foster this learning by taking field trips, having discussions, and reading literature about the effects of tornadoes, hurricanes, tsunamis, and earthquakes on the environment. Learning how climatic processes alter the earth promotes children's understanding of how communities may be affected by natural forces such as storms, tornadoes, and floods. Discuss stories about children's experiences during a storm and the changes that take place. Changes may include water flooding a child's basement or driveway or a pile of debris deposited in their yard. Introduce the concept of taking care of our environment by protecting spaces.

3. **Human-Environment Interactions:** Relationships between humans and the environment dictate actions and activities, including how different communities interact with others. Ways in which people modify their environment reflect their cultural values.

   Related concepts: human settlement, including population densities and communities; animal habitats; environmental resource use and protection.

Talk to children about their family members. Discuss human effects on the environment. Show children how different environments are transformed. For example, taking a field trip to land being transformed into a park, to space where new buildings are being constructed, and to farms where crops are growing, as well as reading books such as *The Great Kapok Tree* by Lynne Cherry, will enhance understanding of how humans impact the environment.

4. **Movement: Movement** encompasses that of people, products, information, and ideas around the world.

   Related concepts: transportation, communication, immigration, transporting goods to markets. Read literature about types of transportation; visit the train station. Use the Internet and various apps (e.g., transportation app on itunes.apple.com) to show different types of movement.

5. **Regions:** A **region** is a convenient unit used to divide the world in order to manage its study. We live in a region. This topic includes studying how regions form and change.

   Related concepts: people habitat, land use, animal habitat (Melendez et al., 2000; Parker, 2005).

6. **Technology and Society:** This topic centers on children's study of how global health, economics, and geography have changed as a result of using methods like air conditioning, dams, and irrigation to modify the physical environment as well as the evolution of basic technologies such as telephones and automobiles (NCSS, 2010, p. 21).

   Related concepts: transportation, technology and its impact on environment and people, media.

   Help children understand that technology can be used to complete tasks. Allow very young children to manipulate technology such as CDs and tapes. Use technology that is not working in the dramatic play area. Avoid the use of media such as TV and iPads with children younger than 2 years of age (American Academy of Pediatrics, 2009, 2010, 2011a, 2011b; Birch, Parker, & Burns, 2011; Campaign for a Commercial-Free Childhood, 2010; Funk, Brouwer, Curtiss, & McBroom, 2009; Institute of Medicine of the National Academies, 2011; White House Task Force on Childhood Obesity, 2010). Model the use of technology by using a computer to write a document or create pictures. A helpful resource for planning technology experiences with young children can be found at naeyc.org/content/technology-and-young-children.

   Highlight the technology that older children interact with on a daily basis, for example, when they listen to tape-recorded stories.

Discuss how new technologies have been used to change their community and to solve individual, social, and global problems. Discuss positive and negative effects of technology. Talk about how media influences us (NCSS, 2010). Allow older children to use computers or iPads to create documents, pictures, and so on, for a geography theme they are learning about. Guidelines for age-relevant technology use are outlined in Chapter 2. Google Earth is another example of technology that has impacted society in useful ways both inside and outside the classroom.

7. **Global Connections:** The topic of global connections is the study of how things that happen in one part of the world impact other parts of the world. Young learners become aware of global connections as a result of their exposure to various media and first-hand experiences.

   Related concepts: Exploration of various types of global connections, cultural exchange, trade, travel, rapid communication through technology, global changes.

   Address the above concepts in terms of how fast changes have occurred and how global connections have been enhanced as a result. Facilitate understanding of how people are connected around the world by establishing e-pals; talk about evidence of the impact of global connections in the community or state (NCSS, 2010).

GEOGRAPHIC TOOLS

Maps in Early Childhood Classrooms

A **map** represents a place or space. A map is a visual representation of the land surface or sea showing physical features such as roads, hills, mountains, and rivers. Maps help us know where we are in the world. Teachers of young children must first teach them about land forms such as mountains, deserts, climate zones, crops, and regions so they may better understand maps or geographic representations or symbols (Parker, 2005). Features such as grids, color, scale, legends, and symbols aid in understanding and interpreting a map or globe. Young children learn to read simple maps by first constructing their own maps starting from their school, to the area around the school, and then to their neighborhood.

Preschoolers may begin map-making with blocks. They may create maps of their neighborhood and their house using blocks; they may also use drawings or pictures. During the primary years children are well able to include more details in their maps and show objects in relation to the particular space they are dealing with. The teacher should give children opportunities to draw maps by taking short field trips. After taking the same short, local field trip several times, the children will draw the route taken on the trip. A floor map works very well for younger children. Children can draw maps of their room, home, classroom, and so on. Not only does the use of concrete objects help elementary age children develop complex, sophisticated concepts and problem-solving skills but it also means that map-making should stem from their own experience, which enhances the learning as they move from the concrete to the abstract.

Pre-mapping Skills: Awareness of Representation and Symbols.

"Before children become visually literate, they must first develop pre-mapping skills (i.e., an awareness of what exists in the physical world, interpretation of **symbols**, and representation from the very simple to the more complex levels)" (Melendez et al., 2000, p. 162). Pre-mapping skills include developing awareness and building knowledge of the following:

- **Physical characteristics of the world:** buildings, bridges, statues, schools, hospitals, churches, residential areas, mountains, rivers, valleys, roads, people, and so forth. Children start to make sense of their physical environment by experiencing their immediate surroundings. Foster learning by bringing to their attention what surrounds them—people and school buildings—then taking walks around the school showing them the physical features.

- **Common pictorial symbols:** traffic signs, traffic lights, commercial symbols, fire alarms, ambulance signs, police cars, gas, phone, hospital, and so on. These symbols represent real objects. Read books that include these symbols. Take walks with young children to see the actual symbol. Use technology by taking pictures, which also allows children to examine symbols further when in the classroom.

- **Directions:** cardinal directions—north, south, east, west; relative direction—close to, over here, over there, far, and near. Introduce young children to directions by reading books that use the terms for relative direction. Involve them in movements that demonstrate these terms. For example, ask Jill to move "close to" Jordan. Then ask Jordan to go "over there" near the teacher's desk. Introduce cardinal directions and the compass rose to older children. Reinforce these terms by using them often and by labeling the classroom walls. Facts such as the sun rising in the east and setting in the west can be used to remind children of cardinal directions. Create a song to act out and practice directionality.

- **Location:** Young children start by learning to locate places they know on simple maps they make in the classroom, such as a layout of the class or the school. Use simple maps and globes for young children. They become familiar with the names and shapes of physical features such as mountains, oceans, continents, and poles. Use literature to introduce young children to these features as appropriate (Bale, 1989, in Melendez et al., 2000; Maxim, 1995; Palmer, 1994).

  - As they advance to primary grades, children can use simple maps with grids and coordinates to locate places (Parker, 2005). To find places on a detailed map, children have to learn to use a grid system. Grids give the absolute location of a place. For maps and globes, longitudes and latitudes constitute the grid system. Young children learn to use grids with simple maps that have lines extending vertically and horizontally. Ask them to find various locations on a simple map (see fire escape maps below). From there they will understand that longitudes are the lines that go up and down and latitudes are the lines that go across on a map or globe. Practice locating places or geographic features on a map with longitudes and latitudes.

- **Natural features and phenomena:** wind and its force, water and floods, weather, climatic changes, shadows. Using resources such as videos will help children become aware of these features and phenomena. The activity of describing weather every morning is an example of fostering learning through daily activities.

- **Environment in other places:** rainforests, beaches, desert, and the plant and human life in such places. Use pictures, videos, and Google maps to compare and contrast the children's environment with that of other places.

Three Stages of Cognitive Mapping

Abstraction in Piaget's developmental stages occurs at the age of 11 to 15. Very young children (younger than 11) are not developmentally ready to deal with mapping because it requires abstractions and representation. Research shows that young children are capable of beginning to form cognitive maps of their immediate surroundings such as home and school. The following are three stages of cognitive mapping that correspond to the preschool, primary, and elementary years (Palmer, 1994).

1. **Topological mapping (preschool years):** At this stage children are able to map using drawings, pictures, and blocks. At preschool age they are able to map simplified versions of places in their immediate environment, such as their classroom, school, and home. Their maps, however, lack scale, distance, and direction. Activities such as creating maps do build their sense about what exists in their environment (Melendez et al., 2000).

2. **Semi-abstract mapping (primary years):** During the primary years children's maps are more detailed. They are able to use symbols that represent elements, such as a cross sign to indicate a telephone pole. At this stage their maps are not accurate; however, by including the elements of perspective, scale, and orientation, we are able to see the children's ability to represent environmental objects (Melendez et al., 2000, p.160).

3. **Abstract mapping (elementary years):** At this stage children are able to use symbolic representation, and their maps are detailed and accurate. Elements are included (Melendez et al., 2000). They are able to draw maps from memory.

Five Elements of Maps

A map can be defined as a way to represent space. Maps have five basic elements:

1. **Perspective:** Part of helping children understand maps is by talking about perspective. This concept underlies maps: They are made by looking at the world from above like a bird in the sky. Take children to the top of a high building and have them look at the surroundings below or, alternatively, use photographs taken from a view above. Point out how small the objects below appear. Ask children (ages 5–7) to draw plane views of normal classroom objects. This can be done either by looking at the object from above and drawing what is seen or by placing the object on an overhead projector and drawing around the silhouette that is projected.

2. **Scale:** Primary age children can learn map scales by helping them understand that "scaling is the process of reducing everything by the same amount" (Parker, 2005, p. 161), that some things are larger or smaller than others, and that maps show the relative size of things. Use pictures and videos of the children and their families to introduce scale. Bring to their attention how small the children look in the photograph or video or even in a drawing.

Maps represent the world, but like pictures they are much smaller. Children can use blocks to make a map of the classroom. Other material like paper can be used to represent roads.

3. **Symbols:** As they use maps and the globe, young children move from understanding common pictorial symbols to map symbols that are more abstract. Symbols represent real objects. Discuss the similarities between picture symbols such as road signs and maps. *Key:* Map keys explain what each symbol represents. The use of map keys is an important skill for children to develop as they move to more complex mapping concepts (see Aberg & Clida, 2003). Have primary age children use map keys as they draw and interpret maps.

4. **Content and purpose:** The content of a map defines its purpose. Maps are used to depict a variety of places and things, such as roads, buildings, water bodies, and urban areas. Help children understand the purpose of a map by asking questions such as the following: What kind of information can we find on a road map? What information can we find on a map of an urban area? What kind of map would allow us to find information about the White House?

5. **Position and orientation:** Establish relationships between objects. **Position** tells the "where" of an object in relation to other objects, that is, the latitude and longitude of given points. **Orientation** tells the specific location of an object, using the cardinal points (north, south, east, west).

Globes

A globe represents the earth as it looks. Explain to children that our world is round and a globe represents that shape. For children in pre-kindergarten and first grade, use a simple globe that displays minimum information. Help children understand that the globe represents a small earth, highlighting the basics such as land and water, rivers, and mountains.

Below are some ideas for using the globe with young children:

1. The globe is a model of the earth.
2. Show and name land—continents and bodies of water such as oceans.
3. Compare the size or space occupied by land and water on the globe.

4. Show children the location of the North and South Poles.

5. Help children find their continent, state, and any other places they recognize.

See the Sample Activities section.

Google Earth and Other Satellite Programs

Google Earth is an excellent resource for teaching about maps and globes. Google Earth (google.earth.com) has free software downloads and instructions on how to use this resource. With this software, a person need only type the name of a city or a street address and then watch. He/she is able to see images of roads, buildings, rivers, and other features through satellite photographs. The software offers zoom and angle options. Primary children in third and fourth grades may be able to operate this system on their own. For children in first and second grades, Google Earth images may be used by the teacher as children watch. In that way the teacher can point out what they need to see and at the same time guide the use of the tool. Here are some topics that students can investigate with Google Earth:

- Students can learn about people's impact on the environment, economics of a natural disaster, and locating places by using directions from other places; students can also discover local events, disasters, places of interest, and local tours. Teachers can use Google Earth to teach geography, history, and many other lessons.

- Students can identify land forms such as mountains, rivers, deserts, lakes, and oceans; after making observations, children can then make models of land forms. For assessment, they can identify land forms specified by the teacher. Through Google Earth, the teacher can mark specific land forms for students to identify.

- Another activity that involves mapping is asking the students to identify the school and the local post office building, write directions, and then draw a map from their school to the post office.

Three-dimensional technological tools, coupled with content preparation and questions that lead to discovery, can help children:

- Understand scale, that is, "that the globe is a model of the earth" (Seefeldt et al., 2014).

- Gain spatial knowledge.

- Develop a more realistic view and understanding of the earth.

Students on computers.

Using Photographs to Make Maps

Photographs of people, especially of the children, and pictures of familiar places are useful in helping them see the concept of representation and scale. The teacher should talk about the photograph and then ask questions such as, "Were you really that small?" She/he can state that, "This picture represents you, only it is very small." Responses or comments such as, "Oh, it's just a picture" and "it is just a toy," when talking about size, demonstrate some level of understanding of scale.

Older children can use photographs to make maps similar to what a teacher would do with Google Earth, as mentioned above. With any suitable aerial photographs, children can draw a map by looking at the photo and reproducing the shapes on paper. An easier way is to place transparent film over the photo and trace the main shapes. The teacher can project Google Maps on a whiteboard and draw over the top of the aerial map, using the whiteboard pen tools. Then the teacher can open the street map in Google and compare. The teacher should model this activity.

Building Geographic Knowledge through Field Trips

Field exploration is one of the best ways to foster concepts about the physical world (Natoli, 1989). It is a concrete experience that sparks children's interest and gives them a chance to interact with their surroundings and ask questions. A successful field trip must make children aware of the goals and objectives in advance. Also, providing questions they can answer during the field trip will help them focus on what they are learning. A question such as, "What road/s did you take to get there?" connects to movement. The teacher should ask questions that relate to the elements of physical places: location, movement, human relationship with places, and regions, for instance. See Figure 7.3 for ideas.

The teacher must consider the following when planning and selecting a site for a field trip: children's interest, community resources, time needed to reach the destination, mode of transportation, number of children taking the trip, safety, length of visit, nature of visit (Melendez et al., 2000), and use of recording equipment such as videos and cameras. For details on field trip organization, see Chapter 2.

Figure 7.3
Ideas for the Types of Questions to Ask.

Movement

Questions related to means of transportation used; roads used to get to destination

Location and Regions

Questions related to the place visited; comparison to familiar places; description of place visited

Place

Questions related to what was seen; feelings about what was seen

People and Places

Questions related to people and their activities

ENVIRONMENTAL EDUCATION AND SUSTAINABILITY ISSUES IN THE EARLY CHILDHOOD CLASSROOM

"If a child is to keep alive his inborn sense of wonder . . . he needs the companionship of at least one adult who can share it, rediscovering with him the joy, excitement, and mystery of the world we live in" (Carson, 1956, p. 45).

Environmental education should start at an early age if children are to grow to respect the natural environment. Early environmental education impacts children's perception and value of, and behavior toward, the environment (Tilbury, 1994; Wilson, 1994). Many children lack the opportunity to interact with the environment in meaningful ways. The school can create such opportunities through interaction with the immediate surroundings, such as the playground, school garden, and plants and animals in the classroom. Additionally, nature and the environment can be brought to children through a variety of technology and interactive media such as the Internet, iPad, video recorders, tablets, and cameras. These tools can be used to help children explore nature through observation, recording, reflecting on their work, and sharing ideas.

When interacting with nature, children first notice what is in their environment through their senses. The teacher must allow them to experience smells, to observe objects and events, to listen to sounds, and to touch. Children are so curious about nature that it becomes a useful vehicle for learning to read and write. In addition, curriculum integration naturally happens when children are studying nature. Thus, nature provides an interesting and valuable way for children to learn. Below are some ideas for activities involving nature:

- Take walks in the school or neighborhood. Observe the environment, pointing out, for example, how people keep the environment clean through putting litter in cans. Discuss plants and buildings the children see along the way.

- Observe insects and take pictures of them. Use a variety of pictures for discussion in class.

- Go to the school playground and allow children to explore what interests them, using a magnifying glass. Use video recorders or iPads with older children. Older children may investigate specific things, while younger children may do more exploring and discovery.

The 3 Rs—Reduce, Reuse, Recycle

An important aspect of environmental education is the 3 Rs concept: reduce, reuse, recycle.

- *Reduce:* The goal is to help children understand at an early age to minimize waste. Explore what this means in terms of classroom items such as books and materials. Discuss ways in which they can use items without wasting them, such as using both sides of paper, sharing materials, borrowing rather than buying new items, making things that are needed instead of buying them, and avoiding the use of disposables.

- *Reuse:* Reuse means using something more than once before disposing of it. Practice borrowing and sharing materials, using second-hand materials, using recycled materials such as containers, and repurposing used art materials. Milk cartons, cereal boxes, and carton boxes work well in creating art and other activities. Start a school garden; then compost it with leftover foods.

- *Recycle:* Recycle means returning a waste product to a factory where it is remade into a new item or prepared for use again. Recycling products include paper, aluminum cans and foil, and milk and juice cartons. Start a recycling project. Label two bins where children can sort the plastic and the cans for recycling. Additionally, visit a recycling plant with primary age children.

PLANNING FOR GEOGRAPHY

Daily/Weekly Planning

The foundation of social studies for children comprises their personal experiences and their understanding of themselves in relation to their families, school, and community. The key topics related to geography discussed in this chapter include location; direction; place; human-environment interactions; movement; regions; technology and society; global connections; and tools such as maps, globes, and photographs. These topics are meant to be taught in developmentally appropriate ways.

Infants and Toddlers

Planning for this age group is based on the teacher's understanding of the kinds of geography activities that children are involved in throughout the day. Daily and weekly planning for infants and toddlers is a function of the teacher's ability to facilitate hands-on experiences that build knowledge and understanding of geography. The teacher should plan to interact with children by asking open-ended questions to scaffold their thinking and problem-solving skills (Pennsylvania Department of Education, 2014). Planning will entail choosing topics as outlined in standards and the curriculum. Teachers can read books, discuss concepts the children are learning, place play items in the dramatic play area, and embark on outside activities such as walks and playground experiences. Teachers should consider the following steps in regard to planning for geography and any topic for young children:

- Identify the topic/concept for the week.
- In planning, outline the skills to be learned and what to look for.
- Observe children's actions.
- Ask open-ended questions.
- Acknowledge and reinforce children's actions relevant to the concept.
- Talk about the concept.
- Read about the concept.
- Provide play items relevant to the concept planned.
- Plan an activity emphasizing the concept.
- Assess children's knowledge and understanding through behavior by observing children in action.

Different topics can take different amounts of time. As a rule, teachers should regularly revisit skills that children are working on even when other topics are taking center stage at a given time.

Pre-kindergarten and Kindergarten Children

Planning for pre-kindergarten and kindergarten children will include some formal instruction. Such instruction may focus on, for example, talking about places where the children live. The children will also be involved in activities that require planning and prior instruction, such as taking field trips around the school and the local community.

Primary Age Children

Planning for children in this age group includes a large portion of formal instruction as well as experiences facilitated by the teacher. The curriculum is more structured. Developmentally, children are ready for more formally organized learning about such topics as weather, urban and suburban places, and human settlements.

As has been mentioned in other chapters, part of planning involves children in the process by finding out what they would like to learn. Then, the teacher goes further by asking what they already know about the topic and what they would like to know. This information aids the teacher in focusing on topics or aspects of a topic about which children have very little knowledge.

Yearly

Yearly planning must be organized by first looking at the standards and the curriculum from an overall perspective before breaking down the concepts expected to be covered. What do the standards directly address with regard to geography? Yearly planning is important, especially for project planning and thematic units. These are teaching styles that are involving and require a large amount of time to plan and execute. Also, other factors have to be considered, such as whether a more suitable time of year is preferred. Yearly planning (long-term planning) gives the teacher an opportunity to look at curriculum requirements in order to budget for materials or decide on which places to visit. It also makes it possible to plan for cross-curricular integration. Some experiences, such as working with the community, involve both school and community cooperation. Yearly planning before the year begins also ensures quality teaching and that whatever needs to be taught is on the calendar. For example, in planning a thematic unit on weather, the teacher must consider when the topic of weather/precipitation is being taught in science and when measurement will be taught in math. Reading and other activities can easily reflect this theme.

Learning Centers

Geography learning centers should include cultural artifacts and other multicultural items. Alternatively, a multicultural center can be set up periodically. Multicultural materials might include multicultural books, dolls, dress-up materials, props, art materials, and posters. Cultural artifacts, such as musical instruments, paintings, and headdresses, can be used when covering topics that fall under human characteristics of places and regions (NCSS standard 3). Children are able to examine

Figure 7.4
Materials to Foster Geographic Knowledge.

Displayed photographs of a variety of places and peoples

A variety of blocks (size—small, large; types—foam, wood)

Measuring tools (ruler, yarn, rope, measuring tape)

Geography instruments (compass, magnifying glass)

Maps and globes (maps of the school, classroom, neighborhood, and town)

Cameras, video cameras

Drawing tools and map-making materials (crayons, pencils, pictures, modeling clay, paper, scissors)

Reference materials (geography books with pictures, atlases, and other information books)

Wooden and plastic figures of animals and people

Store items (cereal boxes, empty packages)

Source: Adapted from Melendez et al., 2000, and Seefeldt & Galper, 2006.

and use the artifacts if they are displayed for long periods of time. Display pictures of artifacts when it is not possible to obtain the actual artifacts.

Figure 7.4 lists various materials that help enhance learning about geography.

HOME/SCHOOL CONNECTION

Involve parents in their children's education by sending home ideas for activities they can do together. Parents can introduce children to a variety of geographic information and features, such as land forms near their home, climate, and weather. Parents can take children for walks around the neighborhood, pointing out signs and landmarks. They can also read specific books that have geographic themes. See Connections to Literacy in this chapter.

ACCOMMODATIONS FOR CHILDREN WITH DIVERSE NEEDS

In teaching geography, it is vital that accommodations be made for children with diverse needs, including those who are English language learners (ELL) (Figure 7.5) and those with special needs (Figure 7.6).

Figure 7.5
Adaptations for ELL.

Adaptations for English Language Learners

Having a multicultural center benefits children from other cultures. Collect authentic items from different cultures to help build a multicultural center by having parents donate cultural items and coming into the classroom as guest presenters. Presentations could include introduction of music, art, authentic food, photos, flags, maps, landmarks, national sports, and so on. Incorporating multicultural experiences frequently throughout the year helps young children better understand geographic diversity. Additionally, children with other language traditions are recognized for their unique experiences and can inform the class in special ways. Encourage ELL students to identify geographic terms in their language and write them next to the English terms. They can also draw pictures of items to reinforce concept learning.

Emphasize academic language by creating a section on the wall for geography words. Place pictures next to those words so students can make connections. Involve ELL students along with the rest of the class in activities in which they have to use those words; an example would be writing in their journals about how they get to school. Younger children will use words such as *left* and *right*. Older children can use the cardinal directions.

Figure 7.6
Adaptations for Children with Special Needs.

Adaptation for Children with Special Needs

Children with diverse abilities and culture may need more support, guidance, or accommodations as they encounter early learning opportunities. Those who do not have mobility can benefit from tactile play with water and sand. Bring the water and sand to those who cannot get on the ground. Children with special needs have the opportunity to work with their peers on various projects. Children may choose how they will complete a project—with the aid of a computer, a peer, or an adult helper, for instance. Using words to describe their actions, combined with tactile play, benefits visually impaired children.

CONNECTIONS TO LITERACY

Books offer a rich source of materials for learning and teaching geography.

Children's Books That Promote Geography

Borreguita and Coyote by Verna Aardema

The Day of Ahmed's Secret by Florence Parry Heide and Judith Heide Gilliland

Down the Road by Alice Schertle

The Earth and I by Frank Asch (Human-Environment Interactions)

The Egyptian Cinderella by Shirley Climo

Here Comes the Mail by Gloria Skurzynski

Johnny Appleseed by Reeve Lindbergh

Kofi and His Magic by Maya Angelou

Snow Day! by Barbara M. Joosse

Taxi! Taxi! by Cari Best

Very Last First Time by Jan Andrews

Wake Up, City! by Alvin Tresselt

Where Does the Trail Lead? by Burton Albert

Location and Place

Animal Architects by John Nicholson

Goodnight, Goodnight, Construction Site by Sherri Duskey Rinker

How Much? Visiting Markets Around the World by Ted Lewin

I Lost My Tooth in Africa by Penda Diakité

Just Like Me by Christine Hood

Make Way for Ducklings by Robert McClosky

On the Same Day in March: A Tour of the World's Weather by Marilyn Singer

On the Town: A Community Adventure by Judith Caseley

P Is for Passport: A World Alphabet by Devin Scillian

S Is for South Africa by Beverley Naidoo

Thomas's Sheet and the Great Geography Test by Steven L. Layne

Movement

Amy & Louis by Libby Gleeson

Apples to Oregon: Being the (Slightly) True Narrative of How a Brave Pioneer Father Brought Apples, Peaches, Pears, Plums, Grapes, and Cherries (and Children) across the Plains by Deborah Hopkinson

From Kalamazoo to Timbuktu! by Harriet Ziefert

Home by Narelle Oliver

Home Now by Lesley Beake

How to Make an Cherry Pie and See the U.S.A. by Marjorie Priceman

The Imaginary Garden by Andrew Larsen

Like a Windy Day by Frank Asch

Mammoths on the Move by Lisa Wheeler

Stinky by Eleanor Davis

Regions

Locomotive by Brian Floca (Movement; Places; Regions)

My Mom Is a Foreigner, but Not to Me by Julianne Moore (Regions)

Year of the Jungle by Suzanne Collins (Regions)

Direction

A Drive in the Country by Michael Rosen

My Farm Friends by Wendell Minor

Rosie's Walk by Pat Hutchins

We're Going on a Bear Hunt by Michael Rosen

SAMPLE ACTIVITIES

Activities for maps and map making should focus on relating the abstraction of maps to reality.

Pre-kindergarten:

- Use blocks, models, and/or Legos to represent buildings and other features of the environment.

- Take class photographs to demonstrate relative size in globes.

- To enable children to experience position in space, encourage them to move in various ways, including climbing, jumping, and rolling. Use positional words like "above" and "below" when giving directions.

Kindergarten through Second Grade

- Make a classroom map. Cut some rectangles out of cardboard to represent tables. Make enough rectangles for the number of tables in your classroom. Draw a basic outline of the shape of the classroom on a piece of paper, and ask the children to arrange the rectangles on the paper so that they match where the tables are found. You could also make other shapes to represent the board, computer, teacher's desk, and so on. When the children have put the shapes into the correct spaces, they can draw around the shapes, and they will produce a map of the classroom.

- Work with learners to build a three-dimensional representation of a familiar environment, such as their bedroom, classroom, or playground.

- Observe and track weather changes by having students record the observations over a period of time.

Third and Fourth Grades

- Have children draw an object first by the way it looks from above and then by the way it looks from a different direction. Have them compare the drawings.

- Use map keys whenever children draw maps and when they interpret them.

- Have children draw, from memory, maps of places they know or have visited in their community. Children can show the route they take from home to school, from home to the supermarket, and so forth. Have them add map keys.

RESOURCES

The list below features sources for material relating to geography and the effective teaching of it.

- National Geographic Association; *National Geographic* magazine; American Automobile Association (AAA); newspapers; United States Geological Service (USGS)

- National Council for Geographic Education website

- National Wildlife Federation: nwf.org

- Magazines, such as *Your Big Backyard* and *Ranger Rick,* newspapers, picture books, poetry books, cameras, empty product boxes and containers, recycled/recyclable materials, boxes, tape, tracing paper, crayons, colored pencils, and so on
- Lesson plans: teacher.scholastic.com/lessonplans/exploreyourearth/

Technology Resources

Technology resources are plentiful and available for download (see below and Figure 7.7).

- Colorado Department of Education. "Results Matter?" Video project: cde.state.co.us/resultsmatter/
- NAEYC Technology and Young Children Interest Forum: techandyoungchildren.org
- Geography Drive USA
- Puerling, B. 2012. *Teaching in a digital age: Smart tools for age 3 to grade 3.* St. Paul, MN: Redleaf.
- Shillady, A., & Muccio, L. S. (Eds.). 2012. *Spotlight on young children and technology.* Washington, DC: NAEYC.
- The TEC (Technology in Early Childhood) Center at Erikson Institute: teccenter.erikson.edu
- Google Earth: google.earth.com
- More apps can be found on Pinterest: pinterest.com/pin

Figure 7.7
Apps for Pre-kindergarten through Grade 4.

Preschool	Kindergarten	First Grade	Second Grade	Third and Fourth Grades
ABC ZooBorns	Britannica Kids: Volcanoes	Barefoot World Atlas	Barefoot World Atlas	The Magic of Reality
Leo's Pad 2: Educational App for Preschoolers	Britannica Kids: Ancient Egypt	Khan Academy	World Atlas by National Geographic	Barefoot World Atlas
Little Farmer	Britannica Kids: Rainforests			Khan Academy

Preschool	Kindergarten	First Grade	Second Grade	Third and Fourth Grades
Peekaboo Barn, Peekaboo Forest, Peekaboo Wild (universal) by Night & Day Studios	Britannica Kids: Solar System		Geocaching	World Atlas by National Geographic
Trucks!! (iPhone) by Wombat Learning Media, LLC			Britannica Kids: Ancient Egypt	Geocaching
Trucks and Tractors (universal) by Literalshore			Stack the Countries	Stack the Countries
			BrainPOP	Stack the States

Assessing Learning Outcomes

- Describe geography in your own words.
- What is the relevance of teaching geography to young children?
- How would you incorporate geography into your daily curriculum?
- Identify geographic tools that should be introduced to young children.
- Create a geography lesson. Include an authentic activity.

References

Aberg, R., & Clida, J. (2003). *Map keys* (Rookie Read-About Geography Series). New York: Children's Press.

American Academy of Pediatrics. (2009). Policy statement—media violence. *Pediatrics, 124*(5), 1495–1503. Retrieved from www.pediatrics.org/cgi/doi/10.1542/peds.2009-21461

American Academy of Pediatrics. (2010). Policy statement—media education. *Pediatrics, 126*(5), 1012–1017. Retrieved from www.pediatrics.org/cgi/doi/10.1542/peds.2010-1636

American Academy of Pediatrics. (2011a, June 13). Council on Communications and Media letter to the National Association for the Education of Young Children. Retrieved from http://pediatrics.aappublications.org/content/early/2011/10/12/peds.2011-1753

American Academy of Pediatrics. (2011b). Policy Statement—media use by children younger than 2 years. *Pediatrics, 128*(5), 1–7. Retrieved from http://pediatrics.aappublications.org/content/early/2011/10/12/peds.2011-1753

Bale, J. (1989). Didactica de la geografia en la escuela primaria. [Geography in the primary school]. Madrid, Spain: Ediciones Morata.

Birch, L. L., Parker, L., & Burns, A. (Eds.). (2011). *Early childhood obesity prevention policies.* Washington, DC: National Academies Press. Retrieved from www.iom.edu/Reports/2011/Early-Childhood-Obesity-Prevention-Policies.aspx

Brophy, J. (1990). Teaching social studies for understanding and higher-order applications. *Elementary School Journal, 90,* 351–417.

Campaign for a Commercial-Free Childhood. (2010, July 26). CCFC letter to Jerlean Daniel, Executive Director, National Association for the Education of Young Children. Retrieved from www.commercialfreechildhood.org/pdf/naeycletter.pdf

Carson, R. (1956). *The sense of wonder.* New York: Harper & Row.

Copple, C., & Bredekamp, S. (2009). *Developmentally appropriate practice* (3rd ed.). Washington, DC: NAEYC.

Funk, J. B., Brouwer, J., Curtiss, K., & McBroom, E. (2009). Parents of preschoolers: Expert media recommendations and ratings knowledge, media-effects beliefs, and monitoring practices. *Pediatrics, 123*(3), 981–988. Retrieved from http://pediatrics.aappublications.org/content/123/3/981.short

Howe, G. (1969). The teaching of directions in space. In W. Herman (Ed.), *Current research in elementary school social studies* (pp. 31–43). Upper Saddle River, NJ: Merrill Prentice Hall.

Hyson, M. (2008). *Enthusiastic and engaged learners: Approaches to learning in the early childhood classroom.* New York, NY: Teachers College Press.

Institute of Medicine of the National Academies. (2011). *Early childhood obesity prevention policies: Goals, recommendations, and potential actions.* Washington, DC: Author. Retrieved from www.iom.edu/~/media/Files/Report%20Files/2011/Early-Childhood-Obesity-Prevention-Policies/Young%20Child%20Obesity%202011%20Recommendations.pdf

Maxim, G. (1995). *Social studies and the elementary school child* (5th ed.). Englewood Cliffs, NJ: Merrill.

Melendez, R.M, Beck, V., & Fletcher, M. (2000). *Teaching social studies in early education.* Albany, NY: Delmar Thomson Learning.

National Association for the Education of Young Children. (2010). NAEYC standards for early childhood professional preparation. Retrieved from www.naeyc.org/ncate/standards

National Council for the Social Studies (NCSS). (2010). *National curriculum standards for social studies: A framework for teaching, learning, and assessment.* Silver Spring, MD: NCSS.

National Geographic Joint Committee. (1994). *Geography for life: The national geography standards.* Washington, DC: Author.

Natoli, S. (Ed.). (1989). *Strengthening geography in the social studies.* Bulletin no. 81. Washington, DC: National Council for the Social Studies.

Natoli, S.J., Boehm, R., Kratch, J., Lanegran, D., Monk, J., & Morill, R. (1984). *Guidelines for geographic education: Elementary and secondary schools.* Washington, DC: Association of American Geographers and National Council for Geography Education and National Council for Geographic Education.

Neuman, S. B., Roskos, K., Tanya, S., & Lenhart, L. (2007). *Nurturing knowledge: Building a foundation for school success by linking early literacy for math, science, art, and social studies.* New York, NY: Scholastic.

Palmer, J. (1994). *Geography in the early years.* London, UK: Routledge.

Parker, W. C. (2005). *Social studies in elementary education* (14th ed.). Boston, MA: Allyn & Bacon.

Pennsylvania Department of Education. (2014). Standard Aligned System. Retrieved from http://www.pdesas.org/Standard.

Piaget, J. (1969). *The child's conception of the world.* Totowa, NJ: Littlefield Adams.

Pica, R. (2013). *Experiences in movement: Birth to age eight* (5th ed.). Belmont, CA: Cengage Learning.

Schoenfeldt, M. K. (2001). Geographic literacy and young learners. *Educational Forum, 66,* 26–31.

Seefeldt, C., & Galper, A. (2006). *Active experiences for active children: Social studies* (2nd ed.). Upper Saddle River, NJ: Pearson.

Seefeldt, C., Castle, S., & Falconer, R. C. (2014). Social studies for the preschool/ primary child (9th ed.). Boston, MA: Pearson.

Sylvester, R. (1995). *A celebration of neurons: An educator's guide to the human brain.* Alexandria, VA: Association for Supervision and Curriculum Development.

Tilbury, D. (1994). The critical learning years for environmental education. In R. A. Wilson (Ed.), *Environmental education at the early childhood level* (pp. 11–13). Washington, DC: North American Association for Environmental Education.

Vygotsky, L. S. (1978). *Mind in society: The development of higher psychological processes.* Cambridge, MA: Harvard University Press.

White House Task Force on Childhood Obesity. (2010). *Solving the problem of childhood obesity within a generation.* Washington, DC: Office of the President of the United States. Retrieved from www.letsmove.gov/sites/letsmove.gov/files/TaskForce_on_ Childhood_Obesity_May2010_FullReport.pdf

Whiting, B. B., & Edwards, C. P. (1988). *Children of different worlds: The formation of social behavior.* Cambridge, MA: Harvard University Press.

Wilson, R. A. (Ed.) (1994). *Environmental education at the early childhood level.* Washington, DC: North American Association for Environmental Education.

Diversity, Anti-Bias, and Multicultural Education

Learning Outcomes

After reading this chapter you should be able to:

- Explain the difference between anti-bias and multicultural education.
- Examine personal dispositions about diversity as a classroom teacher.
- Use a variety of ways to create classroom environments that promote diversity in planning social studies activities for each child.

Big Ideas for Chapter 8: Diversity	Classroom Application	Standards Met
Anti-bias curriculum	Integration of anti-bias guiding principles into classroom with regard to planning holiday celebrations, choice of books, language used, and so on	Knowing about and understanding diverse family and community characteristics (NAEYC 2a)
Culturally responsive classrooms	Understanding the home culture of each child and the benefits of connecting to families	Knowing about and understanding diverse family and community characteristics (NAEYC 2a)
Multicultural education	Use of appropriate multicultural topics and activities throughout the year	Supporting and engaging families and communities through respectful, reciprocal relationships (NAEYC 2b)

Standards Addressed
in this Chapter

NCSS Standards

The National Council for the Social Studies (NCSS) has organized social studies into 10 broad interrelated holistic themes. Those addressed in this chapter are in bold:

1. **Culture**
2. Time, continuity, and change
3. People, places, and environments
4. **Individual development and identity**
5. **Individuals, groups, and institutions**
6. Power, authority, and governance
7. Production, distribution, and consumption
8. Science, technology, and society
9. **Global connections**
10. Civic ideals and practices (NCSS, 2010).

NAEYC Standards

The following NAEYC Standards for Professional Preparation Programs are addressed in this chapter:

Standard 2: Building Family and Community Relationships

2a. Knowing about and understanding diverse family and community characteristics.

2b. Supporting and engaging families and communities through respectful, reciprocal relationships.

Source: NAEYC Standards for Early Childhood Professional Preparation http://www.naeyc.org/files/naeyc/files/2009%20Professional%20Prep%20stdsRevised%204_12.pdf

DEVELOPMENTAL BASIS FOR LEARNING ABOUT DIVERSITY AND CULTURE

The NCSS standard on culture and cultural diversity states that social studies teachers should possess the knowledge, capabilities, and dispositions to organize and provide instruction at the appropriate school level for the study of culture and cultural diversity.

Understanding diversity, anti-bias, and multicultural education issues for young children and families is a complex process. This process is ongoing but should begin or be refined during the teacher preparation period. Listed below are some ethical principles that may guide the teacher during this process.

Ethical Principles

1. First, do no harm. In other words, don't mis-educate children or create environments that do not support children's home language, family, and culture.

2. Welcome each child and family. This means that every child who comes through the classroom door must be treated with respect and dignity.

3. The teacher's language and interactions are important. The words used or not used will influence children's thinking. In addition, personal interaction with children affects their understanding of the social studies content.

The following sections of this chapter expand and support these ethical principles. Cultural competence, **diversity**, **dispositions**, and understanding of family diversity, and engagement strategies will be further developed as part of the preparation for teaching with knowledge of the **anti-bias approach**, a foundation of diversity information, and an appreciation for the complexity of **multicultural education** in a social studies curriculum.

YOUR CULTURAL COMPETENCE

A first step in understanding culture is to examine some defining characteristics. Cultural characteristics include the following components:

1. The ways individuals and groups live and interact with each other
2. The ways that communities are formed and how they work
3. The moral and ethical practices that guide their behaviors and actions (including laws, regulations, policies, and so on)
4. The signs, images, and symbols that reflect the interests and values of communities
5. The common practices that are shared by most members of the culture (language use, family interactions, jobs/work/career options, music, religious ceremonies, recreation, food preparation, and so forth)
6. The perspectives or points-of-view of the members of that culture

These characteristics reveal that culture is a complex set of knowledge, beliefs, and practices. This is very important to remember in planning social studies lessons and working with young children and their families. Simplifying activities about culture is risky with young children because that may later lead to misconceptions about people, language, and regions. Understanding and appreciating culture provides tools

Benjamin LaFramboise/Pearson

for furthering children's knowledge of the academic content. This, in turn, will increase their retention (memory) and therefore boost the chances of success in school.

Here are some questions to ask yourself—you, the teacher—as you plan:

1. What do you know about your own culture?
2. How do you think it has influenced you?
3. What do you know about the culture of most children in your community?
4. Can you identify at least three areas of cultural competency in which you could grow?
5. Identify any bias you may have about race, ethnicity, language, etc. (*Note:* Although this may be difficult, it is an important task for your professional development.)

To further your understanding of culture in early childhood classrooms, consider how Derman-Sparks and Edwards (2010, p. 56) differentiated surface culture and deep culture:

Surface culture: artifacts, costumes, foods, and holidays

Deep culture: language, values, extended family relationships, migration, work (who does what and where), housing arrangements, community connection, intergenerational relationships, ideas about education, health care, recreation, gender roles, role of children, religion, showing emotion, historic events

This differentiation can guide planning for classroom activities, special days, bulletin boards, parent-teacher conferences, and so forth.

CRITICAL RACE THEORY

Another helpful framework for considering matters related to culture involve issues expressed in what is called the critical race theory. Here is a general definition:

Critical race theory: The examination of everyday interactions to find the racial component in them. By looking carefully at what sociologists call *micro-aggressions*, classroom teachers can help to see and then avoid racist practices (Wisegeek, 2014). For example, micro-aggressions could include words or terms that you or children use about groups or individuals, the books that are selected (or not selected) in the curriculum, posters or pictures in the classroom, community members who are invited (or not invited) as guest speakers, and so forth.

Banks (2012) outlines in the "Total Education Environment" a further application of some places or processes in which the concepts included in multicultural education, critical race theory, and anti-bias can be utilized. These include, for example, policies, institutional and hidden curriculum, assessment, and staff attitudes, beliefs, and actions. Doucet and Adair (2013) give some very specific strategies for dealing with race and inequity for preschool through the primary grades. They cite numerous sources of research supporting the idea that young children are often very aware of racial and social justice issues. They provide classroom teachers a variety of ways to plan, have conversations, and work with children and their families in regard to anti-racist themes used in the classroom.

Here is one example of racism in a third-grade class:

Jason was new to the school and was clearly not happy with the change. In his second week in school he told Anna that she should "go back to her country." Anna went to the teacher and repeated what Jason had said to her. The teacher explained to Jason in a private conversation that Anna's family was from the United States and that it was hurtful and disrespectful for him to say those words. Jason seemed to understand and returned to his normal activities, but a similar incident happened again the next week with another discussion; this time the teacher invited the building principal into the

Suzanne Clouzeau/Pearson

discussion. The following day the principal, librarian, and school counselor met to work on a planned series of readings for Jason to help him understand Anna's culture. Jason and the counselor then had discussions about the readings, about what it means to use racist language, and about how to look at the world from other people's perspectives. Eventually Jason and Anna began to meet together with the counselor to read stories and talk about what they learned from the stories. Jason's racist comments no longer happened in the classroom.

Cultural Competence Check:

Do you agree with the statements in the Big Ideas for Chapter 8 chart?

How would you implement a social studies curricula with these statements in mind?

How could you plan and implement social studies activities that relate to the deeper cultural themes, rather than surface themes?

Anti-Bias Curriculum Goals

In 1989, Louise Derman-Sparks and colleagues published the *Anti-Bias Curriculum: Tools for Empowering Young Children.* One of the major tenets of this text was the criticism of widely used practices they called a **"tourist approach."** Tourist curricula are usually identified as activities in early childhood classrooms that are introduced for a short time and show only a shallow, inauthentic, and inaccurate view of the topic and often contain artifacts of a culture that are misrepresented. Holiday celebrations, posters, and plastic dolls typify some of the activities and materials most often used in tourist-approach curricula.

Conversely, the anti-bias approach emphasizes a critique of discrimination in all its forms: race, social class, gender, sexual orientation, age, and abilities. It emphasizes engagement in social activism to respond to injustices. Here are the four goals of an anti-bias curriculum (Derman-Sparks & Edwards, 2010) that could guide classroom practice:

Goal 1

- Each child will demonstrate self-awareness, confidence, family pride, and positive social identities.

Goal 2

- Each child will express comfort and joy with human diversity; accurate language for human differences; and deep, caring human connections.

Goal 3

- Each child will increasingly recognize unfairness, have language to describe unfairness, and understand that unfairness hurts.

Goal 4

- Each child will demonstrate empowerment and the skills to act with others or alone, against prejudice and/or discriminatory actions.

Cultural Disposition Check:

> *Do you agree with these goals?*
>
> *How would you implement a social studies curricula with these goals in mind?*

These goals have significant implications for how classrooms operate throughout the year. They also deeply relate to how individuals and groups feel while in those classrooms. Furthermore, these goals also affect how programs for children and schools function and how decisions that affect children are made.

MULTICULTURAL EDUCATION GOALS

Multicultural education is usually included in a social studies curriculum. The National Association for Multicultural Education (NAME) lists six goals: (1) to respect and appreciate cultural diversity; (2) to promote the understanding of unique cultural and ethnic heritage; (3) to promote the development of culturally responsible and responsive curricula; (4) to facilitate acquisition of the attitudes, skills, and knowledge to function in various cultures; (5) to eliminate racism and discrimination in society; and (6) to achieve social, political economic, and educational equity (Klefstad & Martinez, 2013). Multicultural education differs from the anti-bias approach described earlier in this chapter because the focus is on learning about particular cultures. Ramsey (2012) has outlined some important categories for creating environments for the study of culture and the practice of respecting cultures in schools and programs:

- Developing culturally responsive practices that enable all children from a range of backgrounds to have a successful start in school and to participate fully in early childhood programs.

- Encouraging children to develop positive and realistic identities that embody their race, **culture**, gender, and abilities as well as their personal, family, and social histories.

- Broadening children's perspectives so that they learn to recognize and appreciate commonalities and differences among people in their communities, countries, and the world and develop a sense of solidarity with all people and with the natural environment.

- Engaging children in critically examining their own assumptions and the inequities in their immediate environment and the larger world.

- Encouraging and supporting children to gain the confidence and skills to be activists for social change.

In 1995, Ogbu provided this overview of how classrooms needed to operate: "To be effective in multicultural classrooms, teachers must relate teaching content to the cultural backgrounds of their students. There is growing evidence that strong, continual engagement among diverse students requires a holistic approach—that is, an approach where the how, what of teaching are unified and meaningful."

CREATING CULTURALLY RESPONSIVE CLASSROOMS

Villegas and Lucas (2002) list several ways that teachers can create environments that are culturally responsive, including the following: affirming the views of students from diverse backgrounds; viewing all students as capable learners who have experiences, concepts, and languages that can be built on; and viewing learners as "builders," not empty vessels. They also advocate for teachers to promote the development of critical thinking, problem-solving, collaboration, and the recognition of multiple perspectives. Gay and Kirkland (2003) emphasize that the teacher's critical consciousness is important for understanding themselves, the context, and their own ability to question their knowledge base and assumptions as they attempt to create a culturally responsive classroom.

Janet Gonzalez-Mena (2014) suggests the following for teachers in establishing cultural response education and care: (1) Discuss with parents the dreams and desires they have for their children; (2) think about, as the classroom teacher, what messages are influencing each child's sense of self, sense of cultural competence, and feelings of belonging; (3) ask yourself what culture or cultures a visitor to your classroom would see reflected there. Could this person tell anything about the diversity of families in the program?

HELPING CHILDREN BECOME GLOBAL CITIZENS

To better prepare children for successful living in the future, it will be important for them to understand the world from a more global and less provincial perspective. Here are some specific suggestions that may help the teacher plan a social studies curriculum:

- Include multiple stories and photos of lifestyles in and across cultures.
- Include discussions about values and beliefs in and across cultures.
- Present varying worldviews and perspectives.
- Include both individual and group similarities and differences in and across cultures. (Note that not every member of a culture has all of the same characteristics or practices of the culture at all times.)

Practical justifications for such a curriculum are based on both economic and social justice rationales. For example, many corporations in the United States are now international in operation and management. The national economy is closely integrated with international markets across the world.

On an ethical level it is clearly important we treat each other fairly and with equity. As teachers we should model those behaviors in the classroom and also in the lessons we prepare. Expanding this to a broader perspective can help children understand how to be citizens in the school and later in the world at large.

GENDER AND DIVERSITY AS PART OF CULTURAL UNDERSTANDING

Gender is another factor in understanding diversity in the social studies curriculum and for inclusion in instructional planning. Below are some specific aspects of the early childhood classroom by which classroom teachers can avoid gender stereotyping and increase gender equity:

1. Use of *books, stories, media, and visual displays* that depict both boys and girls in leadership roles, working in a variety of jobs, and doing various tasks at school, at home, and in the community.
2. Use of *learning centers and stations* that provide opportunities for both girls and boys to experience a wide variety of tools, language, materials, and clothing, as well as to practice skills.

Pearson ECE shoot

This is exemplified by a dramatic play area of the classroom where all children are encouraged to play (e.g., camping centers, fix-it shops for pretending to repair appliances, fishing centers with boats and rods). These types of centers are gender neutral and can provide all children with opportunities to act out the roles and to use language and cognitive problem-solving related to each theme in the center.

3. Throughout the *daily schedule*, and especially during transitions and routine times, avoid the use of stereotypical language. Figure 8.1 lists some examples.

Figure 8.1
Examples of Inappropriate and Appropriate Phrases.

During:	Avoid saying:	Instead use:
Lining up	Boys line up first	Color of shirt or first letter of their name
When moving something in the room	I need some strong boys to help me.	I need some strong people to help me.

Language Diversity: Supporting English Language Learners

Ovando (2012) has written that English language learners (ELL) are a complex group. Many are from families whose ancestors have inhabited what is now the United States for thousands of years. But they also include some of the most recent immigrants to the United States from all over the world. Their lives have been shaped over time by assimilation and **acculturation**, resulting in myriad sociocultural and linguistic patterns. The important task that lies before public schools in the United States is to provide ELL students with an equitable and challenging curriculum while offering sociocultural, linguistic, developmental, and cognitive support.

Research by Cummins (2000) and Nieto (2002) indicates that teachers who are aware of the processes of acculturation are better able to support the successful transition from home to school. They have found that teachers' attitudes about their students' communities and their understanding of the transitions students experience across distinct cultural practices can open opportunities for students to develop multicultural and multilingual identities.

Research on language has also shown the following: All languages and language varieties are equally complex, and although they may differ in various ways, those differences do not imply that one language or language variety is superior to another. It is widely argued that by placing language varieties on a hierarchy, the cause of social inequities experienced by speakers of nonstandard varieties of English is often located in the speech patterns of those individuals, as opposed to in the larger social structures that are truly at the root of such iniquities (Baker, 2012).

Goldenberg (2006) has recommended the following instructional supports for ELL students:

1. Strategic use of the primary language
2. Consistent expectations, instruction, and routines
3. Extended explanation and opportunities for practice
4. Physical gestures and visual cues
5. Focusing on the similarities/differences (cognates) between English and home language
6. Building on home language skills
7. Targeting vocabulary and checking comprehension frequently
8. Paraphrasing students' language and encouraging them to expand

Teachers should consider what these findings from research indicate for classroom practice, especially regarding literacy and reading instruction. For example, both the home language and the academic language (or school language) could be used for instructional time and for routines throughout the day.

One ELL teacher in a school district in Pennsylvania used an app to create directions for open houses in Spanish, which was the home language of many families. She sent directions home ahead of time along with the invitation to the open house to let families know they could tour the school using their smart phones (which many families had access to). Information about the school day was posted around the room and in the hallways so that families could learn about their child's school.

Figure 8.2 presents an idea for an interview tool for new ELL students that was adapted from an activity in *A How-to Guide for Teaching English Language Learners in the Primary Classroom* (Dragan, 2005).

Dragan (2005) has also recommended some strategies for the first 20 days of school for ELL students in the primary grades, including the assignment of buddies, parent volunteers, and older grade helpers. These strategies can help students with transitioning into a new class to learn routines and procedures that may be unfamiliar.

Understanding of Family Diversity

Researchers Luis C. Moll and Norma Gonzalez modified the concept of household funds of knowledge from anthropologists James Greenberg and Carlos Velez-Ibanez. Through home visits, discussions,

Figure 8.2
Sample of an Interview Tool for New ELL Students.

Child's name:	Age	
	Favorite color (have color samples from which to choose)	Favorite food (have magazine pages with different types of food from which to choose)
	Favorite game (have photos of popular games)	Favorite toy (have pictures of popular toys)
Teacher's notes from interview:		

and research, Moll and Gonzalez found that families had extensive amounts of knowledge and experience that could be useful in classroom instruction (Moll & Gonzales, 2004; Moll and Spear-Ellinwood, 2012).

The **"funds of knowledge"** is a useful tool for classroom teachers. By building relationships with families, teachers can scaffold the knowledge that each child brings from his/her home culture into the lesson or school activity. Using the fund gives the teacher a resource for both planning and instruction that are more meaningful to each child.

Suggestion for your teaching: *Think of the funds of knowledge as a checking account from which you can withdraw money. Recognizing that children bring knowledge and concepts from home gives you a basis from which to expand children's understanding of a lesson's content.*

Diversity, Families, and Holiday Suggestions

Because holiday celebrations vary widely from family to family, it is important that teachers carefully plan activities during the school day. Here are some guidelines to consider:

1. Be clear about your goals for including holidays in the curriculum. If one goal is to expand an anti-bias curriculum, learning about and/or experiencing a wide variety of holidays can affirm cultural identity in some children and help others appreciate traditions that are different from their own.

2. Get to know the families of the children in your class or group, and discover how each feels about holidays before you move forward with a holiday curriculum. Be sensitive to and respectful of families who don't celebrate any holidays, or families who worry about their children being exposed to holidays other than the ones their family celebrates.

3. Connect all holiday activities and/or lessons to real people rather than making generalizations, which can lead to stereotypes. Make sure you have accurate information (based on ideas from Gonzales-Mena, 2014).

Incorporating these planning suggestions into lessons is an important way to build communities that are inclusive and avoid the use of stereotypical content or depictions. In Figure 8.3, reminders are provided for planning lessons and running the learning centers.

Figure 8.3
Guidelines Related to Holidays.
Learning Center and Lesson Planning Guidelines Related to Holidays

Topic	Issue to address or avoid	Suggested practice
Halloween celebrations or activities	Do not assume that all families celebrate this day.	Check school or program policies. Avoid stereotypical images (e.g., witches) if celebrations are permitted.
Thanksgiving activities and visual displays	Avoid "cutesy" displays, props, and materials of Native Americans and Pilgrims.	Select books, bulletin board posters, and so on that depict historically accurate scenes, including (authentic) clothing, food, and housing.
Religious celebrations	Avoid celebrating or focusing on only one religion or religious tradition.	Invite many families and members of the community to share a wide variety of family customs and traditions throughout the year.

HOME/SCHOOL CONNECTION

1. Invite families to participate throughout the year in class activities.

2. Plan special events that celebrate family traditions and interests.

3. Invite community members to participate in the social studies lessons by bringing in examples of their work, hobbies, or traditions.

4. Ideas for resolving conflicts or disagreements: (a) Actively listen (think about why families are expressing their views); (b) affirm that you have listened and will work on solutions; (c) consult with resources (e.g., school counselors, principal, ESL teacher); and (d) be as flexible as possible and be willing to compromise to accommodate family and cultural differences.

Suzanne Clouzeau/Pearson

ACCOMMODATIONS FOR CHILDREN WITH DIVERSE NEEDS

Diversity, anti-bias, and multicultural education by its very nature must provide accommodations for children with diverse needs, including those who are English language learners (ELL) (Figure 8.4) and those with special needs (Figure 8.5).

Figure 8.4
Adaptations for ELL.

Adaptations for English Language Learners

To better understand how to teach social studies concepts to English language learners, use the following strategies:

<u>For preschool and kindergarten:</u>

Use real objects in addition to words or pictures.

Provide time to play with materials.

Use language from their culture that describes the same social studies concept.

<u>For first grade through third grades:</u>

Use role-playing to make abstract concepts concrete.

Create analogies to help students link the unfamiliar with the familiar.

Pre-teach reading assignments to help struggling readers.

Create opportunities for jigsaw (cooperative) learning to provide reading and study support.

Be a considerate speaker (instructor) to help struggling listeners.

Examples (Teaching English Language Learners, 2013): Use graphic organizers, speak slowly and distinctly, and write key concepts and vocabulary on the board or on a flipchart. Use simple, familiar language whenever possible, and pause frequently to ask and answer questions. Use pictures and other visual cues to aid conversation.

Note: The use of *academic language* (words and terms used primarily in schools) is typically a challenge for English language learners. This can be a cultural barrier for succeeding in schools. Using explicit reminders, memory strategies, pictures, and symbols to explain and remember these school terms can give English language learners the tools they will need to succeed in the school environment.

Source: Examples listed above are excerpted and adapted from www.glencoe.com/sec/teachingtoday/subject/teaching_ell.phtml, retrieved on March 21, 2013.

Figure 8.5
Adaptations for Children with Special Needs.

Adaptations for Children with Special Needs

For better understanding of how to teach social studies to children with special needs, the following was excerpted from *Social Studies Education for Students with Disabilities* (Sunal & Haas, 2008, pp. 232–233). Appropriate classroom strategies for teaching these children include the following:

- Activity-oriented instruction
- Instruction related to students' everyday experiences
- Interesting social studies activities, such as authentic games of the time period or cultural group
- Appropriate linguistic and conceptual social studies content demands
- Efficient classroom management, establishing ground rules and procedures for social studies activities
- Focus on skills development throughout social studies activities
- Examination of textbooks for the impact they may have on students

CONNECTIONS TO LITERACY

In the area of diversity, anti-bias, and multicultural education, books offer a rich source of materials for learning and teaching.

Boys and Girls of the World: From One End . . . to the Other by Nuria Roca

Desert Is My Mother/El Desierto Es Mi Madre by Pat Mora, illustrated by Daniel Lechon

Don't Call Me Special: A First Look at Disability by Pat Thomas

Friends from the Other Side/Amigos Del Otro Lado by Gloria Anzaldúa

The Glory Field by Walter Dean Myers

Hairs/Pelitos by Sandra Cisñeros

The Journey: Japanese Americans, Racism, and Renewal by Sheila Hamanaka

Katie Henio: Navajo Sheepherder by Peggy Thomson, photographs by Paul Conklin

Lift Ev'ry Voice and Sing by James Weldon Johnson, illustrated by Jan Spivey Gilchrist

Molly's Pilgrim by Barbara Cohen, illustrated by Michael Deraney

¡Viva México!: The Story of Benito Juárez and Cinco de Mayo by Argentina Palacios

Other sources of multicultural literature for social studies in pre-kindergarten–third grade

African American Images website

American Indian Reference Books for Children and Young Adults

Big Multicultural Tales

Children's Book Center at University of Wisconsin

Hispanic Books Children's Catalog

Horn Book Guide

Japanese American Curriculum Project

Multicultural Review

Multicultural children's picture books. In Klefstad, J. M., & Martinez, K. C. (2013). Promoting young children's cultural awareness and appreciation through multicultural books. *YC Young Children, 68*(5), 74–81.

Multiethnic Children's Literature (Gonzalo Ramirez and Jan Lee Ramirez)

Through Indian Eyes: The Native Experience in Books for Children

SAMPLE ACTIVITIES

The teacher can find a variety of worthwhile and effective activities and methods to build rich experiences that promote understanding of diversity. In their classroom practice, teachers can use two strategies to individualize (Gartrell, 2013):

1. Get to know each child's interests, abilities, skills, language, culture, family, and other unique characteristics.

2. Use knowledge of each child to provide materials, activities, and interactions that support learning.

Activity Based on a Sample Lesson

The following sample activity is based on one created by Neuman and Roskos (2007, p. 144):

> *Learning Objective.* To begin to understand similarities and differences among people.

> *Whole Group.* Have shoeboxes with mirrors glued to the inside lids. Tell the children they are going to see something different. Ask questions such as, "What do you think you are going to see?" "What could be in the box?" Ask children to look at the mirrors and share what they see. Then read the book, *We Are All Alike . . . We Are All Different* (1991), a book written and illustrated by the Cheltenham Elementary School Kindergarteners.

Discuss with the class how everyone is alike, and then discuss some differences, while looking again at the mirrors.

Additional Tools for Planning Learning Centers and Projects

The Checklist for Assessing the Visual Material Environment (*Anti-Bias Curriculum*, Derman-Sparks, 1989) is of value to teachers as they set up learning centers and design projects for their students.

As a further aid, teachers should consider the following questions as they think about planning lessons and activities for teaching social studies content:

1. Is the planned activity historically accurate?

2. Is the activity culturally complete? Does it include social justice issues in age-appropriate ways?

3. Does the lesson or activity mislead, misrepresent, or misinform children in any way? For example, is the lesson or activity historically accurate? Does it contain "cutesy" representations of racial/ethnic groups? Or stereotypical pictures? Or posters of gender roles?

RESOURCES

The following resources offer the teacher various types of material to help children understand diversity, anti-bias, and multicultural content in the social studies curriculum.

Websites

- **Cooperative Children's Book Center** offers bibliographies of children's books on a variety of diversity issues: education.wisc .edu/ccbc

- **Starting Small**, Teaching Tolerance project of the Southern Poverty Law Center, Montgomery, AL: tolerance.org/kit/starting-small

    The vision of community that the early childhood classroom provides can color children's expectations about equity, cooperation, and citizenship for a lifetime. This training kit for early childhood educators profiles seven innovative classrooms in which teachers are helping children practice fairness, respect, and tolerance.

    Starting Small includes a 58-minute DVD featuring Vivian Gussin Paley and a companion text (PDF) highlighting classroom profiles, reflection prompts, and activities.

- **National Opportunity to Learn website: Restorative Practices Toolkit:** otlcampaign.org/

From NAEYC: *Teaching Young Children*

- **Activity Planning Form:** naeyc.org/tyc/files/

- **English Language Learners:** naeyc.org/files/tyc/file/

- *Getting It Right for Young Children from Diverse Backgrounds* (Espinosa, 2010).

Assessing Learning Outcomes

- What did you learn about anti-bias and multicultural education?

- What did you learn about your personal disposition and thoughts regarding diversity?

- What did you learn about diversity in planning for social studies activities?

References

Baker, S. (2012). English language speakers, fluent and limited. In J. A. Banks (Ed.), *Encyclopedia of diversity in education.* Thousand Oaks, CA: Sage.

Banks, J. (Ed.). (2012). Total education environment. In *Encyclopedia of diversity in education.* Thousand Oaks, CA: Sage.

Cheltenham Elementary School Kindergarteners (1991). *We are all alike . . . we are all different.* New York, NY: Scholastic.

Cummins, J. (2000). *Language, power and pedagogy: Bilingual children in the crossfire.* Clevedon, UK: Multilingual Matters.

Derman-Sparks, L., and A.B.C. Task Force. (1989). *Anti-bias curriculum: Tools for empowering young children.* Washington, DC: National Association for the Education of Young Children (NAEYC).

Derman-Sparks, L., & Edwards, J.O. (2010). Anti-bias education for young children and ourselves. Washington, DC: National Association for the Education of Young Children (NAEYC).

Doucet, F., & Adair, J. K. (2013). Addressing race and inequity in the classroom. *YC Young Children, 68*(5), 88–97.

Dragan, P. B. (2005). *A how-to guide for teaching English language learners in the primary classroom.* Portsmouth, NH: Heinemann.

Espinosa, L. (2010). *Getting it right for young children from diverse backgrounds: Applying research to improve practice.* Upper Saddle River, NJ: Pearson.

Gartrell, D. (2013). Supporting all children in a gender-friendly classroom. *Teaching Young Children*, Feb/Mar 2013, *6*(3), 8.

Gay, G., & Kirkland, K. N. (2003). Developing critical consciousness and critical reflection in pre-service teacher education. *Theory into Practice, 42*(3), 181–187.

Goldenberg, C. (2006). Improving achievement for English learners. What research tells us. *Education Week, 25*(43), 34–36.

Gonzalez-Mena, J. (2014). *50 Strategies for communicating and working with diverse families.* Upper Saddle River, NJ: Pearson.

Klefstad, J. M., & Martinez, K. C. (2013). Promoting young children's cultural awareness and appreciation through multicultural books. *YC Young Children, 68*(5), 74–81.

Moll, Luis C., & Gonzales, N. (2004). Engaging life: A fund of knowledge approach to multicultural education. In J. A. Banks & C. A. M. Banks (Eds.), *Handbook of research on multicultural education* (2nd ed., pp. 699–715). San Francisco, CA: Jossey-Bass.

Moll, Luis C., & Spear-Ellinwood, K. (2012). Funds of knowledge. In J. A. Banks (Ed.), *The encyclopedia of diversity in education.* (pp. 938–939). Thousand Oaks, CA: Sage Publications.

National Council for the Social Studies (NCSS). (2010). *National curriculum standards for social studies: A framework for teaching, learning, and assessment.* Silver Spring, MD: NCSS.

Neuman, S., & Roskos, K. (2007). *Nurturing knowledge: Building a foundation for school success by linking early literacy to math, science, art and social studies.* New York, NY: Scholastic.

Nieto, S. (2002). *Language, culture and teaching: Critical perspectives for a new century.* Mahwah, NJ: Lawrence Erlbaum.

Ogbu, J. U. (1995). Understanding cultural diversity and learning. In J. A. Banks and C. A. M. Banks (Eds.), *Handbook of research on multicultural education.* New York, NY: Macmillan.

Ovando, C. J. (2012). English language learners. In J. A. Banks (Ed.), *Encyclopedia of diversity in education.* Thousand Oaks, CA: Sage.

Ramsey, P. G. (2012). Early childhood multicultural education. In J. A. Banks (Ed.), *Encyclopedia of multicultural education.* Thousand Oaks, CA: Sage.

Sunal, C. S., & Haas, M. E. (2008). *Social studies for the elementary and middle grades: A constructivist approach* (Haas 2008 edition, pp. 232–233). Upper Saddle River, NJ: Pearson.

Teaching English language learners. *Teaching Today.* Glencoe, retrieved from www.glencoe.com/sec/teachingtoday/subject/teaching_ell.phtml

Villegas, A. M., & Lucas, T. (2002). *Educating culturally responsive teachers: A coherent approach.* Albany, NY: SUNY Press.

Wisegeek. (2014). Definition of critical race theory. Retrieved from www.wisegeek.com

9

Assessment

Learning Outcomes

After reading this chapter you should be able to:

- Explain ways in which children show progress in understanding social studies concepts at their particular ages.
- Describe how you would use assessment to guide lessons.
- Create a variety of activities that would allow children to demonstrate their understanding of a particular social studies concept and describe a common assessment you could use.

Big Ideas for Chapter 9: Assessment	Classroom Application	Standards Met
Developmentally appropriate assessment	Using developmentally appropriate assessment embedded in appropriate activities	(Suggested by authors as meeting NAEYC standards 1,3,4,6)
Understanding the many ways you can assess children	Incorporating a variety of assessments through observations, projects, anecdotal records, and portfolio building	(Suggested by authors as meeting NAEYC standards 1,3,4,6)

NCSS Standards

The National Council for the Social Studies (NCSS) has organized social studies into 10 broad interrelated holistic themes. This chapter addresses appropriate assessment of the following themes:

1. Culture
2. Time, continuity, and change
3. People, places, and environments
4. Individual development and identity
5. Individuals, groups, and institutions
6. Power, authority, and governance
7. Production, distribution, and consumption
8. Science, technology, and society
9. Global connections
10. Civic ideals and practices (NCSS, 2010)

NAEYC Standards

The following NAEYC Standards for Professional Preparation Programs are addressed in this chapter:

Standard 1: Promoting Child Development and Learning

Standard 3: Observing, Documenting, and Assessing to Support Young Children and Families

Standard 4: Using Developmentally Effective Approaches

Standard 6: Becoming a Professional

Source: NAEYC Standards for Early Childhood Professional Preparation http://www.naeyc.org/files/naeyc/files/2009%20Professional%20Prep%20stdsRevised%204_12.pdf

DEVELOPMENTAL BASIS OF ASSESSMENT GOALS

Assessment is measurement: measuring what children know, what they understand, what they can apply, and what they need to know. This entails monitoring development and learning, using assessment information to guide planning, providing support and services to those in need, and reporting to families and others (McAfee & Leong, 2009).

The NCSS standards all require some measurement of understanding for teachers to build upon. Allowing children the opportunity to demonstrate their perceptions and giving them authentic opportunities in the classroom to act on their understandings enables teachers to build lessons accordingly.

In an early childhood classroom, this means having the opportunity to demonstrate and practice skills in a real world way. Infants and toddlers cannot respond to direct questioning about history or identity, but they can learn routines and the qualities that make them unique. They may not know the term *civic ideals*, but they can learn about taking turns, helping one another, and sharing. As early childhood teachers present these opportunities in their classrooms every day, they can apply this new purpose of helping children become part of the community of their classroom. They see the teacher as their model of leadership, someone who guides them, helps them problem solve in peaceful ways, and offers them a variety of new experiences. Through carefully watching children and paying attention to how they demonstrate understanding and ability, teachers can meet their individual and specific needs. Sharing this information with families helps teachers and families work together through common goals for children. To ensure that assessment is developmentally appropriate, teachers must pay attention to children's ages and developmental characteristics as a group, individually, and culturally (Copple & Bredekamp, 2009).

Suzanne Clouzeau/Pearson

Building a Safe Environment

The very foundation of being able to see and understand what children know is providing them with a safe environment in which to play with, explore, and practice new concepts. The ability to relax in their learning, to take risks, and to experience, yet not fear failure, is the basis of tenacity, persistence, and sustained effort. Social learning opportunities are another aspect of a safe environment. Engaging with others, sharing ideas, and working toward a common goal, while negotiating through trial and error, allow children to further their understandings of concepts.

Providing Developmentally Appropriate, Engaging Materials for Exploration

Children need to make meaningful connections in their learning. The only way for them to accomplish this is to be immersed in materials and activities that are purposely connected to the lesson. For example, very young children may begin by exploring with water. Water tables are common in early childhood classrooms and allow children to feel water, try to capture water, pour water, and often splash with water! While they are playing, they are learning the properties of water. They are able to recognize water in many places—the bathtub, the sink, the water they drink, the rain in the sky, the puddles they like to walk through, rivers, lakes, and so on. As they gain experience, they can build on this under-standing by mixing it with other materials, using it in cooking, examin-ing snow, and much more. Still later, children can begin to understand the need to conserve water, to realize that many people do not have access to clean drinking water, to find ways to recycle water, and to learn about both the environmental and the societal impacts of a drought. They cannot immerse themselves in learning about these concepts by having teachers read from a book; they must be able to explore, to see and feel, and engage in their own research in order to create meaning. These sensory experiences additionally solidify learning and support re-tention (Pica, 2006), an ultimate goal in the learning process.

Similarly, children can create projects using the concepts they are being taught. As they learn about the Liberty Bell as a symbol of free-dom, they may be tasked with creating their own symbol of freedom and connecting it to an historical event they have examined on their own. The class might display their symbols in a class museum, inviting families to attend, and then follow up with a class book that includes photographs and writings about their freedom symbols. Teachers may use a **common assessment** to examine skills while allowing for a variety of ways for children to demonstrate individual levels of understanding.

Family Contributions

Families are an integral part of the classroom. Teachers who build posi-tive relationships with families are more effective and more aware of their learners overall. Families can provide information beyond what a teacher is able to collect, such as information about routines, fears, dislikes, interests, and other key preferences that allow the teacher to reach the children with additional possibilities. For example, knowing that a child loves racecars instantly provides the teacher with a strategy for teaching symbol recognition. By using small toy cars and placing a sticker with a number on each car, the child is drawn into the activ-ity and the two can begin to talk about the "number 3 car passing the number 2 car," building skills while engaging in a favorite activity.

When working with families, teachers need to see a triangular effort, that is, the child, the family, and the teacher all working toward the

Suzanne Clouzeau/Pearson

Assessing – Teacher with Child.

success of the child. Teachers also must embed themselves in the goals and plans for the child. By using phrases such as "Our goal for the up-coming weeks . . . " and "We are going to work on . . ." emphasizes for the family that the teacher has a well-thought-out plan and an active role in it.

ASSESSMENT OPTIONS

Assessment can be accomplished in a variety of ways, including the use of **observation**; **anecdotal records**; **checklists** and **rating scales**; talking and exploring with children; and written summaries, quizzes, and tests.

Observation

Being able to watch children closely allows teachers to better under-stand how and what children think about their surroundings and the expectations placed on them. When teachers are responsible for in-structing a roomful of students, it is impossible to focus on just one. Through practice and the use of a variety of assessment tools, teachers are able to collect quite a bit of information about their students while teaching and supervising a classroom of them. Practice makes this a routine part of the flow of the classroom and helps teachers become keenly aware of the many factors that can impact a child's learning.

Using Observations

By taking the information gained from observations, checklists or rating scales, and anecdotal records, teachers can adjust their lessons to meet children "where they are." This ability to adjust increases understanding by providing additional opportunities and carefully re-teaching foundational concepts. It further allows teachers to weave lessons into day-to-day activities. For example, the teacher who is helping children learn about patterns will point out a child's striped shirt and recite the pattern to the children: "I see a pattern on Grant's shirt, let's look at the stripes, green, blue, green, blue, green, blue! Wow, patterns are everywhere!" Connect this finding to the stripes on the flag: "What do you notice about the stripes on our flag? Red, white, red, white, red, white, yes, that *is* a pattern!" Children can line up according to their shoes—sneakers, sneakers, sandals, sneakers, sneakers, sandals—and then discuss the matter when they run out of what they need to continue the pattern. Children are engaged in the activity while teachers are taking note of their individual levels of understanding. At this level

David Kostelnik/Pearson

Engaging and Observing.

they are broadening their understanding to their environment, further connecting them to their surroundings and to other people and places.

Anecdotal Records

Teachers of young learners should become well versed in using anecdotal records, which allow them to capture a moment in which a child demonstrates some level of understanding, unique thinking, an unexpected response, or any expression or event worth noting (Figure 9.1). Anecdotal records are quickly recorded and added to a child's portfolio for later analysis. The record may enable the teacher to see a pattern develop or may represent a random moment that is not repeated again. These simple recordings are written on anything available: sticky notes, a predesigned form, or scrap paper. What is most important is that it is documentation recorded in the moment of the learning environment.

These recordings are especially helpful during conferences with families; it is much more effective to be able to share a moment such as that in Figure 9.1 than to say to a family, "T.J. is helpful." Families

Figure 9.1
Anecdotal Record.

Child's name: T.J.   Date: March 8   Time: 9:17   Setting: At the store center

While working on choosing and purchasing items at a classroom store, T.J. noticed Zachary struggling with the concept of paying for items. He said, "Do you want help? I can help you." When Zachary said "Yes," T.J. explained that Zachary would need to count his coins to know if he had enough money to pay for what he chose. T.J. asked, "Are you trying to buy two apples?" Zachary said, "Yes and they are .23 each." T.J. said, "You need to add .23 plus .23 to see if you have enough." Zachary responded that the total would be .46 and he did not think he had enough money. T.J. said, "Then you could just buy one, and when you count what's left you can pick something else . . . maybe." Zachary put 1 dime, 2 nickels, and 3 pennies on the table. As he laid each coin down, he would look at T.J., who would give a reassuring nod. When all the coins were counted, the boys exchanged a high-five! They then returned to the store items to see if there was anything else Zachary was interested in buying.

---

appreciate and need the clarity provided by these records, and teachers need the recorded documentation. Anecdotal records can include anything the teacher believes is worth noting and remembering; they can be as short as one or two sentences or a little longer. For example, they may include the help offered by a child to a peer who becomes frustrated with a puzzle: The teacher would record what the helper said, how the peer responded, and how the two followed up the exchange.

Records might also include a child's sharing a creative way to solve a problem, such as a suggestion to switch computer time with recess in order not to miss outdoor recess because of rain, or a child's declaration at morning meeting that he saw a full moon in the sky the night before and that means the moon in the next phase will be getting smaller.

Watching Anecdotally

Watching children closely enables teachers to see how children demonstrate their perception of the concept being learned. What is their understanding of what they are working with? Are they using the materials in a variety of ways? How are they exploring the materials and/or activity? Are they demonstrating some level of success (this would be

David Kostelnik/Pearson

Assessing growth: observing child's use of materials.

different for different children)? When teachers purposely watch children in their interactions and play, they gain important insights into children's thoughts, ideas, and understandings. Through careful recording of these brief notations, teachers can look for patterns, growth, and unique expressions of thinking.

Checklists and Rating Scales

Checklists and rating scales are commonly used when assessing basic facts and developmental milestones. Initially, as children begin to develop symbol recognition, teachers in early childhood classrooms use checklists to record the letters and numbers children are recognizing, while rating scales record where children are on a continuum of learning. In social studies content, these forms of assessment may be used to document how children demonstrate levels of understanding of a concept such as economics. Are they able to explain the difference between wants and needs? Historical dates and events? Natural and human resources? The design of the rating scale reflects levels of mastery on a continuum of acquisition. From introductory levels to more complex thinking, the rating scale would allow the teacher to mark the individual student's levels of demonstration. It is the ranking of the child's level of information.

Talking *to* and Exploring *with* Children

While engaging with children within the context of their activities, teachers are able to ask questions about and build on understandings in ways that will allow children to grow in the authenticity of the moment, meaning they are able to further explore the concept through trial and error and with ideas constructed through the teacher's guidance. This sharing of thoughts about their work, along with ideas for further challenges, allows teachers to understand where children are in the process of acquiring and using new information. Dynamic assessment recognizes children on the verge of acquiring a new skill (McAfee & Leong, 2009). With minimal scaffolding from the teacher, they have that "aha" moment. This is narrowing down to the instructional level that guides teachers in building the most helpful lessons for the child. In addition to discussions during exploration, teachers can conduct mini-interviews with children to gain even greater understanding of children's interests and thought processes (Wallace, 2006).

Written Summaries, Quizzes, and Tests

Written summaries, quizzes, and tests should be used sparingly with children and must be carefully aligned with developmental levels and abilities. When provided with activities that build meaningful connections and historical concepts, children are more likely to be successful in writing about their new knowledge. When built into projects—for example, creating a brochure or a blog about a famous landmark—children are able to incorporate important dates and details that will be recalled more readily and more purposefully on upcoming tests.

Approaches to Avoid

As noted in Figure 9.2, some approaches to gathering information about children's learning are not developmentally appropriate and fall into this category of approaches to avoid. Descriptors for what to avoid, key points to remember, and actions to take follow:

Avoid: Having the same expectations for all children.

Remember: When teachers understand child development, they realize that children go through different stages of development at different times and in different ways. Although there is an expected sequence of development, children typically reach milestones at different times, and many components of their development need to come together to allow them to achieve these milestones. Children are also developing in a variety of ways. They are developing cognitively as they understand increasingly complex thoughts and can put a series of ideas together in a meaningful way. They are developing physically as they grow and develop a coordinated coming together of gross and fine motor skills. They are developing socially and emotionally as they

Figure 9.2
Appropriate Assessment Expectations.

Developmentally appropriate	In-contrast
Recognizing individual strengths, needs, and progress while also understanding the variety of experiences and prior knowledge children will naturally have	Having the same expectations for all children
Providing lessons and experiences in play and social environments that foster children's need for making meaning of what they are learning	Presenting lessons in drill and skill fashion, isolated from their real world, and therefore preventing them from making important connections
Using a variety of authentic assessment opportunities to evaluate children's understanding (including anecdotal records, performance assessments, authentic assessment, and developmental checklists/rating scales)	Expecting children to be able to produce work through tasks that are not developmentally appropriate

gain skills in the give and take of conversing and working with others. With all the combinations and levels of these three components of development, there are countless results for the current status of any individual child. This is why teachers cannot maintain the same expectations for all children; they are simply too different from one another in their developmental processes.

Action: It becomes the teacher's responsibility to understand how each child's strengths and needs in these areas impact individual progress along the path of acquiring knowledge. Teachers must design lessons that meet and allow for this diversity.

Avoid: Presenting lessons to children in drill and skill fashion, isolated from their real world, and therefore preventing them from making important connections.

Remember: Children need to have hands-on experiences with materials and activities in order to understand how things work, to see what connects with prior knowledge and therefore adds depth to their understanding. Children need repeated opportunities to practice and learn new skills (Henniger, 2009).

Action: Exploring with materials in an authentic way provides meaning, especially for young children. For example, children need many interactions with different groups of items that demonstrate an amount before they can understand an abstract number symbol. As another example, children using a topographical map to explore physical characteristics of places and regions are able to feel the map and follow the terrain of land formations. This represents learning a concept while building meaning. Hearing about locations on maps and comparisons of physical features is very different from being able to visually compare oceans and rivers, or highways and streets, on a map. Such an experience, combined with virtual visits, builds understanding and comparisons of concepts. This is a necessary step to true learning. Eventually creating their own map, children are replicating a specific region based on research gathered through inquiry. Additionally, social studies perspectives involve experiences such as visiting a farm and playing store to understand production, distribution, and consumption, as opposed to reading facts from a book. Children learning about law and governance can examine a societal need and actually work through the steps to establish a policy.

Avoid: Expecting children to be able to produce work through tasks that are not developmentally appropriate.

Remember: Teachers need to use caution in the ways they collect information about children's levels of understanding. By combining a thorough understanding of child development with hands-on learning opportunities, teachers build authentic assessment opportunities to watch, listen to, and guide children in their learning. Some of the testing being used in early childhood classrooms requires children to fill in bubbles positioned in front of a correct response or decide the best possible answer out of a series of three or four options. These tasks may have more to do with a child knowing "how" to follow the format of the particular test and complete the selection process accordingly than with providing an accurate reflection of their thoughts about a skill or assessing their problem-solving skills. Therefore, it is quite possible that a child possesses a skill but is merely unable to complete the testing format.

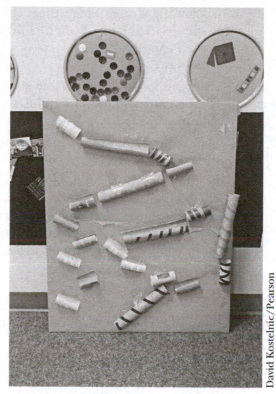

David Kostelnic/Pearson

Individualized Activity.

Action: The teacher must maximize opportunities for children to demonstrate
their knowledge in authentic ways. Use observational techniques to collect
information about children's understandings. Offer a variety of ways for children to engage in project-based learning. For example, when children are
learning about different cultures, they need to be immersed in the "feeling"
of that culture through authentic music, food, dances, clothing, languages,
and traditions. Allowing children to research, replicate, and share components they find intriguing will have a lasting impact.

SOME WAYS CHILDREN MIGHT DEMONSTRATE UNDERSTANDING

Just as children develop in different ways at different times, so, too, do
they show their understanding of concepts in various ways.

1. Engaging in an activity that fosters understanding (e.g., placing
   events in a sequential order)
2. Expressing levels of understanding in their own ways (e.g., recording
   tally marks in comparing city [urban] and country [rural] features)

3. Explaining strategies to others (Much like the anecdotal record earlier in the chapter, when children are able to explain how they work through a task, they are demonstrating knowledge in a concrete way.)

4. Using understanding outside a particular lesson/activity (e.g., a child creates a replica of an historical monument while exploring with materials)

5. Maintaining understanding over time (recalling and expecting the routine of the classroom)

6. Building on the current level of understanding, developing connections, and adding complexity (asking questions, posing possibilities that demonstrate a developing depth of understanding and a need for more information; e.g., a child may ask how mountains are represented on a map)

INCORPORATING INTO PLANNING

It is important that teachers understand the developmental needs and capabilities children have as learners. Teachers must provide activities that allow children to practice skills in a way that builds meaning and

Assessing using manipulatives.

Benjamin LaFramboise/Pearson

HOME/SCHOOL CONNECTION

- Include families as an important part of your teaching team; make sure they are aware of your appreciation of their input, ideas, questions, and concerns.
- Make yourself easily accessible to families to ensure an open line of communication.
- When sharing assessment information, help families understand how you collect information; have materials in front of you and provide work samples and photographs in an effort to enable them to see how you documented information from their child.
- Listen closely when they explain how their child demonstrates understandings at home.
- Plan goals together, helping them know about and use developmentally appropriate approaches; use words like "together," "we," and "our" when outlining strategies.
- Be clear about the goals you have for their child, turning needs into a specific plan of action, with goals spread out over time.

understanding. When children can engage with materials, they are able to show teachers how they are thinking; through manipulating materials and trying ideas, they can see how things work and relate to one another. When they are socially involved at centers, children can use new skills as they discuss, problem solve, and play with peers. This activity further strengthens their understanding as they consider others' thoughts and ideas.

Teachers must also use the information they collect to guide current lessons and plan future ones. Assessment information will indicate children's levels of understanding, allowing a teacher to individualize teaching or to slow down, accelerate, review material, or try new teaching strategies for the entire class (McMillan, 2011).

ACCOMMODATIONS FOR CHILDREN WITH DIVERSE NEEDS

In assessment processes, teachers must provide accommodations for children with diverse needs; these children include English language learners (ELL) (Figure 9.3) and those with special needs (Figure 9.4).

Figure 9.3
Adaptations for ELL.

Adaptations for English Language Learners

Children for whom English is not their primary language especially benefit from teachers' close observations and engaging with materials to demonstrate their understanding. Pictures offer additional support, as does dramatic play. Children are often able to communicate between themselves with little spoken language; therefore, social learning opportunities are essential. This enables them to connect through play and begin to build language connections. The arts are another way for children to communicate and begin to connect through language.

Figure 9.4
Adaptations for Children with Special Needs.

Adaptations for Children with Special Needs

Key to inclusive education is planning a way of assessing that allows all children opportunities to express their levels of understanding. This begins with the classroom environment as a whole. Just as assessment must always stay connected to the objectives of a lesson, inclusion must be woven through every facet of the day, equally as embedded and purposeful. And, everyone must be part of the thinking and problem-solving of the class. All children must be actively helping to figure out how all of their peers can be included (Sapon-Shevin, 2007), as this sets the tone that "we are in this together," we share ideas, and we leave no one behind.

Opportunities for hands-on experiences allow children with special needs to interact with materials in a variety of ways. This further ensures their ability to find meaningful connections. **Sensory experiences** provide children with additional learning opportunities. Texture, smell, sound, taste, and visual connections may provide memorable sensations.

Examining a student's educational needs and goals, along with her abilities, will guide a teacher in knowing what is an appropriate expected outcome for that student as well as how she is best able to express knowledge.

Summary

Here are some questions to consider in thinking about planning and connecting assessments:

- Are we using developmentally appropriate teaching strategies?
- Following that, is the **assessment** aligned with how children learned the concept and also **developmentally appropriate**?
- When planning a lesson, are we using assessment to look at children's prior knowledge, therefore guiding our instruction to re-teach or move forward with a concept?

Assessing Learning Outcomes

- Using the social studies strand of production, distribution, and consumption, create and describe two different activities that would allow children to develop an understanding of these categories. Describe a common assessment that would allow you to review each activity with the same set of criteria.
- Explain how children at different early childhood ages develop an understanding of time, continuity, and change.
- Describe how you would use assessment results to guide your teaching.

References

Copple, C., & Bredekamp, S. (2009). *Developmentally appropriate practice in early childhood programs. Servicing children from birth through 8* (3rd ed.). Washington, DC: National Association for the Education of Young Children (NAEYC).

Henniger, M. L. (2009). *Teaching young children: An introduction (4th ed.).* Upper Saddle River, NJ: Pearson.

McAfee, O., & Leong, D. J. (2009). *Assessing young children's development learning.* Boston, MA: Pearson.

McMillan, J. (2011). *Classroom assessment: Principles and practice for effective standards-based instruction.* Boston, MA: Pearson.

National Council for the Social Studies (NCSS). (2010). *National curriculum standards for social studies: A framework for teaching, learning, and assessment.* Silver Spring, MD: NCSS.

Pica, R. (2006). *A running start: How play, physical activity and free time create a successful child.* New York, NY: Marlowe & Company.

Sapon-Shevin, M. (2007). *Widening the circle: The power of inclusive classrooms.* Boston, MA: Beacon.

Wallace, M. (2006). *Social studies: All day, every day in the early childhood classroom.* Clifton Park, NY: Thomson Delmar Learning.

Glossary

Abstract A broad or general understanding of a concept.

Abstract mapping Detailed mapping by elementary age children.

Acculturation The process of learning about and functioning in a culture.

Affective Processes in social-emotional development that involve forming attachments, establishing relationships, and learning to live in families, classrooms, and communities.

Anecdotal records Short narratives/descriptors of a moment in the classroom worth noting.

Anti-bias A method and philosophy of planning environments, daily schedules, and interactions in programs that promote attitudes and actions that are not biased or stereotypical. This approach includes issues and interactions about age, race, ethnicity, gender, orientation, and so on, of both children and families.

Arts and creative expression Activities, space, and materials that promote children's exploration of their thoughts and feelings through painting, play dough/clay, dance, music, and so on.

Attachment The process by which young children gain intimacy with at least one caregiver to build foundations of long-term, caring relationships.

Autonomy Development of independence in young children.

Change Creating difference.

Checklists A predetermined list of skills in which the teacher checks "yes" or "no," depending on whether the child is demonstrating that skill right now or not, respectively.

Civic ideals Basic freedoms and rights of a just society.

Class meeting A time when a class meets to establish community, solve problems, and set routines and expectations for the smooth running of the classroom.

Class meeting The coming together of a group to share ideas and thoughts.

Classroom community The process of supporting children in their development to work and live with others, fostering self-regulation and prosocial skills.

Cognitive Processes in thinking, reasoning, problem-solving, and conceptualizing in child development.

Common assessment Using one format of assessment to assess a variety of pieces demonstrating one set of objectives.

Community A group that lives and works in close proximity to one another.

Community helpers Those people working in the community who act as models to help children grow in their sense of community and expanding relationships.

Concrete A very specific, tangible representation of a concept.

Consumer A child or adult who uses goods and services.

Continuity Consistency over time; with fluidity.

Critical race theory A deep and thoughtful process to eliminate bias and stereotypical actions, words, and policies in schools and programs.

Culture All of the characteristics that combined form a cohesive representation of a population of people (including beliefs, practices, life styles, religion, language, and so on).

Decentering Development of mental capabilities to enable children to think from another perspective.

Demand How much of something people want.

Developmentally appropriate assessment Assessment that is aligned with children's capabilities in their current level of growth and development.

Differentiation Planning that involves assessing children, in authentic ways, to determine the best match with their current abilities, learning profile, and interests.

Direction The lateral movement of an object or the body.

Dispositions Attitudes or patterns of thought that may affect interactions in programs, with families and with individual children.

Distribution The way goods reach consumers.

Diversity An understanding that families and children are not all the same, even if they are members of the same culture, and that cultures vary from each other in some ways and are the same in others.

Dramatic play The type of play in which children are given time, space, and freedom to develop interactive scenarios that build on their ideas and understanding of how the world works (familiar stories, family situations, etc.). This type of play builds both executive functioning and self-regulation abilities.

Egocentrism Stage of development in which most thoughts concern one's own needs or interests.

Exchange The way in which people acquire products, trading among communities and countries through the use of money.

Funds of knowledge Research term indicating that children from other cultures had some concepts and ideas that were not readily accessible due to language differences. Unlocking or reducing this barrier helps teachers find children's strengths and knowledge base.

Geography The study of people, places, and the environments and the relationships among them.

Goods Any kind of products that children can touch.

Historical learning Lessons and activities that use historical understandings as the objective.

Historical understanding Having the ability to comprehend historical concepts, times, and events.

Identity and family Children typically have opportunities to explore who they are, first within families and then increasingly in out-of-home situations.

Integration Activities and strategies that combine multiple standards and content areas into a planned lesson.

Learning centers Areas of a classroom where different materials, props, books, and so on are arranged for children's play (e.g., art, music, movement, table games, dramatic play, discovery, library, blocks).

Learning preferences Understanding and appreciating that young children learn differently from each other (listening, moving, constructing, problem-solving, interacting with others, and so forth).

Location Positions of people, places, and things on the earth.

Map Representation of places or space.

Model Demonstrating routinely through authentic and genuine actions.

Moral development Understanding of how children begin to make decisions for themselves and others.

Movement The change in location or flow of people, products, information, and ideas around the world.

Multicultural education Activities, curricula, and materials that promote understanding of other cultures and societies.

Needs The things children and adults require to survive.

Observation Purposefully watching children in an effort to gain their levels of understanding/mastery of skills.

Ordinal Of an organized rank.

Orientation Tells the specific location of an object, using the cardinal points (north, south, east, west).

Perspective A map element; it is the concept that maps are made by looking at the world from above.

Place Physical and human characteristics of a place or where we live.

Position The "where" of an object in relation to other objects.

Production An attempt to meet the wants of consumers.

Project approach A specific method of curriculum development by Lilian Katz and Sylvia Chard that supports children's investigation of ideas, materials, resources, and research over an extended period of time that is based on their interests.

Psychomotor Processes in physical skill development, such as coordination, eye-hand movements, locomotor (skipping), fine motor (cutting with scissors), and non-locomotor areas (hopping in place).

Rating scales A predetermined list of skills with categories for levels of attainment the teacher uses to identify where the child is on a continuum.

Region A convenient unit used to divide the world in order to manage its study.

Responsibilities Planning both the daily schedule and the room arrangement to support young children's growth in sharing in the operation and management of the materials and equipment in the room and program.

Restorative justice Types of interactions that promote increasingly deeper understandings of the complexities of racism and bias.

Routines A pattern of doing things.

Scaffold Interact with learners to build on the parts of a concept they are understanding and guide them to the next level.

Scale A map element; it is the process of reducing everything by the same amount.

Scarcity The concept that resources can be limited.

Schema In Piagetian theory, the mental structures that develop in relationship to children's concepts, language, and processes of thought about the world, themselves, and others.

Semi-abstract mapping More complex mapping by primary age children.

Sense of belonging Intentionally working with children in ways that communicate that they are welcome and that the environment (including the teacher) is trustworthy, consistent, and dependable.

Sensory experiences Activities that engage the senses.

Sequence A particular order of events.

Services Anything done for people by somebody else to satisfy their needs is a service.

Supply How much of something is available.

Sustainability Understanding of the ways we can help children support practices that protect the environment through daily routines and actions.

Symbol Pictorial representation of the real object, event, and so on.

Thematic unit Topics that are selected to focus on one area of study using common words, props, and materials (e.g., frogs).

Time Using the increment measurements of a clock and/or calendar.

Timeline A sequential representation of a series of events for a specified time.

Topological mapping Simplified map-making using drawings, pictures, or blocks by preschool children.

Tourist approach The type of planning that promotes a shallow understanding of culture and diversity, leading to misunderstanding and misconception. It is the opposite of an anti-bias approach.

Wants The things children and adults would like to have.

Index

Note: Page references followed by *f* refer to figures; page references followed by *n* refer to notes.